ARTHUR C. CLARKE'S

JULY 20, 2019

LIFE IN
THE 21ST
CENTURY

ARTHUR C. CLARKE'S

JULY 20, 2019

LIFE IN THE 21ST CENTURY

AN OMNI BOOK
MACMILLAN PUBLISHING COMPANY
NEW YORK

Macmillan Publishing Company
866 Third Avenue, New York, N.Y. 10022
Collier Macmillan Canada, Inc.

Library of Congress Cataloging-in-Publication Data
Clarke, Arthur Charles, 1917–
Arthur C. Clarke's July 20, 2019.
"An Omni book."
Includes index.
1. Twenty-first century—Forecasts.   I. Title.
II. Title: July 20, 2019.
CB161.C515   1986   303.4′9′0905   86-12618
ISBN 0-02-525800-1

Macmillan books are available at special discounts for bulk purchases
for sales promotions, premiums, fund-raising, or educational use.
For details, contact:
Special Sales Director
Macmillan Publishing Company
866 Third Avenue
New York, N.Y. 10022

This is a work of historical speculation; the appearance of certain historical figures is therefore inevitable. All other characters, however, are
products of the author's imagination, and any resemblance to persons
living or dead is purely coincidental.

10 9 8 7 6 5 4 3 2

Printed in the United States of America

CONTENTS

ACKNOWLEDGMENTS

I want to thank the following for their contributions: Robert Weil (Apollo history), Patrice Adcroft (medicine), Douglas Colligan (robotics), Richard Wolkomir (eduction), T. A. Heppenheimer (transportation, space, war), Tim Onosko (movies), Mark Teich and Pamela Weintraub (sports), Erik Larson (housing), G. Harry Stine (office), Judith Hooper (psychiatry), Dick Teresi (sex), Kathleen Stein (death), Owen Davies (general science), and photo editors Robert Malone and Fran Heyl for acquiring and coordinating all the illustrations.

ARTHUR C. CLARKE'S JULY 20, 2019

2019

LIFE IN THE 21ST CENTURY

INTRODUCTION: LETTER FROM A LUNAR INHABITANT

The best book ever written about the future opens with these words:

> *There are two futures, the future of desire and the future of fate, and man's reason has never learnt to separate them.*
>
> —J. D. Bernal, *The World, the Flesh and the Devil*, 1929

A strict logician, of course, would say that the first four words are nonsense. There's not even *one* future, let alone two, because the future, by definition, does not yet exist.

Nevertheless, we all know what Bernal meant. There *does* "exist," somewhere in every thinking person's mind, a vague image of the future that he or she would like to happen. It is seldom indeed that the real future—the "future of fate"—coincides with human aspirations. Indeed, with billions of conflicting desires and hopes, how could it? Not even an omnipotent God could create such an impossibility. As I write these words, the Iranians and the Iraqis are each praying to Allah for victory, doubtless with equal devotion. . . .

Yet even if it doesn't exist, it is important to think about the future; as has been so often pointed out, we'll spend the rest of our lives there. Some aspects of the future are easier to deal with than others; let me quote from the *second*-best book on the subject:

> *All attempts to predict the future in any detail appear ludicrous within a few years . . . with a few exceptions, I am limiting myself here to a single aspect of the future—its technology, not the society that will be based upon it. This is not such a limitation as it may seem, for science will dominate the future even more than it dominates the present. Moreover, it is only in this field that prediction is at all possible; there are some general laws governing scientific extrapolation, as there are not (pace Marx) in the case of politics or economics.*
>
> —Profiles of the Future, 1962

In a comment carefully designed to cause equal displeasure in Washington and Moscow, I went on to say, "Politics and economics are concerned with power and wealth, neither of which should be the primary, still less the exclusive, concern of full-grown men." And to my displeasure, I've just noticed that the cover of the revised 1984 edition refers to *Profiles* as "prophetic," which is just what it isn't. As the subtitle carefully explained, it's "An Inquiry into the Limits of the Possible." And that's all that any book on the future—including this one—can ever hope to be.

Still, such inquiries can be extremely useful, whether they take the form of science fiction or think-tank computer studies. Although SF requires no justification (as long as it's well written), it does have great social value as an early warning system—something none of us who have survived the year 1984 is likely to forget. It is often difficult to distinguish between "futures scenarios" produced by such organizations as the late Herman Kahn's Hudson Institute and synopses of science-fiction novels—quite a few of which, I hope, will be generated by this volume.

Round about 1970, I suggested a motto for that noble body, the Science Fiction Writers of America: "The Future isn't what it used to be." (I still don't know whether I made this up, or stole it from somewhere—probably the latter.) Certainly I am always changing *my* future, and have done so again while writing this preface.

I'll be only 102 in 2019, which by then will be no unusual age. My great-grandfather Arthur Heal barely missed the century mark, dying in the year I was born and passing on his name to me. Even more to the point, he was still riding horseback when he was as old as I'll be—not in 2001, but *2010*. We farm boys have good genes.

So who knows: The following "Letter from Clavius" may be a self-fulfilling prophecy. Stay tuned.

And if this book is successful enough to demand a sequel (another "future of desire"), may I suggest to my editors a title that Alvin Toffler kindly gave me many years ago: *After the Future—What?*

LETTER FROM CLAVIUS

Clavius City, 20 July 2019

It doesn't *seem* like fifty years—but I cannot be sure which memories are false, and which are real.

Present and past are inextricably entangled. The monitor screen has just shown the ceremony at Tranquillity Base, culminating with the *third* hoisting of the American flag. It was blown down, of course, by the blast of *Eagle*'s ascent stage, and lay there on the trampled Moon soil for thirty-six years until the Apollo Historical Committee reerected it. Then the big quake of 2009 knocked it down again; this time, we're assured, it would take a direct hit by a fair-sized meteor to lower it. . . .

Now, immediately after the live transmission from Tranquillity, they've put on a grainy old tape—yes, *tape*, not vidule!—from exactly half a century ago. And there I am back in the CBS Studio on West 57th Street with dear old Walter Cronkite and wise-cracking Wally Schirra, watching Neil Armstrong take that first step off the ladder. . . .

For the hundredth time, I strain my ears. Neil Armstrong once told me (and by then he must have been heartily fed up with the whole subject), "What I *intended* to say was: 'That's one small step for a man, one giant leap for mankind.' And that's what I *thought* I said."

Sorry, Neil—you fluffed! The "a" got short-circuited between brain and tongue. But it doesn't matter; this time, at least, history has been correctly reedited.

Did I ever imagine, back in 1969, that I would reach the Moon myself? I very much doubt it; yet I'd anticipated the circumstances more than twenty years earlier. If I may be allowed the modest cough of the minor prophet—

(AUTOSEC MARK III: THAT PHRASE ALREADY USED IN LAST THREE DOCUMENT FILES.
Shut up, Hal, or I'll reprogram you.)

—as I was saying before I was rudely interrupted, I'd already thought of a very good reason why I might be on the Moon for my hundredth birthday.

In the summer of '47, writing in exercise books "liberated" during my Royal Air Force days from a bombed-out school in the East End of London, I concluded my first full-length novel, *Prelude to Space*, with these words:

> The great medical discoveries made at the lunar base had come just in time to save him. Under a sixth of a gravity, where a man weighed less than thirty pounds, a heart which would have failed on Earth could still beat strongly for years. There was even a possibility—almost terrifying in its social implications—that the span of human life might be greater on the Moon than upon the Earth.
>
> Far sooner than anyone had dared to hope, astronautics had paid its greatest and most unexpected dividend. Here within the curve of the Apennines, in the first of all cities ever to be built outside the Earth, five thousand exiles were living useful and happy lives, safe from the deadly gravity of their own world. . . .

Had I thought of it, I could have added another reason. Some thirty years after those words were written, Earth's "deadly gravity" killed my own mother. A very common cause of death among old people is complications following the breaking of bones after a fall. Such an accident is virtually impossible here on the Moon.

"Five thousand" was, I am afraid, a wildly optimistic figure: The present population at Clavius is only one thousand, and that includes administrative and technical staff. But in 1947, very few people would have bet on more than zero.

And if I may switch to my "minor prophet" mode again, I'd like to refer to "Out of the Cradle, Endlessly Orbiting . . . ," written in June 1958 (the summer of the first satellites). It began: "Before we start, I'd like to point out something that a good many people seem to have overlooked. The twenty-first century does *not* begin tomorrow; it begins a year later, on January 1, 2001. . . . Every hundred years we astronomers have to explain this all over again, but it makes no difference. The celebrations start just as soon as the two zeros go up. . . ."

That could be my first mention of 2001—ten years before "Also Sprach Zarathustra" blasted from a thousand speaker systems. (Hello, Stanley—were you involved in putting up that big 1 by 4 by 9 black slab in Tycho on my hundredth birthday? I'm delighted to hear that you're finally shooting *Napoleon*. But what's this rumor about a happy ending, with the French winning at Waterloo?)

(IRRELEVANT TO SUBJECT.
Phooey. INTERRUPT OVERRIDE. *That'll* fix you!)

Where was I? Oh, yes—"Out of the Cradle . . ." It takes place during a very tense moment on the Moon—the first test of the thermonuclear engine for the Mars expedition. Then, to the great annoyance of the narrator—the Russian in charge of operations—everything suddenly stops. The secret has been very well kept: He had no idea. . . .

> There was a click as the circuit was rerouted, followed by a pause full of indeterminate shufflings and whisperings. And then, all over the Moon and half the Earth, came the noise I promised to tell you about—the most awe-inspiring sound I've ever heard in my life.
>
> It was the thin cry of a newborn baby—the first child in all the history of mankind to be brought forth on another world than Earth. We looked at each other in the suddenly silenced blockhouse, and then at the ships we were building out there on the blazing lunar plain. They had seemed so important a few minutes ago. They still were—but not as important as what had happened over there in Medical Centre, and would happen again billions of times on countless worlds down all the ages to come.
>
> For that was the moment, gentlemen, when I knew that Man had *really* conquered space.

Well, that was fiction, back in 1958; now it's fact—though it took a little longer to happen than I had imagined. This is always a problem with technological extrapolation: short-range forecasts tend to be too optimistic, long-range ones usually underestimate. Who could have dreamed how many cars or telephones there would be in the world, a mere fifty years after they were invented?

Certainly none of us early Space Cadets imagined that, after the United States's six landings on the Moon, it would be more than a generation before men returned there. Yet with the twenty-twenty foresight that history gives, that now seems inevitable; we should have learned a lesson from the two closest parallels in the past.

The South Pole was first reached in 1911 by the most primitive of means—skis and sleds. Then it was abandoned; not until almost half a century later it was *inhabited*. When men returned to the Pole, they used aircraft, radio, tractors, nuclear energy. And they settled there in comfort; there was even a sauna at the American base. My old friend Wernher von Braun once told me he'd rolled naked in the snow at the South Pole, which would certainly have astonished Scott and Amundsen. . . .

The other historic parallel is much less famous, but in some ways it's even more instructive.

In 1930, Dr. William Beebe and Otis Barton made the first descent into the ocean abyss. Enclosed in a tiny steel sphere suspended from a cable, a "bathysphere," they eventually reached a depth of almost a kilometer. Beebe was acutely aware of the similarity to space exploration. In his 1935 book *Half Mile Down*—my copy was too battered (and too heavy) to bring with me, alas—he wrote: "Until I am actually enclosed within some futuristic rocket and start on a voyage into interstellar space, I shall never experience such a feeling of complete isolation from the surface of the planet Earth as when I dangled in a hollow pea on a swaying cobweb a quarter of a mile below the deck of a ship rolling in mid-ocean."

But the bathysphere was a dead end—a pioneering experiment never to be repeated. A quarter of a century later, the Piccards developed the free-diving bathyscaphe, which by 1960 had reached the maximum ocean depth of almost eleven kilometers in the Marianas Trench.

Superb technological achievement though it was, the Saturn V rocket that took the first men to the Moon was also a technological dead end; someone once compared it to an ocean liner that carried three passengers and sank at the end of its maiden voyage. Before space travel became practical, it had to be superseded by the fully reusable shuttles and interorbit ferries that we have today.

And their development required more resources in money and engineering skills than any single nation—even the United States—could possibly muster. More than these, it demanded political will, and a degree of international cooperation that we now take for granted but which, back in the dangerous decade of the eighties, often seemed impossible of achievement.

Looking back now, I think I can pinpoint the exact day when the tide began to turn—though it still took many years for the era of sterile confrontation to end. The date was October 30, 1984, when President Reagan signed Senate Joint Resolution 236, "Relating to cooperative East–West ventures in space." I still have the copy that the resolution's sponsor, Senator Spark Matsunaga, presented to me in Hawaii a few weeks later.

It opens with the words:

> Whereas the United States and the Soviet Union could soon find themselves in an arms race in space, which is in the interest of no one. . . .

and ends with:

> *Resolved by the Senate and House of Representatives of the United States of America in Congress assembled*, That the President should—
>
> (1) endeavor, at the earliest practical date, to renew the 1972–1977 agreement between the United States and the Soviet Union on space cooperation for peaceful purposes;
>
> (2) continue energetically to gain Soviet agreement to the recent United States proposal for a joint simulated space rescue mission; and
>
> (3) seek to initiate talks with the Government of the Soviet Union, and with other governments interested in space activities, to explore further opportunities for cooperative East–West ventures in space including cooperative ventures in such areas as space medicine and space biology, planetary science, manned and unmanned space exploration.

Those were noble aspirations, and I am happy that, despite many disappointments and setbacks, the president lived to see them fulfilled. . . .

I'm afraid I'll have to finish this later—the monitor's just switched to Neil and Buzz and I want to hear what they've got to say.

At eighty-eight and eighty-nine, respectively, they both look in pretty good shape.

Considering they stayed on Earth.

Opposite page: A permanent space station will be the first step toward setting up way stations from which to explore other worlds.

JULY 20, 1969:

A 2019

INTERPRETATION

OF THE

APOLLO

MOON LANDING

THE PATH TO 2019
An excerpt from the inaugural speech delivered by the President of the United States in January 1993

America's space movement has been touched by tragedy on numerous occasions over the last three decades. In January of 1967, a tragic pad fire at Cape Kennedy not only took the lives of three of NASA's finest astronauts, but also jeopardized the very future of this nation's space program, halting Apollo spaceflights for a period of over twenty-one months. Then, in 1986, again in the month of January, the shuttle ship *Challenger* exploded seventy-three seconds into its voyage, killing seven brave American explorers, including a high school teacher who had, in vain, prepared her lesson plans for space. Who cannot remember, only seven years ago, this terrifying spectacle—the sickly stream of black smoke, the burst of angry white and orange flames, the hail of debris that fell over the Atlantic Ocean, the funerals for our fallen heroes?

Today, as I speak to you, we are in the midst of another space tragedy of far more terrifying proportions. The astronauts who perished in 1967 and in 1986 at least died in the furtherance of a cause: the exploration of space, the discovery of celestial bodies, the scientific understanding of our universe's origins. The tragedy that afflicts us today is not the stuff of bold newspaper headlines; it produces neither flames that sear the morning sky nor the anguished sighs of relatives that make the news at six. This tragedy's victims are not bodies, but a nation's extinguished spirit. Apathy rarely, in fact, makes news at all. The last two decades, an era stretching from 1973 through 1993, has produced no tangible progress in space exploration. This record constitutes a tragedy of the greatest national proportions.

I'm deeply saddened by many of our senators and representatives in Congress who question the need for a manned space station, even with the knowledge that the Soviet Union has been expanding its *Mir* space station ever since it was placed in orbit just days after our *Challenger* astronauts died. It's imperative—for medicine, for industry, and for reasons of national pride—that America send its own perma-

Previous page: The Apollo 11 expedition. "Apollo," said astronomer Thomas Gold, "was buying a Rolls-Royce, but leaving it in the garage because you can't afford the gas."

nently manned space station into orbit before the end of this century—an event that I hope to witness while still in office. I'm also quite appalled at people saying that America cannot land on Mars before 2035. That's absurd. In 1969, the greatest scientific minds of our age predicted that by the end of the Vietnam War, we would have sent a manned mission to Mars—by 1985 at the latest. That mission would have provided an appropriate new focus for American industry and technology. Today, in 1993, we have sadly to revise this schedule. I'm confident that if we renew our efforts to probe the Martian soil, we'll be able to do it by 2010.

And finally, I'm saddened that we have no current plans to return to the moon. Can it really be that astronaut Gene Cernan was the last American to walk on the Moon? "We leave the Moon as we came," he said, "and God willing, we shall return, with peace and hope for all mankind." An entire generation of Americans has been born since the explorer from Apollo 17 uttered those words twenty-one years ago, and *man* is still not willing.

Distinguished Cornell astronomer Thomas Gold described our space malaise more succinctly. "Apollo," he said, "was buying a Rolls-Royce, but leaving it in the garage because you can't afford the gas." The term I begin today will be dedicated to finding the fuel that is needed to establish a permanent lunar base, a fuel that comes as much from the collective mind and will of the American people as it does from the national budget. It will be a term consumed by a national mission to refocus America's sights on space. In undertaking this brave agenda we will bring to an end the era of space apathy that has laid waste to so much native promise and ambition. And if we are indeed successful in our plans, we will not only have sent a space station into orbit and a manned probe to Mars, but also returned to the Moon with a permanent lunar base and settlers, on or before July 20, 2019, the fiftieth anniversary of our first Apollo Moon landing."

LOOKING BACKWARD
A historian of 2019 interprets
the first Moon landing.

In the distant summer of 1969, the first Apollo Moon landing seemed to validate the American character at a time when national esteem was on the wane. The Moon walks of NASA astronauts Neil Armstrong and Buzz Aldrin could be celebrated as something quintessentially American, a triumph that brought the spirit of the westward migration out of a previous century and into the age of space. The Apollo 11 Moon mission stirred as much national pride as the Bicentennial celebration that would come seven years later; it generated as much fanfare as the dawn of the new century in the year 2001. But the Apollo triumph was not appreciated only by Americans; it was celebrated by millions of people throughout the world, who had shared the dreams of such space prophets as Galileo, Jules Verne, and H. G. Wells of sending men to the Moon. On that momentous Sunday, July 20, 1969, the Moon landing seemed to alter the course of human history far more profoundly than any international hostilities ever could, for it spoke of change, of peace, and of a future that seemed almost limitless in its grand design.

Despite the ambitious visions that the Apollo mission inspired, the successful landing came at a time, ironically, when interest in space in the halls of Congress was on the decline. The Apollo program represented the last triumph of the American space movement for a period of close to three decades.

President John F. Kennedy's declaration that the United States would land on the Moon "before this [the 1960s] decade is out" was a prophecy that came true with but five months to spare. But was there a future beyond these trips to the Moon? How would NASA survive once Apollo was done and gone? Throughout the mid-1960s, the Apollo missions had all along benefited from the ultimate romantic allure of a Moon landing. Any effort to thwart the path of NASA would have been considered almost unpatriotic, the repudiation of a fallen saint who had prophesied a Moon voyage two years before his fall in Dallas.

Yet there were those who anticipated a Dark Age for space exploration in the thirty-year period following the triumph of Apollo. A few experts, even in 1969, pondered whether the enthusiasm could be sustained to facilitate a similar landing on Mars or even a permanent lunar base. Wernher von Braun, the renowned twentieth-century pioneer of space rocketry, questioned how long federal funding would survive in a post-Apollo age. The United States had poured over $36 billion (in 2019 dollars, $720 billion!) into the exploration of space since the beginning of its race with the Soviets; von Braun predicted in July 1969 that without the national goal of another space conquest and without a continued Soviet space threat, the cajolery of NASA administrators would no longer sway the policy-makers of Washington. The space movement, without a large budget, would, like Carnaby Street boutiques and Lyndon Johnson's Great Society, become a victim of its time, a fleeting triumph of the culture of the 1960s.

Yet the crowds that came out to watch the blast-off at 9:32 A.M. on July 16 reflected the frenzy of the moment. Close to a million people, in addition to three thousand reporters, lined the highways leading to Cape Kennedy, forming a procession that snaked for miles. Observers likened the scene to a religious pilgrimage from the Crusades. So intense was America's interest in the Apollo mission that the discovery of a twenty-eight-year-old secretary's body trapped underwater in an Oldsmobile (a car model still popular in the 1960s) driven by a senator bearing the name Kennedy hardly made the front page.

Five days after blast-off, *The New York Times*, then still printed on paper, devoted its entire front page to the Moon landing, recording the more mundane events of July 20, 1969 on an inside page. It was, by all appearances, a normal summer Sunday. Melvin and Myra Goldberg, the *Times* reported in its slice-of-life profile of the nation, drove from suburban Scarsdale to visit their children in summer camp in New York's Adirondack Mountains. In New Orleans, Miss Ella Allen celebrated the Apollo landing by hurling herself from the ferry landing at Jackson Avenue into the waters of the Mississippi River. "Dear Lord, here I come," she cried just before two policemen halted her journey to her maker.

Yet it is difficult to claim that life on that languid Sunday continued at a normal pace. The Moon landing produced a nationalistic passion in Americans not seen since the end of World War II, and it inspired pride and keen interest from countries throughout the world. The Apollo 11 success came in the midst of the Vietnam War—perhaps the most controversial and internally divisive war in American history—and seemed to validate the American character as much as the war's napalm bombings had sullied it. Like the nineteenth-century exploration of the American West, the Moon landing fulfilled the notion of Manifest Destiny, for the Earth, in 1969, had been fully charted, and space represented the last frontier. The Apollo 11 mission, then, was a twentieth-century revival of the frontier drama of a forgotten age, with astronauts Armstrong, Aldrin, and Collins heirs to the grand legacy of Christopher Columbus, Lewis and Clark, and Charles Lindbergh.

In contrast to the Spanish, French, and English who had settled in the New World, the heroes of 1969 seemed hardly motivated by self-interest or colonial greed. A 1967 treaty, signed by nearly a hundred countries, protected the international sovereignty of the Moon, and a belief grew that space would remain free of the colonial, Cold War passions that had divided the planet. Konstantin Tsiolkovsky, the Russian space theorist, had, in fact, believed as early as the late nineteenth century that space would be free of the petty rivalries that afflicted the Earth. The 1969 Apollo venture represented the zenith of such idealism. Scientific pursuit in space, it was then believed, would transcend the pettiness and strife on Earth, and would ultimately deliver man onto a new level of human consciousness. The Moon landing ushered in a fleeting era of idealism that attempted to resurrect a patriarchal image of the United States that had been tarnished in the twenty-four years since the end of World War II.

This excitement reverberated not only through the corridors of NASA, but also through the entire nation. A revolution was in progress on many levels. The United States, in 1969, was undergoing profound social and cultural changes.

As the Apollo 11 mission culminated the American space revolution, the Woodstock concert of 1969 idealized the spirit of the so-called sixties youth movement. Woodstock was a nonstop, three-day affair that featured the top rock musicians of its day and attracted over 300,000 enthusiastic young spectators to a dairy farm in upstate New York. Buried under the dozens of Moon landing stories that ran in *The New York Times* on July 20, 1969, was an understated advertisement for the Woodstock Music & Art Fair, an "Aquarian Exposition" promising "three days of peace and music." Most of the newspaper's Sunday readers, spellbound by the breaking news from the Moon, concentrated on the heroics of Armstrong and Aldrin, only glancing at the Woodstock announcement that included such names as Joan Baez, Arlo Guthrie, Janis Joplin, and the Grateful Dead—musicians popular in our grandparent's generation. Yet the dizzying spectacle of the Woodstock concert, held three weeks later on the meadows of dairy farmer Max Yasgur, mirrored the revolutionary culture of the 1960s as accurately as the Moon landing reflected the goals of the American space movement.

Many senior citizens, especially those now over seventy, can recall the social import of the legendary festival. It's difficult to imagine that our grandmothers wore mini-skirts that revealed the bottom of their buttocks, that our grandfathers' hair once cascaded down their backs, and that their states of consciousness seemed eternally altered by LSD, then an illegal recreation. But to that generation the concert was the apotheosis of a rebellious spirit that swept the age, and the era—the Woodstock Generation—actually drew its name from the three raucous days of music and revelry that punctuated the humid summer of 1969. Those youths believed that the white male power structure that had existed in the United States since the founding of the Union was about to crumble, yielding to a communal society that stressed love over war, socialism over materialism, drugs over sobriety, and orgies over abstinence. About the generation's pacifist nature, the Sullivan County sheriff, Louis Ratner, commented after the concert, "I never met a nicer bunch of kids in my life."

This announcement from a festival ad in *The New York Times* of July 20 reveals the mood of the 1960s:

> **Art Show**—Paintings and sculptures on trees, on grass, surrounded by the Hudson Valley, will be displayed. Accomplished artists, "Ghetto" artists, and would-be artists will be glad to discuss their work, or the unspoiled splendor of the surroundings, or anything else that might be on your mind.

> **Crafts Bazaar**—If you like creative knickknacks and old junk, you'll love roaming around our bazaar. You'll see imaginative leather, ceramic, bead, and silver creations, as well as Zodiac Charts, camp clothes, and worn-out shoes.

Every forty years, as if cyclically programmed, our nation seems to undergo a crisis of values that threatens its most sturdy social foundations. In the 1920s, the proliferation of assembly-line automobiles and the explosive growth of the city threatened the moral fiber of a small-town America that had predominated since colonial days. The flapper of the Roaring Twenties tore off her corset as defiantly as the hippie of the late sixties burned her bra, as vehemently as the greenie of 2011 rejected her mother's synthetic clothes.

The antitechnological anticomputer revolution—the so-called War for Humanity—that began in this country around 2005, exactly forty years after the first student protests against the Vietnam War, must be viewed in light of the unrest of the 1920s and 1960s. Millions of youths—the greenies—rejected the pervasiveness of computers and robots in their lives, took to the streets to protest the corporate values that they saw as strangling everything virtuous and human. Indeed, the generation that comprises America's grandparents—the hippies—has more in common with its grandchildren—the greenies—than the parents corseted uncomfortably in between.

Reflecting on the vanished summer of 1969, the events of the Apollo Moon landing and the Woodstock concert seem disparate and disconnected, to say the least. The one, man's momentous arrival on the Moon, reflected the crowning accomplishment of the American scientific establishment. Here was a group of men who had used the most sophisticated aerospace and engineering technology to send man away from his home planet. It was a group that had the patina of the military—men dressed in starched white shirts, men with stiff crew cuts, men engaged in brusque, now archaic, dialogue that always ended with "Roger." The other event, the three-day, rain-soaked mud frolic at Woodstock, which culminated in Jimi Hendrix's hard-rock rendition of "The Star-Spangled Banner," projected the antithesis of a Houston Mission Control room. The hippies who frolicked naked in the lily ponds at Woodstock that August preferred Navajo beads to NASA spacesuits, a marijuana "joint" to a cool glass of Tang. To them, the military was a national anathema, responsible for forty thousand deaths in Vietnam, and the Pentagon was the hated symbol of the war they all dreaded.

Yet the two events converged in a way few would recognize even today. In wholly different ways, both events affirmed the peaceful nature of humanity and acted to unify a divided people. Citizens in their seventies or older can remember quite distinctly these two events, even without the aid of the memory-enhancing vasopressin drugs that have become so popular in recent years. Along with the Kennedy assassination of 1963, the July Moon landing seems to remain the most vivid memory to people born before the year 1960. Of course, the Moon landing altered the course of human history far more profoundly than any band performing on Max Yasgur's farm could have hoped to, but both spoke of change, of peace, and of a future that then seemed, after many barren years, finally imbued with a far-reaching vision.

To modernists of the twenty-first century, the spirit of 1969 seems charmingly naive, akin perhaps to Woodrow Wilson's belief that he could "save the world for democracy" or Neville Chamberlain's declaration of "peace in our time." But who can fault our grandparents for having possessed this spirit? Caught up in the excitement of an event that was being compared to Columbus's discovery of the New World, who would have known in 1969 that the Apollo mission would leave man unchanged? Who could have known that the international euphoria would not linger beyond summer's end? And who would have known that space in the decades that followed would become as armed and as colonially fractured as the African continent in the nineteenth century?

The astronauts—Neil Armstrong, Buzz Aldrin, and Mike Collins—lacked such insights on July 20, 1969. They were, quite understandably, excited about landing on the Moon, but theirs seemed solely a scientific mission. The Apollo flight easily could have not come off at all. Following the tragic Apollo 1 fire in January 1967, no missions were attempted for twenty-one months. When the next Apollo mission was launched in 1968, the national view of space had changed substantially. By that time the budget had become a key issue. The astronauts would have to demonstrate tangible scientific results if funding were to continue.

"The emphasis had shifted from the time of Kennedy's term," Buzz Aldrin remembered. "It had shifted from an American putting a flag on the Moon to a *human being* bringing back rocks. Because the public in 1969 wanted more justification for the expenditure, we had to change the reason for going. Nor was our reason to beat the Russians," Aldrin said. "Yes, Kennedy had committed us to a race, but we had uncommitted ourselves, and the new causes were for science and the understanding of Earth's evolution."

The Apollo mission had, in fact, several scientific goals. The astronauts would attempt to measure solar wind and trap atmospheric particles, calculate the distance from the Moon to the Earth by an accuracy of six inches, set up equipment that would search for tremors or quakes on the Moon's surface, and bring back about eighty pounds of lunar dust, soil, and rocks for analysis by over a hundred scientists from nine participating nations.

The flight was marked by tension, most of it unanticipated. Unknown either to the astronauts or to their commanders at NASA, an unmanned Soviet craft had been launched on Sunday, July 13, three days before the Apollo blast-off. What was Luna's mission? Was it to observe the Apollo landing? Could the robotic craft rescue American astronauts if they became stranded? The trouble was that the Soviets had on record the trajectory of the Apollo mission, but the Americans had no inkling of the path of the robotic Luna probe. Frank Borman, who had been an astronaut and had top scientific connections in Moscow, called the head of the Soviet Institute of Science in the middle of the night. Even he was unable to get a satisfactory answer. "What damn near happened that is realized by very few people is that a Russian spacecraft crashed onto the Moon in the vicinity of our own landing site. Had Luna 15 been successful in removing rocks from the Moon's surface and returning them to Earth, the story would have been quite a bit different," Aldrin explained years later.

The actual landing occurred on the evening of July 20, and brought tensions of a different sort. The LM, or lunar module—called *Eagle*—carried two days' worth of oxygen and food in its shell, weighed 52,000 pounds, and measured twenty-two feet in length. On the far side of the Moon, Aldrin fired the LM's engines to begin the landing. The lunar craft slowed and dropped about twenty-six nautical miles in its final descent. One hundred feet short of landing, Armstrong and Aldrin spotted a crater the size of a football field, and Armstrong had to steer the craft manually another two hundred to three hundred feet to avoid rocky terrain that was unfit for landing.

Had the craft descended atop a pile of boulders, as appeared imminent, the men's return would have been imperiled. The LM could have easily tipped over. Despite the presence of the robotic Soviet craft, there could be no rescue from the Moon's surface. Thomas Paine, director of NASA in 1969, said, "The landing operation on the Moon was by far the most critical task of the mission," a belief seconded by Buzz Aldrin, who felt that his and Neil Armstrong's lunar walk was an anticlimax to the landing of the lunar module.

At precisely 4:18 P.M., on July 20, the module made physical contact with the Sea of Tranquillity. The American craft scattered lunar dust in

Opposite page: Artist Norman Rockwell's vision of man's first step on the Moon.

all directions. The soil, the two men would soon discover, was like malleable clay or sand. "Tranquillity Base here. The *Eagle* has landed," reported Commander Armstrong. In the Bronx, New York, the Yankees halted their play and sixteen thousand people sang "The Star-Spangled Banner." In Washington, D.C., President Richard Nixon, four years before his fall from grace, communicated with the astronauts by radiotelephone. Across the world, more television viewers watched the landing and the subsequent walk than any other single event in the history of the planet, before 1969.

The actual walk began at 10:56 P.M. on the evening of July 20. Hundreds of millions of people followed the event with spellbound intensity. Neil Armstrong, a child of the depression, the son of a state auditor from Wapakoneta, Ohio, the commander of the Gemini 8 space-docking flight, took nine steps down an aluminum ladder. Planting his feet solidly on the lunar surface, Armstrong declared, "That's one small step for man; one giant leap for mankind." Armstrong's words, among the most famous and often quoted phrases of America's post-war era, would be repeated by millions of schoolchildren in that time. There have been historical parallels, but it had been almost a complete century since an exploration event so totally stirred the public's imagination. Like Dr. David Livingston and Henry Morton Stanley in the nineteenth century, Armstrong and Aldrin were the heroes of their time. Armstrong seemed a modern-day Christopher Columbus. His *Eagle* was a high-tech reincarnation of the *Santa Maria*, and his crew had not merely opened a virgin continent to a race of Caucasians, but the entire Moon to all of man.

Even today, as we approach the end of this second decade of the twenty-first century, the Moon remains frontier territory, like the continent of Antarctica in the 1980s, the realm of only a few scientists. So many questions have yet to be answered. The Moon's geographic and atmospheric qualities are only now being demystified, so one can imagine the trepidation that Armstrong and Aldrin felt on July 20, 1969. Since the Moon's gravity is only one-sixth that of Earth's, an astronaut who weighed 210 pounds in Houston would weigh only thirty-five pounds in the lunar environment. As Aldrin and Armstrong learned, mobility was very easy, since the body used less oxygen and water. Stopping and turning—motions that involve traction—were far more difficult. Also, the lunar soil, as scientists in more recent voyages can verify, proved far harsher and more inhospitable than NASA had anticipated. Aldrin, in fact, had so much trouble with the Moon's soil that he was unable to plant his equipment deeply enough to carry out a solar wind test. Armstrong encountered similar difficulties in staking a mylar-constructed American flag into the lunar ground.

In spite of these obstacles, the Moon landing proved to be an enormous technological triumph in many respects, not the least of which was satellite transmission. One has to remember that commercial television was barely twenty years old then. It was a cultural phenomenon that had not even existed at the end of World War II. Color television had just begun to enter American homes in 1964, while cable television, home satellite dishes, VCRs, and holograms were simply unfathomable. But here, on July 20, close to 202 million Americans, not to mention millions of others around the world, were watching *on a live television transmission* this lunar pas de deux. How were Armstrong and Aldrin coming in so loud and clear? Each man had a microphone attached to his space helmet that relayed sounds into the receiving equipment in the lunar module. Not only sounds, but also atmospheric pressure, module information, and even heartbeat measurements were then relayed from *Eagle* via satellite to a radio telescope—an Earth satellite dish, of sorts—in Goldstone, California, where it was then passed on to the Goddard Space Center in Maryland. Had John Kennedy realized how intricate and sophisticated the technology would have to be to land a man on the Moon, would he still have issued his challenge, before Congress, in 1961?

On the day after the landing, July 21, the lunar explorers prepared for their departure from Tranquillity Base. "You're cleared for take-off," spoke the voice of Mission Control. Aldrin replied, "Roger, understand. We're Number One on the runway." It was 1:54 P.M. as the top portion of the *Eagle* module lifted off from the Sea of Tranquillity. The engines had been tested over three thousand times, for there could be no failure. The lower section of the lunar craft remained where it had alit just $21\frac{1}{2}$ hours before—now a permanent monument on the Moon, inscribed with the words:

HERE MEN FROM THE PLANET-EARTH

FIRST SET FOOT UPON THE MOON

JULY 1969 A.D.

WE CAME IN PEACE FOR ALL MANKIND

Neil Armstrong's footprint on the Moon, July 20, 1969: Even as he took this first step on the lunar surface, Congress already was preparing to scale down America's space program.

An astronaut who weighs 210 pounds in Houston weighs but thirty-five in the lunar environment.

As *Eagle* lifted off that afternoon, the American flag that Armstrong had planted toppled over. Its stars and stripes rested impassively on the Sea of Tranquillity's soil, an image that suggested not so much America's pusillanimity but the Moon's feral and indomitable will. About four hours later, *Eagle*, now a passive vehicle, rendezvoused with the mother ship, *Columbia*, on the far side of the Moon.

July 20, 1969: One small step for man . . . (©NASA)

Left: Man has created the robot as a tool . . .
(© Robert Malone)

Below: . . . but that tool may become his successor.
(© Robert Malone)

Opposite: Meet the employee of the future. No pension needed, and it has a résumé as long as your actuator.
(© Dan McCoy)

Following: The robots of 2019 will be able to see, feel, and in general have a keener sense of their world.
(© Robert Malone)

The hoopla that had surrounded the lunar landing of July 20 would continue for several weeks. Having survived reentry, *Columbia* first appeared as a tiny orange speck in the Pacific sky, several hundred miles southwest of Hawaii, on the morning of July 24, 1969. "Gee, you look great!" President Nixon exclaimed from the U.S.S. *Hornet* as he looked through the window of the astronauts' quarantine compartment. "This," the president added, "is the greatest week in the history of the world since the creation." It was a political irony, not entirely lost on his Democratic opponents, that Nixon was able to take credit for the spectacular Moon landing, a national experiment that had been launched eight years earlier by a liberal Democrat from Massachusetts. But in this moment of triumph, not even the liberal press of 1969—those hundreds of reporters and editors who had, according to Nixon, unfairly savaged his career since the late 1940s—dared write unkindly about the head of state. Like the Armistices of 1918 and 1945, the Moon landing acted as a healing agent, an event that unified the nation's divided people in a display of celebration and unabashed patriotism. The seemingly endless war in Vietnam had blessedly been banished from the front pages. Its victims' stories would be rendered silent, for at least a month or two, by the feats accomplished on the twentieth of July.

While the three astronauts celebrated in their quarantined Lunar Receiving Laboratory, administrators at NASA were far less sanguine about the future of space. There was every reason to believe that Wernher von Braun's fears about funding in the post-Apollo age would sadly be realized. The Apollo landing of July 20, as spectacular as it was, seemed like a "flash in the pan," for the mission came when NASA's budget had been sharply curtailed. Without a space schedule that included the constant display of new fireworks, the public would grow restless, and Congress would divert the funds to other projects.

True to course, the next twenty-five years proved disappointing in space exploration. The intense fervor that enveloped that day in July dissipated in the subsequent years. The original Moon landing became like a beacon whose brightness was shrouded each passing year by a thicker layer of fog. The public's fascination with space lay dormant throughout the 1970s and 1980s, momentarily awakened here and there with the blaze of a comet or the explosion of a shuttle, but lacking the commitment to sustain the spirit of July 20, 1969. In fact, the predictions made by space experts in 1969 were far too optimistic. Sir

Bernard Lovell, for example, writing in the *Bulletin of the Atomic Scientists* in August 1969, predicted that the United States would send a manned mission to Mars between 1980 and 1985. Lovell's contemporaries, commenting on the post-Apollo age, were certain that a space lab would be in orbit before the end of the seventies, and that a permanent lunar base—a closed environment, a habitat made partly of lunar materials—would be a virtual certainty before the end of the century.

No one could have foreseen, on that historic Sunday in 1969, that only twelve Americans would set foot on the Moon before the year 2000, and that Apollo 17 would make the twentieth century's last manned lunar landing. The spirit of July 20, 1969 was not, in fact, revived until the President's inauguration speech of 1993. Like Kennedy's speech in 1961, it spoke of commitment to space and set the country on a course for the future. Space itself became the vehicle of political power, space's mandate the mandate of the president. The universal excitement in 1969 was carried forth by younger generations, so that the costs of the space laboratory and the manned mission to Mars no longer seemed prohibitive.

While America's new lunar base brings new hope to space exploration, one goal of that 1993 speech remains unrealized even in this twenty-first century. Imagine if Columbus had discovered the New World in 1492 and no settlers had returned? Imagine if the words of the first navigator of Australia, who said, "I've now mapped this continent so thoroughly that no one need ever go back there again," had been heeded?

But the Puritans and the Quakers made the perilous journey to the American colonies, and to the Australian continent came prisoners and brave pioneers. Why should our own twenty-first century be different? Our planet is infinitely more crowded today than it was at the beginning of the seventeenth century. Political oppression and religious persecution have hardly been tempered over the last four hundred years. Overpopulation threatens to destroy the planet over the next decade. The need for emigration to distant terrains is, in fact, more pressing than it has ever been.

"We shall return, with peace and hope for all mankind," were the departing words of the last Apollo astronaut on the Moon in 1973. That's already forty-six years ago. It's 2019, and a permanent lunar base is hardly sufficient. We must return not only with a hardy band of research scientists, but with thousands of settlers, and plant the flag more firmly this time, so that the spirit of the explorers in that summer of 1969 can be celebrated as we approach July 20, 2019.

C H A P

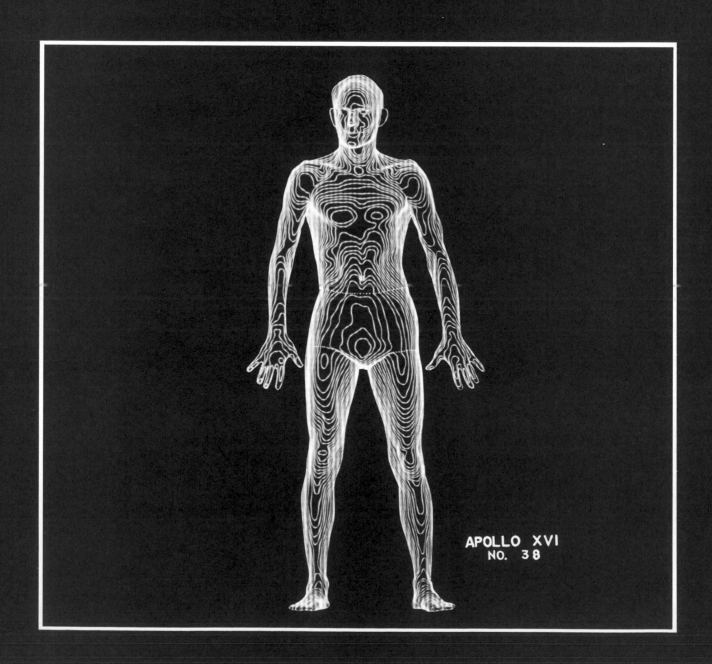

APOLLO XVI
NO. 38

A DAY IN THE HOSPITAL

Commonwealth of California
Department of Health's
Vital Records

CERTIFICATE OF LIFE

Subject:	Baby boy, Miller
Date of Conception:	November 15, 2018; 12:15 P.M.
Place:	Comprehensive Fertility Institute, Beverly Hills, California
Number of Parents:	Three, including surrogate mother—mother donated egg, father sperm
Method of Conception:	In vitro fertilization followed by embryo transfer. Mother's body had rejected her artificial fallopian tube. After 8 days on pergonal tablets, mother produced 2 eggs. Both were removed during routine laparoscopy and screened for possible defects. Eggs united with father's sperm. After 48 hours in incubator, embryos were removed from growth medium and placed in surrogate's womb. Only one embryo attached itself to uterine wall.
Prenatal Care:	Ultrasound at 3 months. Fetal surgery performed at 5 months to correct small defect in bone of right foot.
Date/Time of Birth:	Jason Lawrence Miller born July 20, 2019; 4:15 A.M.
Father:	Jason L. Miller, Sr.
Mothers:	Amy Wong (natural), Maribeth Rivers (surrogate)
Birth Method:	Newly lifed in Morningstar Birthing Center, division of Humana Corporation. Natural delivery after 5-hour labor. Labor pains controlled though acupuncture. Therapeutic touch used for last hour of labor. Child's father, adopted sister, and natural mother attended the delivery.
Weight/Length:	10 lb.; 25 in.

Previous page: Thermographic map of the human body, showing "hot" and "cold" regions. Such research will lead to the super-diagnostic tests of 2019.

Eye Color:	Green
Genetic Profile:	Yunis Test shows missing sub-band on chromosome 5, indicating premature graying of hair. Will be totally gray by age 22.
	Bands on one chromosome upside down; could have fertility problems.
	Nicked chromosome indicates a greater than average vulnerability to lung cancer.
High-Risk Professions:	Any career that would expose individual to possible lung damage: painting, mining, etc.
Body Type:	Mesomorph. Build well suited to contact sports, such as football. To maximize muscle development and athletic ability, should begin exercise program by age 4.
Projected Life Span:	82 years

At one end of the complex there is the flailing of limbs followed by some heavy breathing. The aerobics class is just about over, and in thirty minutes the room will serve as a lecture hall. "Eating Your Way to Good Health" is the topic on the evening of July 20, 2019. On the second floor two new parents share an intimate candlelight dinner, fresh shark with shallots and wild rice. Just around the corner a group of elderly men and women watch the Marx Brothers' *A Night at the Opera*.

Though it resembles a leisure community, this is in fact a hospital. Here, people come into life, their birth certificates bearing enough biological information to form a blueprint of their future. But the hospital has also become a place for the cultivation of wellness, a place where people can rejuvenate themselves, take control of their lives, even restore their spirits.

Beyond this, it is a commercial unit, a business with an eye toward the bottom line, an enterprise that vies with other medical establishments for customers, rather than a social institution intent upon ministering to the physical needs of both rich and poor. The surplus of physicians, the improved health of most Americans, the oversupply of hospital beds, and the escalating cost of high-tech diagnostic tests, as well as a reduction in government funding, has forced the hospital to reevaluate its role in the community.

With some thirty-five years to go, the hospital of 2019 is already taking shape. Consider these projections for the mid-1990s, reported in a study conducted by Arthur D. Little, Inc., for the Health Insurance Association of America:

- The shift of care from inpatient to ambulatory settings will accelerate.
- Hospitals will integrate into corporate structures.
- More companies will offer multiple Health Maintenance Organization (HMO) options.
- Consumers will become increasingly responsible for their own health care, thus putting pressure on insurers to design benefits that reward good health habits and penalize poor ones.

The winds of change have already touched us. Investor-owned firms own or operate one hospital in five: The Humana Corporation owns and runs more than eighty for-profit hospitals worldwide; Hospital Corporation of America owns 250 hospitals and manages two hundred more. A half dozen corporations are making a foray into other areas of health care as well, teaming up with insurance companies and hospital supply houses. According to Dr. Paul Ellwood, former president of the health research group called InterStudy, by the year 2000, six out of every ten Americans will have all their health-care needs, including hospital care and health insurance, provided by perhaps a total of ten companies.

At the same time, the number of hospital admissions will continue to drop, and the average length of stay decrease. Outpatient clinics will carry out much of the surgery performed in this country, eliminating many hospital stays altogether. Using lasers, doctors can now speedily and safely remove warts, moles, even skin cancers in their offices, as well as perform delicate eye surgery without admitting the patient to the hospital.

People who enter the hospital for critical procedures, such as liver and kidney transplants, will recover far more quickly than transplant recipients once did. In fact, in St. Paul and Minneapolis, the average hospital stay for the most common problems has already dropped from 5.3 days in 1983 to 4.3 days in 1984. Doctors are slowly cutting down on the number of tests patients must endure and are discharging patients earlier. When possible, people are recuperating at home.

With such progress, suddenly the very institution committed to bestowing good health finds itself ailing. To bolster their hospitals' flagging income, administrators are going to unprecedented lengths to attract "clients." To make a patient's surroundings more pleasant—even therapeutic—hospital planners are consulting with interior designers. The hospital environment is now seen as a medical tool capable of speeding recovery. Furthermore, fitness courses and diet and alcohol clinics are being added to the roster of hospital programs.

To be sure, the hospital of 2019 will still perform such profound procedures as brain surgery and artificial heart implants. But virtually everything else about it will have changed, including the structure itself. Gone will be the scrubbed and sterile buildings fashioned in the 1950s. In fact, the patient entering a hospital thirty years from now may have a hard time remembering when hospitals weren't aesthetically pleasing. The halls will be bathed in sunlight that streams through dozens of skylights and windows circling the main atrium. Sprays of fresh greenery will decorate the rooms, all of which boast a view of either an atrium or well-groomed grounds. Festive paintings will deck the walls, and in the common areas guests will be greeted by aquarium tanks filled with colorful tropical fish.

The first medical establishments to offer patients quality care in a homelike setting were birthing centers. Some are independently operated, others are affiliated with hospitals. All provide kitchens, rockers, playrooms for the baby's siblings, and basic medical equipment, such as IVs and incubators. Spurred on by the centers' popularity as well as by increasing evidence that factors such as architecture, lights, and furnishings can influence healing, planners have begun to pay more attention to the hospital's form in addition to its content.

At the Planetree Model Hospital Project, an experimental wing located in the Pacific Presbyterian Medical Center in San Francisco, patients enjoy a hotel-like environment. The rooms have bedspreads, potted plants, paintings, and track lighting; patients and their families can prepare snacks or meals in the project's well-stocked kitchen. Even the nursing station, in an effort to break down barriers between patients and staff, is open and indirectly lit.

"Planetree is setting the stage for the future of hospital care," predicts Dr. John Gamble, Pacific Presbyterian's chief of staff. "The incorporation of modern medicine and technology in a setting that upholds the full rights and dignity of the individual patient will add immeasurably to healing."

One study in particular lends weight to Gamble's argument. For eight years, nurses at a Pennsylvania hospital kept detailed notes on patients undergoing gallbladder surgery—the amount of pain that followed the operations, any minor complications that occurred, and the length of the patients' recovery. The researcher who analyzed the data found that one group recovered more slowly and seemed to suffer more pain: the group whose rooms had no view. By contrast, patients who had stayed in rooms overlooking a stand of trees generally went home about a day and a half earlier than the "no-view" patients.

By the year 2019, patients will comparison shop for a hospital, taking into consideration such varied factors as the institution's appearance,

The University of Utah's "thinking" artificial arm: The wearer's thoughts control its every movement.

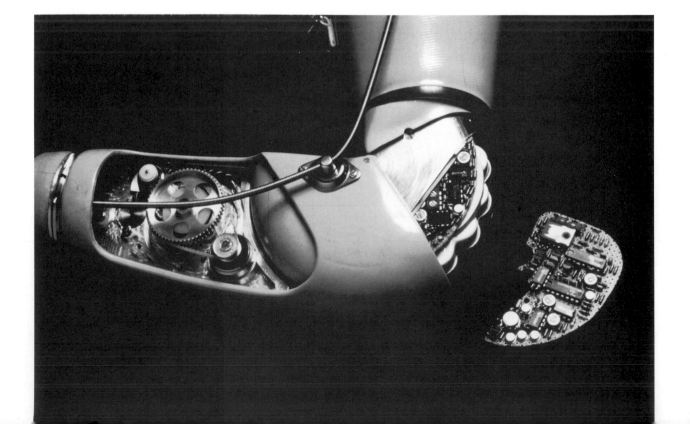

extras it offers, and the costs of certain procedures. In the Columbus, Ohio, region, for example, twenty hospitals joined forces and published a cost comparison guide for patients, listing such diverse offerings as the price of hip surgery and coronary bypass. Across the nation, hospitals are hiring "guest relations" representatives, who see to it that patients receive certain amenities—from gourmet fare to fresh flowers. A few medical centers, hungry for patients, have already begun to tout such items as large-screen televisions, video recorders, and hospital "suites." (One reporter dubbed this competition "the invasion of the bodysnatchers.")

In some cases, the existing amenities will simply be improved. Instead of a candy striper pushing around a rickety little cart supplied with half a dozen Readers Digest Condensed Books and a year's worth of magazines minus their front covers, hospitals will offer a congenial, well-stocked library with extensive files on diseases and their treatment, as well as audio tapes of best-selling novels and special large-print editions of newspapers and literary classics. In the waiting room, soft blue-tinted lights, said to have a soothing effect, will calm anxious patients and their families. As limited visiting hours become a thing of the past, special rooms with extra beds to accommodate family members of critically ill patients will appear in many institutions.

And as Americans take increasing responsibility for their own health, and work to avoid diseases such as cancer and heart disease, hospitals will add wellness programs to their list of offerings. By capitalizing on the national obsession with staying fit, administrators will succeed in finally broadening the hospital's function in the community. The hospital of 2019 will be a resource for those interested in keeping their good health, not simply a sanctuary for the ill.

Administrators have, in just the past few years, looked to Madison Avenue to sell their services and solve the problem of vacant beds and underutilized equipment. There are newspaper advertisements for birthing centers—"design your own private miracle"—and for "hospitels," a hybrid of hospital and hotel. Couples in the twenty-first century will watch late-night television commercials for "feel good" weekends—package deals available from their local hospitals: "While away the three-day weekend in our whirlpool. Consult with our top-notch C-V experts. Heal your body—and mind—at Midvalley Memorial." Clients will check in for a workup that includes a battery of painless tests, a consultation with a nutritionist and three specially prepared meals a day, an antistress program tailored to the client's particular needs, and a workout in the physical therapy facilities. The weekend might be spent doing aerobic exercises, eating low-cholesterol fare, and producing more alpha waves.

A less obvious—though more far-reaching—change will be the complete computerization of the hospital. In hospital billing departments, nurses' stations, medical labs, and at patients' bedsides, the ever-present computer will process, monitor, record, and retrieve all vital information, in effect becoming the "collective conscious" of the entire hospital. To date, more than a hundred hospitals in the U.S. rely on multimillion-dollar computer systems.

Imagine having millions of bits of information basic to the hospital's operation at your fingertips. For nearly every department, from housekeeping to administration, the advantages are innumerable. Manufacturers of software that links clinical data with financial reports contend that such packages will allow hospitals to be run more efficiently and with fewer staff members.

Dozens of systems already exist, each one tailored to the needs of a particular department. For example, one program gives the physician all the available treatments for various illnesses, from pneumonia to gallstones. It breaks down cost of treatment, provides information on expected recovery time, and tells the physician what other physical problems may ensue. Another system, with shades of Big Brother, allows administrators to monitor nurses'—and doctors'—performance and issues an alert when the staff seems to be ordering unnecessary tests or when a patient is not released on schedule.

Until recently, most hospitals have limited the computer's role to the billing department. But doctors, nurses, unit clerks, and other employees are seeing how computers can enhance patient care. Ulticare, a system being tested in a few hospitals throughout the country, replaces one of the most antiquated, yet vital, components of patient care: the patient's chart. Developed by Health Data Sciences Corporation, the program works like this: A nurse slides a specially coded card into the patient's terminal, and the computer kicks up the same information that would be recorded on a chart, plus what must be done next for the patient. The computer also stores information that would normally be scattered throughout the hospital, such as results of lab tests, X rays, and other procedures.

Once a nurse types in the tasks she's performed and makes any other necessary notations, she removes the card. According to physicians who use the system at William Beaumont Hospital System in Royal Oak, Michigan, Ulticare reduces hospital costs and the chances of transcription errors. In addition, the system frees nurses from paperwork, allowing them to spend more time caring for their patients. It even warns personnel of possible medication problems. "It hooks up all start and stop orders for medicine, and broadcasts a panic alert if a lab test shows, for instance, exceptionally high blood sugar," says Mary Ann Keyes, Beaumont's assistant director.

It seems as if the computer's abilities are almost limitless. If so, will the computer eventually replace the practitioner? Are we swiftly approaching the day when a robot will take our temperature and blood pressure, listen to our lungs, swab our throats and do the blood workup, and then feed its data into a computer, which will in turn spit out the diagnosis?

More likely, the computer will be used as a consultant of sorts, the source a doctor turns to for a second opinion, or at least for additional background on a disorder. According to Dr. Robert Wigton, associate professor of medicine at the University of Nebraska, the computer will put a vast amount of medical literature at the physician's disposal—instantly. Wigton envisions a day when a doctor will simply request a patient's X rays, and a voice-activated computer will produce them on a screen alongside the patient's bed. Physicians stumped by a medical mystery will type in all of the clues—results of the patient's tests, his complaints, and his general condition—and ask the computer for its "opinion." Because the latest medical literature will also have been programmed in, doctors will be privy to new treatments that have met with success at other institutions.

Wigton's dream will soon be a reality. Computers are already giving doctors quicker access to X rays and CAT (computerized axial tomography) scans. PACS (picture archival communications systems) promise to save radiology departments time and reduce hospital costs in addition to making patients' medical images and files simultaneously available to physicians in different parts of the hospital. AT&T's Commview, a type of PACS, features computer workstations—in the hospital, as well as in neighboring clinics—that hook into a central image-processing system. A doctor treating the victim of a car accident, for instance, could view the results of a CAT scan at the same time a specialist miles away examines them.

The downside of this technological advance is that some clerical and maintenance jobs will be eliminated as computers take on those tasks that humans once performed by rote. Computer mavens, however, will find openings in medicine, as their skills are needed not only to set up systems, but also to maintain them. Staff members in each department will be trained to feel comfortable referring to, even relying on, the hospital's computer's consciousness.

Just as computers will become the hospital's mind, robots will become the hospital's hands. In the twenty-first century, each hospital will be outfitted with a team of capable, tireless robots to help with duties ranging from emptying bedpans to assisting in brain surgery. Some will be simple instruments resembling the industrial arms used in the auto industry; others will be more sophisticated, able to move about, even "speak," like the lovable C-3PO of *Star Wars* fame. And in every area of the hospital, robotic helpers will ease the work load of their human coworkers. Larry Leifer, a mechanical engineer at Stanford University, predicts that these machines will follow preset paths to hand out meals and drop off fresh linen; do tedious—and often distasteful—lab work, such as processing urine and fecal samples; aid patients undergoing physical therapy by flexing stiff joints; and help out in the operating room, passing instruments to surgeons. They will listen to patients' problems, and in the case of quadriplegics, act as an extension of the patient's own body.

A robot's invulnerability to disease and to the radioactive materials used in nuclear medicine make robotic aides particularly appealing. A robot on wheels could, for instance, deliver radioisotopes from a generator housed in a lead vault to the patient's doctor. Placing an empty vial in the generator, the robot would collect the correct dose and carry it to the physician, minimizing human exposure to the radioactive material. Likewise, mechanical arms could process infectious bacteria and viruses without ever coming down with an illness. Robotic lab assistants could transfer suspected herpes infections to culture tubes or sputum from a tuberculosis victim to a microscope slide.

But not all of the hospitals' robots will be doing the drudge work. The world's first neurosurgical robot, Ole, made his debut in January 1985 when he assisted surgeons at Memorial Medical Center in Long Beach, California. Brain surgeons use the six-jointed mechanical arm as a kind of intelligent hand during certain operations. Locked into

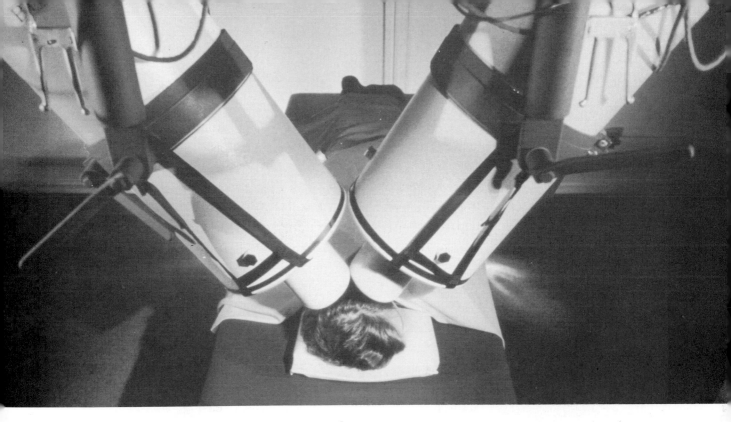

position, Ole holds the drill for the surgeon, allowing the doctor to be accurate to 1/2,000 of an inch when draining cysts or removing tumors.

By the year 2019, mechanized "surgeons" will be a vital part of the operating room (OR) team, responsible for implanting tiny radioactive pellets in the center of tumors, guiding surgical lasers to their targets, applying clamps to the surgical site. Human surgeons may eventually have their own robotic assistants, each trained to respond to its master's voice and to take over the more routine tasks, such as closing an incision, when his human counterpart becomes tired, or work in sync with the surgeon when a steadier hand is needed. Because the surgeon will have programmed his skills, even his personality, into the robot's brain, it will be as if the doctor himself were completing the procedure.

The surgeon of 2019 will not only have a robot as an aide, but thanks to more highly developed diagnostic equipment, he will have a far better idea of his patient's condition and the possible outcome of surgery long before the operation begins. The ideal diagnostic tool for any doctor would be a "feinberg," the hand-held device that made Bones McCoy of *Star Trek* fame look like a Nobel laureate. Passed over the body like a magic wand, the feinberg instantly gave McCoy a diagnosis of the patient's condition. Though not as comprehensive as the feinberg, one experimental instrument, the Dynamic Spatial Reconstructor (DSR), will provide the surgeon with far more critical

Super brain scanners, coupled with computers, seek out human malfunctions and diagnose instantaneously.

information than is currently available without first opening the patient up.

The surgeon performing open-heart surgery or even an artificial heart transplant will first use the DSR to produce a three-dimensional X ray. This device, which was recently developed at the Mayo Clinic in Rochester, Minnesota, allows the physician to do "exploratory surgery" without ever touching the patient. It provides so many pictures of the body that all sides of an organ can be examined before surgery begins.

The operating theater will remain the stage for dozens of latter-day miracles. Virtually every body part will have an artificial counterpart. Prosthetic technology will offer hope to accident victims whose limbs have been smashed beyond repair. Custom-made bones will replace hips ravaged by cancer; bionic arms will respond to the thoughts of their owners. Women who are infertile because of a faulty fallopian tube will conceive with the aid of an artificial one. The deaf will hear; the lame will walk.

Long before 2019, pumps that dispense insulin will be planted under a diabetic's skin, ending the discomfort of daily injections. Eventually, this procedure will become as common as implanting a pacemaker. Artificial hearts, powered by a tiny battery pack worn on a belt, will beat in their owners' chests indefinitely. Transplants will seem nearly as ordinary as tonsillectomies.

The patient of 2019 will expect to participate in decisions about his own care. This goes well beyond seeking a second opinion for certain surgical procedures or choosing the hospital with the best prices. The sagas of coma victim Karen Ann Quinlan and birth-defected baby Jane Doe have tugged at the heartstrings of millions of Americans, prompting them to ask questions about quality, rather than length, of life, and to want control of their own treatment in the event a tragic accident leaves them dependent on a life support system. A growing number of individuals are writing "living wills," which state that under such circumstances no extraordinary measures should be taken to extend their lives.

Patients are also learning to depend on their own healing powers when undergoing treatment for cancer and other life-threatening disease. Evidence is mounting that attitude often affects healing, and those patients physically and mentally able to do so will tap the healer within themselves. The best-known example of this is author Norman

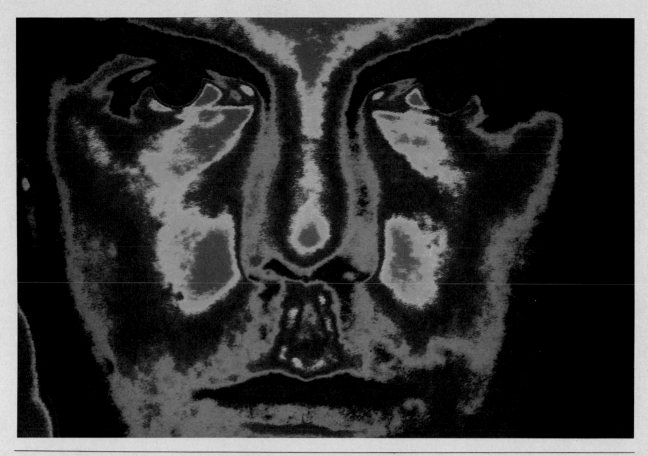

Medicine in 2019 will certainly be high-tech, but hospitals will be humanized to make people feel less like machines. (*Above* © Dan McCoy; *below* © Walter Nelson)

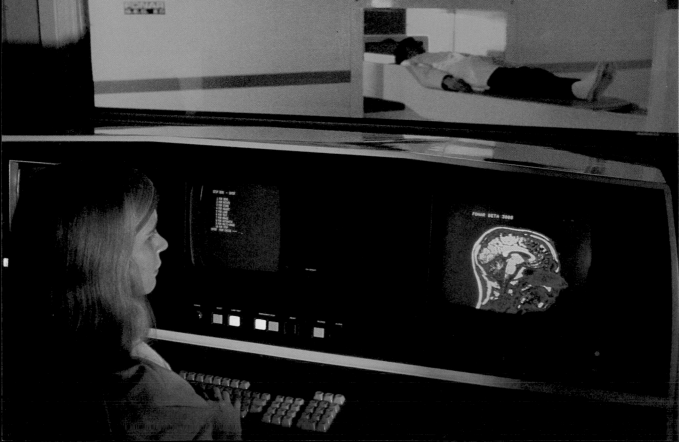

A robot surgical arm takes aim on a dummy patient. (© Dan McCoy)

Man-made skin may revolutionize plastic surgery in 2019. (© Dan McCoy)

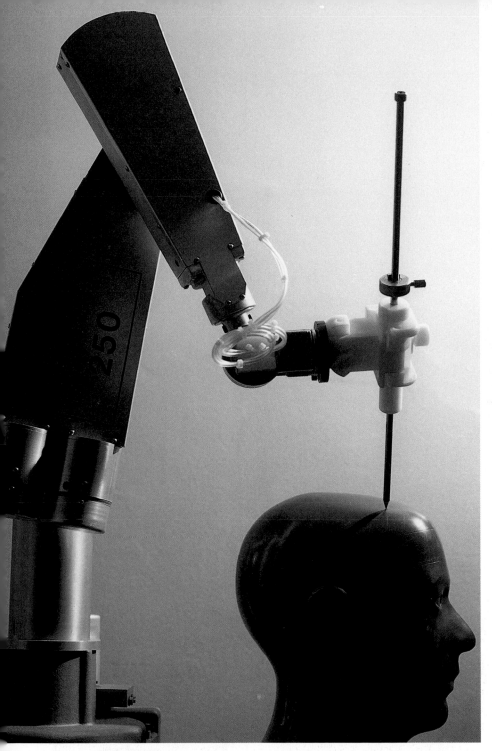

Opposite: Superscanners will ferret out malfunctions in a four-color flash, thereby eliminating today's tedious and painful medical exams. (*Above* and *below* © Phillip A. Harrington)

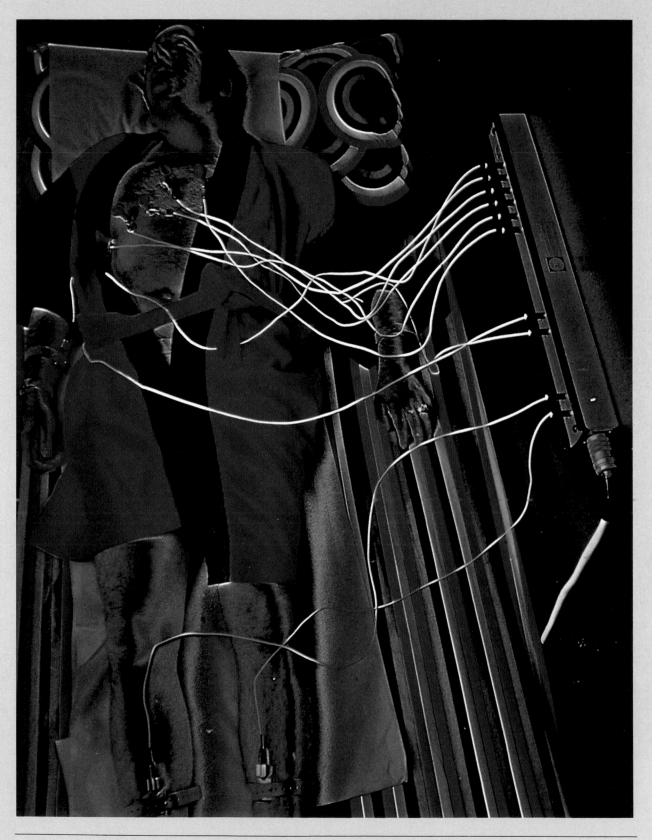

Advanced diagnostic tools are already supplementing the phyician's standard references. (© Hank Morgan)

Cousins, who, felled by a serious illness, decided to prove that laughter was indeed the best medicine. Hospitalized for a crippling degenerative disease and given little hope of recovery, Cousins conducted his own Marx Brothers film festival. To the amazement of his doctors, Cousins became well. Researchers subsequently found that patients who feel more in control of their illness are quicker to recover than those who show little interest in their therapy.

Other factors will help to make the patient feel in control, not the least of which is the public's changing attitude toward doctors. No longer considered omnipotent, physicians are more likely than ever to be challenged by those patients who grew up with consumerism. Better informed than their grandparents, the patients of 2019 will not only know more, but will demand more of their practitioners. Suddenly, physicians are more accountable for their actions—and for their errors, as witnessed by the skyrocketing cost of malpractice insurance.

The physician glut expected in the twenty-first century will also help upgrade the level of medical care. Patients will be able to select from several physicians, all eager to administer their services and, because they have fewer patients, able to spend more time with each. Increasing numbers of doctors will belong to group practices and receive a salary. As a result, they will be expected to maintain certain levels of excellence.

Physicians themselves will have changed a bit as their training becomes more varied. Both Rochester University Medical School and Johns Hopkins in Baltimore have dropped the Medical College Admissions Test from their list of requirements in an effort to open their doors to students with a liberal arts, rather than a science, background. Slowly, medical schools have been incorporating nutrition courses into their curriculum; by 2019, the medical student will have logged a good many hours in nutrition classes, as well as in classes on robotics and computers. Finally, women will be better represented in the medical profession. With record numbers of them entering medical schools, the proportion of female physicians will grow to 20 percent of all doctors by the year 2000.

A concomitant effect will be the entry of more men into nursing. The demand for nurses with specialties, in intensive care and surgery for instance, will rise sharply. Whereas the physician of 2019 will still concentrate on diagnosing the patient's illness and prescribing the proper treatment, the nurse will become more intimately involved in the healing process, helping the patient to hasten good health through biofeedback, meditation, and other holistic methods.

Opportunities for nurses will increase appreciably in the twenty-first century as they start their own corporations. One of the first of these, the Health Control Centers in Denver, Colorado, is run exclusively by nurses, who provide patients (often referred by physicians) with such self-healing tools as biofeedback. Using a device called the Mind Mirror, which is similar to an electroencephalograph (EEG), nurses monitor the rhythms of both hemispheres of the brain. Electrodes attached to the patient's head pick up brain activity; a display panel then reveals the type of rhythms being generated: Beta waves are typical of the conscious mind, alpha waves of daydreams, theta waves of subconscious activity, and delta waves of deep sleep. The Denver nurses use this tool to help patients reach a state of deep meditation, which they believe promotes the body's healing properties.

Slowly, health insurers will begin to recognize the validity of such procedures and will be more willing to provide coverage for holistic methods. In fact, medical consumers will have an alphabet soup of health-care plans from which to choose. HMOs (Health Maintenance Organizations), PPOs (Preferred Provider Organizations), and other health plans are gaining acceptability partly because of the spiraling price of hospital care. Employers, crippled by the cost of providing their workers with health insurance, are demanding that health-care providers come up with alternative methods of medical coverage. Some experts calculate that by the late 1990s, nearly half of the people in the U.S. may use HMOs and similar plans. For-profit hospitals have also devised health plans, and corporations like Humana and Hospital Corporation of America are offering a variety of insurance options in an effort to bring more patients into their institutions.

HMOs provide free services to those consumers who enroll in their medical plan for a flat yearly fee. Members select a physician from a list, and use only those hospitals chosen by the HMO. Because these organizations operate on a strict budget, enrollees are carefully screened before they receive approval for hospitalization. With a PPO, a subscriber gets a discount when he sees a physician who is on the insurer's roster. Usually, it's the employer who contracts with a group of doctors and a hospital to which employees have access. In this way a hospital is guaranteed a certain number of clients. Should an employee decide to go elsewhere or to see a doctor not listed with the PPO, he foots the bill himself.

As employers have more of a say in their employees' medical care, they may be the ones to decide whether the group insurance pays for heroic procedures, such as heart and kidney transplants. For example, Honeywell, Inc., which is among the first companies to approve heart, lung, and liver transplants for its workers, has consistently reviewed these major operations on a case-by-case basis. The question will no longer be, "Are we doing everything possible for the patient?" but rather, "Is this procedure really necessary, and will it enhance the patient's quality of life?" Americans could eventually see the rationing of high-tech costly procedures, such as open-heart surgery. (Already, medical ethicists are wrestling with the idea of limiting availability of certain operations. Said one expert, "The only way to cut costs will be to deny benefits to some people.") Great Britain has used such a rationing system for many years. Waiting lists for elective surgery are typically several years long.

Even the most optimistic social prophets concede that the poor and unemployed will suffer under the evolving health-care system. In the twenty-first century, the medical system may treat the poor one way and the affluent another. Medicare may curtail funds for heroic procedures altogether. Several states already use a gatekeeper system for Medicaid recipients in which a general practitioner determines whether a patient will have access to a specialist. This trend is likely to continue.

The federal government's health-care policies also jeopardize medical care for the elderly. The prospective payment system, put into effect in October 1983, ushered in the era of diagnosis-related groups (DRGs). This system, which applies only to Medicare patients, assigns a fixed rate for a particular illness. If complications arise, or if a patient takes longer to recover than the average, the hospital is not reimbursed for the "extra" fees. Critics of this system claim that it forces hospitals to release patients prematurely, and that it reduces a hospital's ability to take on charity cases.

Social, as well as governmental, forces will cut into hospitals' operating capital. People once turned to the local emergency room for the treatment of minor "emergencies," such as nosebleeds, bee stings, and sprained ankles. Now, in many parts of the country, they have the option of visiting the local walk-in clinic or "Doc-in-a-Box." These are

springing up along the nation's highways, wedging themselves between the Color Tiles and Burger Kings, the K-Marts and Carvels, all tributes to high traffic volumes. Suburban malls even boast their services. Open seven days a week, these centers offer medical treatment at prices often below that of the emergency room and sometimes even below that of the private physician. And there's never more than a ten-minute wait. More than three thousand free-standing clinics in the U.S. provide treatment for relatively minor health problems. By the year 1990, that number will double.

Occasionally, these McMedicines are started by a physician with an entrepreneurial leaning; most are owned by such supermed corporations as Humana. Many are headed up by former emergency-room physicians. Centers are staffed with at least one licensed physician and a registered nurse, and maintain basic medical equipment, including X-ray machines and defibrillators. There's also lab equipment to process blood and urine samples—a measure that saves time and cuts costs.

Some clinics, called surgicenters, cater exclusively to patients who need minor, sometimes elective surgery, such as tonsillectomies, hernia repairs, biopsies, even face-lifts and tummy tucks. As bloodless laser surgery becomes more commonplace, these outpatient operating rooms will take over most minor operations. Patients will spend a few hours in a recovery room and then head for home. Even the critics of such centers admit there's a psychological bonus to one-day surgery: People tend to regard the procedures as simple "repair work" rather than as treatments for an illness.

Although walk-in clinics are a relatively recent development in the medical world, hospitals are already feeling their impact: They have diverted paying patients from the emergency rooms, which are now crumbling under the weight of caring for the poor and indigent, and have reduced the number of operations performed in hospitals. Throughout the country, many hospitals have begun to close down one or more wings. In fact, the National Health Plan Guidelines issued in 1978 suggested that the supply of nonfederal, short-term hospital beds be reduced.

Eventually, as these clinics become more widespread, they may begin teaming up with the local hospital system. Instead of scattering the various sectors of health care, some of the major hospital corporations will consolidate physicians' offices, outpatient surgery services, diag-

Opposite page: The most elite residency in 2019 will be space science. Accidents in zero-g will require specially trained physicians to treat the injured.

nostic centers, fertility clinics, pharmacies, wellness centers, and hospital quarters into a mall-like structure, built around common dining and lounge areas.

The Carter County Medical Mall in Elizabethton, Tennessee, slated to open in late 1986, will hold only a hundred beds. But proponents of the plan say the extra space means that departments like physical and respiratory therapy can be expanded to accommodate a higher volume of outpatients.

Medical malls will also house a diversity of specialty health centers. Periodontists and nutritionists, radiologists and physical therapists will have offices under the same roof. Visitors will shed pounds and learn to change their eating patterns at the obesity clinic, dry out at the alcohol center, and learn how to quit smoking at something that could be called "HabitBreakers." Phobias will be cured at a storefront dubbed "Fear-Less."

But not everyone will have to travel to the neighboring medical mall to receive diet counseling or find out if a sore throat is actually a strep infection. In 1982, Americans bought upwards of 50 million home medical tests in an attempt to evaluate their own conditions. Home pregnancy tests, for example, which account for the biggest share of the market, allow women to begin prenatal care earlier than ever before. By the year 2000, home tests for bladder infections, diabetes, venereal diseases, and asthma will have become so sophisticated—even fail-proof—that patients will be able to diagnose their own ailments.

Ideally, a patient would type the results of such a test into his personal computer, which would then relay the information to a computer in the doctor's office. The doctor would then determine whether or not she need see the patient to prescribe the correct treatment.

Equipment once synonymous with the hospital will be miniaturized and simplified for use in the home. A new, pocket-size heart monitor that measures blood flow to the heart will alert cardiac patients to dangerous arrhythmias. A portable transcutaneous electrical stimulator, which can be plugged into an ordinary outlet, will heal broken bones quickly and thoroughly by guiding the cell repair mechanisms. Children suffering from scoliosis—curvature of the spine—will also be treated at home with an electrical stimulator.

Despite such revolutionary developments, people will continue to need the type of medical care that can only be administered in a hospital. Architects and medical experts have already pooled their talents to produce today the hospital of the twenty-first century in the form of a one-thousand-foot exhibit that is currently touring the country. First presented at the annual American Hospital Association's 1984 meeting, the project was three years in the making.

Before putting the diorama and multimedia presentation together, researchers at Auburn University in Alabama, and members of the architectural firm Earl Swensson Associates, analyzed such factors as an aging population, alternative health-care systems, communication technology, and other changes that will dictate the shape of the twenty-first-century hospital. They took into consideration the fact that new drugs and vaccines will certainly eliminate some diseases, while environmental hazards and sexual habits will spawn others.

All of the technology highlighted in the exhibit is either currently available or in the prototype stage. There are wrist computers that keep nurses abreast of patients' conditions, specially designed metal detectors that scan an accident victim's body to see if he has any artificial parts, and "high touch" recovery rooms that help a patient get well quickly.

Human life, from the miracle of birth to the mystery of death, will be enhanced in countless ways by these technological achievements, by the robot hands performing precise surgical tasks and computers that instantly analyze and comprehend a welter of confusing symptoms. But even more important, in the year 2019, we, the human masters of such devices, will have gained a greater understanding of ourselves. Peering into our bodies with CAT scans and Mind Mirrors, we will also have seen the wonder of the ways in which we work and are built—all of us the same. The hospital of the future will house and promulgate the ultimate truth: Health is a balance of mind and body and can best be achieved in an environment carefully attuned to both. A visit to the hospital may never surpass a week in the Bahamas, but in thirty years it will certainly have lost most of the dread with which it is greeted today. And that alone, we have recently discovered, may be half the battle.

A DAY
IN THE LIFE
OF A
ROBOT

RÉSUMÉ

Name: Universon Robot
Social Security Number: None
Marital Status: N/A
Age: 58 years old
Sex: Three choices (male, female, asexual)
Height: 5 feet
Weight: 60 to 2,800 pounds (depending on job requirements)
Present Health: Excellent
Medical History: Lost hand (now replaced) in a forge accident; lost memory (restored by tape); blinded in a kiln explosion (new, improved stereoptic vision since installed)
Life Expectancy: 29 man-shift years
Special Abilities/Training: Industrial/heavy-duty outdoor model: Fluent in three robot languages; instantly retrainable with memory replacement module; three-jointed arm has 6 degrees of movement and is capable of lifting up to 2,000 pounds with one end effector (hand). Precise—can work within a tolerance of $1/1000$ of an inch; works 24-hour shifts.
Personal model: Available in either stationary or mobile configurations; can learn to respond to owner's voice; comes with Level I Conscience, the program of protective ethics, factory installed (not available in warrior mode).
Work Experience: Assembly-line worker, welder, painter—Ford, General Motors, Chrysler
Materials handling—Pittsburgh Plate Glass
Domestic—Engelberger household, Danbury, Connecticut
Operating room nurse/attendant—Long Beach Hospital, Long Beach, California

References supplied upon request

Previous page: A robot in motion designed by sculptor Clayton Bailey.

A few years ago, Joseph Engelberger, the cofounder of Unimation, the world's first industrial robot company, dreamed up this robot résumé to impress upon people the wide ranging abilities of his company's industrial drones. It's been updated slightly to reflect the variants in the kind of intelligent and semi-intelligent machine workers we can expect to see in the twenty-first century. By 2019, more and more of the descendants of those factory drones, like the descendants of immigrants who came to the New World, will be working at more upscale jobs: They will be undersea explorers, heavy-construction workers, crime fighters, nuclear power plant inspectors, cybernetic companions, and astronauts.

By 2019, the machine will be in the first phase of a tremendous evolutionary leap. No longer will the robot be a simple-minded, dumb, insensate machine found only along factory production lines. The machine will have moved out of the cloistered manufacturing plant and into our world. We will work alongside the machines, relax with them, live with them.

Roboticized homes will become more and more common. A first-time visit to one of these homes might be a disappointment. No robot butler will greet you at the door, and there'll be no little androids scurrying about. In the household of 2019, the first phase of home robotization will not be a single robot but a small family of intelligent appliances.

First of all, the house itself could be a kind of robot, an automated building with a central intelligence. The house's various systems—heating, cooling, lighting, security alarms, ventilation, closed-circuit television, light control—would all be subject to the direction of the home's central computer, a kind of automated majordomo. Buyers will assume their new home comes equipped with a central computer as standard equipment the way houses now come with indoor plumbing and fully wired for electricity. (See Chapter 10, "House Arrest," for more details on the home of the future.)

Futurists at the Massachusetts think tank/consulting firm of Arthur D. Little, Inc., suggest that the roboticized home will have automated centers where appliances are linked together into intelligent work teams. Getting a meal ready, they say, could be simplified with a dual unit that's part refrigerator, part microwave oven. In the morning you would preselect a frozen meal stored in your freezer. At the appropriate time that meal package would slide out a door into the microwave oven. By the time you walk in the door at night, a hot meal would be waiting. If you are going to be late, you simply call home and tell your home computer to delay the meal.

Even simple meals could be automated. You might be able to order a sandwich in the same way. In fact, a grocery store in Yokohama, Japan, has a prototype of a robot sandwich maker. The Ham Slicer is a refrigerated meat container with a robot slicer and scale inside. A human customer simply walks up to it, taps a few buttons on the control console, telling the machine the kind of meat, the thickness of slices, and the weight he wants, and the machine cuts, slices, weighs, and wraps the meat in a matter of seconds. With a little adaptation, the same design could produce a masterpiece of a Dagwood sandwich as well.

Parked out of sight in a closet would be your robot vacuum cleaner. According to a preprogrammed schedule, it would roll out of the closet, cruise over a premapped course on the floor, and do the week's cleaning. The Japanese electronics firm Hitachi already has an experimental model of a robot vacuum cleaner that looks like a sleek, driverless car of the future. It sits quietly in the closet, foraying out to perform its functions. Still experimental and costing ten times what current vacuum cleaners sell for, the robot vacuum will no doubt be part of some of the more upscale, gadget-conscious homes in a 2019 suburb.

Training the machine is relatively simple, and it most likely mirrors how we will housebreak our own helpmates of 2019. First, the human reads off a word list to the robot. From this exercise the robot learns to recognize its master's or mistress's voice. Then the human tries out the voice commands, fine-tuning her ability to control the robot hand. Leifer's robot understands about 90 percent of the commands it hears.

The Stanford helper, like all companions, has three types of duty to perform. One type is the chores of daily living: getting meals and brushing teeth, for example. The second is small jobs or errands, called "vocational tasks": turning the pages of a book, opening a drawer or door. Third is recreational activities: playing a game of chess, for example.

These helpers are precursors of the electronic companion-valet, a robotic module with mix-and-match components. A basic industrial robot today can be outfitted with a wide selection of distinct attachments. For example, there are as many as fourteen different kinds of hands and several different styles of fingers customized to pick up different-shaped objects. Similarly, the homebot would seek out its utility closet and pop on a new hand or a new tool or even a new set of sensors with the same ease with which we change our clothes.

And there will be more and more things for these smart machines to do as they grow more adept. Although few homes have enough work to keep a robot working at the fever pitch of his industrial counterpart, we will no doubt find new tasks for this automated slave to perform. Artificial intelligence (AI) pioneer John McCarthy of Stanford University offered a little insight into what life with an intelligent machine would be like: "If you had this robot to work twenty-four hours a day, you would think of more and more things for it to do. This would bring about an elaboration in standards of decoration, style, and service. For example, what you would regard as an acceptably set dinner table would correspond to the standards of the fanciest restaurant, or to the old-fashioned, nineteenth-century standards of somebody who was very rich. People ask: 'What will happen when we have robots?' And there is a very good parallel. Namely, what did the rich do when they had lots of servants?"

As we get used to the luxury of having slaves at our beck and call, we may want them around for companionship as well. For those who care, robo-dogs and robo-cats will be a luxury we will all be able to afford. Computer game designer and entrepreneur Nolan Bushnell has designed a line of microchip powered, fuzzy animals—Petsters—that gurgle in response to a human voice. "Think of it as replacing biological animals. You get the good things without the bad. It's companionship without the kitty litter," he has said.

By 2019, these little creatures may be walking as well as talking and even coming at the beck of their master's or mistress's call. "There will be a time when you will be able to reconstruct Fido, the family dog, after it dies," suggests Bushnell, "and program the new version with Fido's personality. We may not be able to program a Fido, but we could have an electronic substitute."

Not all robot canines will be just cute pets. After reviewing the ingenious, but inadequate, machines devised as seeing aids for the blind, roboticist Susumu Tachi, of the Mechanical Engineering Laboratory (MEL) in Japan, decided that what the blind really need is a mechanical version of a guide dog. (In Japan, the need is pressing: With over 300,000 blind individuals, there are only about 350 guide dogs available.) By 2019, we may start seeing the first of Tachi's MEL dogs out on the street. He envisions them as compact walking machines with a handle on their backs so they can be picked up and carried onto a bus or up a flight of stairs. They can't be too small, otherwise they might get stepped on. A good size would be about the bulk of a portable vacuum cleaner. Each would be equipped with a set of sensors and a built-in memory map. A blind person would simply tap a few of the braille-coded buttons on the back of his robot to tell it where it is and where he wants to go. The robot would get a fix on its current location and set off in the right direction, its footsteps premapped in its memory.

To be truly helpful, robots will have to be able to find their way around and to be able to manipulate the world around them. Industrial machines work in areas that have been custom designed for them—work spaces cleared of all extraneous debris and with materials set up within the precise reach of mechanical arms and hands. There is no clutter, nothing decorative. Military pick-and-place robots are now being designed to tolerate battlefield chaos, and this technology may well find its way into the home. But initially, at least, the home of 2019 will probably have to be made "robot friendly."

Today, the average house is a robot's nightmare of obstacles and unexpected challenges: stairs to climb; chairs, tables, and other furniture randomly scattered around; variable surfaces, from shag rugs to wooden floors; pets and small children wandering by at random; and hundreds of objects of varied sizes, shapes, colors, and weights.

A home that is comfortable to a robot domestic will have to correct at least some of these problems. And such rooms as the kitchen and bathroom may have to be customized for robot cleaning and maintenance. Tile walls and floors with a drain in the center would make it easy for a machine to scrub them down. Main rooms in the house would have to be uncluttered or at least cleaned up before the robot vacuumed. The rooms would be spare but airy, with as much built-in furniture as possible. Perhaps the floors would be of a type that a robot machine could spruce up easily, such as short-napped carpeting. Delicate furniture and breakables would be out of sight, perhaps in a family room that a human would clean on occasion. In a two- or three-story house, it might be practical to own a cleaning machine for each floor so you don't have to buy one of those new, very expensive wheeled robots with little extensor legs that let you walk them to another floor like an obedient dog.

By 2019, people may first start buying personal robots—(as distinguished from the domestic housecleaning machines)—simply for the novelty of it and for doing simple fetch-and-carry jobs. These small and unthreatening machines will be able to do such things as take out the garbage, carry items, set the table.

We could control these machines in a variety of ways. The house computer might supervise the comings and goings of all the smart machines. Or we could push a few buttons on a small control unit on our digital watch or the machine's torso to activate a preprogrammed behavior. A simple way to instruct your family robot would be with voice control. Already, today's personal machines have voices, computer memories, and even abilities like voice recognition. One very expensive (close to $7,000) personal robot, called Gemini, can recognize up to three different voices, then say a few well-chosen words itself.

For some people, voice control will be a valuable option. In devising a helper robot for the handicapped, Stanford University researcher Dr. Larry Leifer has already proved that we can make a robot do our bidding. His robot is a small off-the-shelf industrial arm with a two-fingered hand, featuring voice or joystick control and the ability to understand fifty-eight spoken words. By waggling the joystick or merely by telling the machine where to move (up, down, etc.), a wheelchair-bound person can have the machine hand things to him and even do a little fetching. With about forty-five minutes of training, a new user can learn, for example, how to teach the robot to get a glass of water. The Stanford group has already tested their robot with over a hundred handicapped people, aged five to ninety, with encouraging success.

Some experimental robot dogs already are wandering around Tachi's laboratory. The machine is tethered to its owner by an electronic leash through which the MEL dog keeps track of its owner's walking speed and adjusts accordingly. Two rearward-looking sensors help the machine make sure the human is directly behind it. Should the person wander too far to the right or left, the robot guide dog sends a brief electronic pulse to a stimulator on the user's right or left wrist as a gentle reminder to move more directly behind the machine.

Life will be equally interesting for the robot outside the home, especially back in the factory where it began. By 2019, it will be the most common factory employee. By the turn of the century, experts estimate there could be as many as one million industrial machines in the United States alone, and their presence would affect as many as 3.8 million factory jobs now held by humans.

Robots of the twenty-first century may come in three models: male, female, and asexual.

A walking robot developed by the University of Wisconsin.

AROK the robot—one of the most famous robot sculptures.

The uniqueness of the roboticized factory will be evident as soon as you drive up to a plant. While most of today's industrial complexes are sprawling acres of warehouses and manufacturing facilities swarming with armies of workers, future factories will be more compact structures. They will have fewer people, and that will mean reduced space requirements: smaller parking lots and a lesser need in general for "people facilities" such as lunchrooms and locker rooms.

Because future factories won't need a lot of people, they can be built anywhere a company needs them: in the middle of a city or in a small, backwoods community—anywhere the plants are accessible by a major road or train line. The traditional business strategy of building where labor is cheap will be irrelevant. If the zoning permitted, manufacturers could just as easily erect a plant on Park Avenue as on the outskirts of Detroit.

The factory of 2019 won't have humans on the production lines. The factory of the future will resemble a more sophisticated version of Japan's Fujitsu Fanuc factory, where a hundred robots and only sixty humans produce ten thousand electric motors every month. Different areas of the work floor will resemble an industrial inferno: suffocatingly high temperatures, deafening noises, toxic fumes, and production lines working at killing speeds. Machines can operate easily in situations that are, literally, inhuman.

Rarely will there be a human in sight. Those who are visible will be there in a strictly subservient capacity: tuning up, adjusting, baby-sitting the steel-collar workers. Of course, no worker will be allowed on the floor without his safety coveralls on. Emblazoned on the front and back will be bar-code patterns that warn the worker machine, "Stop! A human is in your area." Since all the machines would have at least rudimentary vision, this is the simplest way of protecting human workers against death or injury. (People will still talk about the so-called robot homicides of the 1980s, when careless workers in both the U.S. and Japan stepped in the way of a blind and dumb machine, with fatal consequences.)

The robots will take many forms: work cells of disembodied arms, roving material-handling smart carts, or multiarmed "jack of all trade machines" that can be moved to a new work area, equipped with a new set of tools, reprogrammed, and put to work. Just as the computer industry began with time-sharing information and computer facilities, we will see time-shared robots, itinerant machine workers moving from job to job and taught in an instant how to perform a new job.

The small army of sophisticated machines will be supervised by machine as well—the centralized factory computers. In a sense, the factory will be one enormous robot, the computer its guiding intelligence, and the machines on the floor parts of the grand design. "As automation becomes more flexible," explains Joseph Engelberger, "robots may lose their distinct character. They may simply be elements of the entire production organism. Science fiction has given us a counterpart of this phenomenon. In *2001: A Space Odyssey*, HAL is a distributed robot that we never see in an embodiment, but that permeates the space vehicle."

We are already seeing the beginnings of that in automotive plants, where a central computer coordinates the complex frenzy of automatic activity with an electronic chain of command called "local area networks," or LANs. Although different intelligent machines understand different machine languages, they can all be made to work together through a computer-translator-manager that makes machine language Babel coherent and efficient.

With this overlay of computer control, the "set-and-forget" factory will become the rule, not the exception. More and more plants will resemble the one run by the Magnesans Corporation in southern Sweden, where robots haul parts to work areas and every machine works at a typically inhumane pace all week long and straight through the weekend. No on-the-spot monitoring is necessary on the weekends, and the nearest human is ten miles away.

Productivity can be tuned like a car engine. When demands are low, different banks of machines would be turned off. When necessary, the output of such a factory could be herculean. Unlike present factories that operate one or two shifts per day, the automated factory could do the equivalent of four shifts.

As our smart machines take over the distasteful jobs inside our factories and homes, they will provide the same relief outside as well. By 2019, we will be able to call on a breed of machine known as the risk-taker, a kind of automated daredevil that will do deadly or deadly dull work: police work, inspecting the interior of a nuclear reactor or the depths of a coal mine, searching for survivors inside a burning building, and helping authorities defuse terrorist bombs, to name a few.

The Japanese government has mobilized an $88-million effort to build a breed of risk-takers by the 1990s. By the turn of the century, they expect to have nuclear power plant robots and rescue robot firefighters, as well as robot miners.

To make such machines possible will require a drastic transformation of our regular robot, a transformation that has already begun. To find its way around in a world of random twists and turns and obstacles of all sizes and types, the risk-taker of 2019 will need sight.

The most obvious choice would be to copy human vision, but it is not the most appropriate. For one thing, it is too complicated to duplicate fully. As vision expert Thomas Binford of Stanford University explains, "The retina of one eye has roughly a hundred million specialized cells and four layers of neurons, all capable of doing about ten billion calculations a second. And this is before any information reaches the optic nerve, which connects the eyeball to the brain." It is his guess that it could take as long as two hundred years to duplicate in a machine what we do every time we open our eyes.

For another, it will probably not be necessary. The eye is a limited sensor. It can detect only a small portion of the spectrum, has a sharply limited range of focus, and can work only under bright light levels.

Because of their specialized work, many of the robots of 2019 will not have anything resembling human vision. And they won't miss it, either. For inspecting radiation leaks, one machine might need "eyes" that are sensitive to gamma radiation. Another machine might function quite well as a roaming sentry with infrared and sonic sensors. (One Massachusetts firm has already built a sentry robot that uses such a system.) Vision will be customized to fit the job.

Outside the factory, on the farm, some Purdue University experts have an experimental model of a weed-killing robot that uses infrared vision to spot plant leaves and identify whether that plant is friendly or hostile before spraying it with weed killer. The University of California at Davis has a lettuce harvester that uses X-ray sensors. The machine focuses a weak radioactive beam at a row of lettuce heads and "reads" the beam that bounces back. In two seconds it can gauge the plumpness and density of a lettuce plant and decide whether the plant is ripe for picking. (In one test it outperformed experienced human lettuce pickers.)

Robots already have hands. What they will have in 2019 is a sense of touch fine enough to cradle an egg or a grip strong enough to pick up an engine block. The secret will be a skinlike covering that has a layer

Opposite page: Employee of the future. Will robots put all blue-collar workers out of work?

of force sensors, the electronic equivalent of our nervous system, embedded in it. Already there are several candidates for cybernetic epidermis. At MIT, researchers have designed a three-layer robotic skin. The top and bottom layer is made of a flexible synthetic hide. Within the middle layer is a fine net of electrical conductors. When an object is squeezed against this skin, the points of pressure produce high and low surges of current that a computer translates into touch sensations.

In a variation of this design, Carnegie-Mellon University researchers have freckled the robot hand with pressure-sensitive dots of polymer film that produce an electrical signal when squeezed. University of Florida scientists have designed a rubber skin with a ridged pattern on it, somewhat like an exaggerated fingerprint. When pressure is applied by a squeeze, the ridges vibrate. Sensors under the skin relay these vibrations to a computer that reads them. And one ingenious Stanford University researcher has even suggested that the inside of a robot hand be lined with electronic hairs. Cheaper than some of the more sophisticated skin designs, the whiskers on the "hairy hand" design, as it is called, serve two purposes: They act like the whiskers of a cat and gently guide the hand so it is centered on an object before it grasps it, and, as the hand squeezes the object, they give pressure readings.

So the robots of 2019 will be able to see, feel, and in general have a keener sense of their world. But how can we bestow truly human capabilities on them? One way is to marry machine brawn with the human brain. It's an old idea, one that dates back at least to 1948, when a technician at the Argonne National Laboratory in Illinois was able to handle the hot debris from nuclear fuel with a pair of remote-controlled hands he designed. AI pioneer Marvin Minsky of MIT calls this field of quasi-robotics "telepresence." With telepresence, a human, using controls attached to his hands and arms, can direct a set of mechanical hands and arms at a distant worksite. Direct sensory feedback—touch and vision—from the machine makes the cybernetic limbs an extension of the human. Extending his reach yards, or even miles, with this technique, man can work remotely almost anywhere— from the ocean floor to the airless vacuum of space.

We have already seen the value of this teamwork of human brain and silicon brawn in hostile environments on Earth. Probably the best example of how well we can work in hostile worlds is the new generation of underwater robots called "submersibles." Humans do not tolerate the depth of the sea well. They can barely go a thousand feet down, are lucky if they can tolerate a few days inside the cramped quarters of a hollow steel diving ball, and the return to the surface is a risky ordeal. As U.S. Navy underwater-robot expert Robert Wernli puts it, "The ocean poses one of the most hostile environments that man can imagine, where extreme pressures, dynamic forces, corrosive attack, turbid water, and other problems usually deal Mother Nature a winning hand. Therefore, it is no wonder that the ocean engineer would rather extend his presence into the ocean remotely, if possible, and remain topside in a warm, comfortable environment next to the coffeepot."

Some robots, like the submersible Argo, developed at Woods Hole Oceanographic Institute, are of the "flying eyeball" variety, equipped to scan the ocean floor only with sonar and television cameras. (It was Argo that helped find the *Titanic*.) Others are hard-working machines. One of the best examples is the SCARAB (Submersible Craft for Assisting Repair and Burial), developed by an international consortium of telecommunications companies. SCARAB is a remote-controlled underwater worker equipped with video and still cameras, a set of electrically powered thrusters, and an on-board tool kit for its two robotic arms. Three people control the machine over a ten-thousand-foot umbilical.

By 2019, more and more people will sit by the coffeepot dispatching their fleets of machines to another hostile environment: space. By the 1990s, some of the first long-term space stations, designed to survive ten to twenty years, will be in orbit. To maintain an orbiting building that long, says NASA administrator Raymond Colladay, will absolutely demand that robots be working out there with humans. By then we will almost certainly begin to see work crews of what he called "expert robots" overseeing the maintenance of the space station.

But they will not work alone. The best space station design is one in which the dominant intelligence is still human, and NASA agrees. Culbertson has said that the ideal space station is one that is manned full time. Man-robot systems simply are more flexible in responding to crises as they occur, and people should be in space to supervise what is going on. Working the robots from an Earth-bound base is feasible, but it has its drawbacks, not the least of which is the time lag of half a second or more between a command issued from Earth and its execution out in space.

The man-robot team is a formidable combination. We already have a preview of what this means in the robot arm, called the Remote Manipulator System (RMS), installed on the shuttle. With RMS, an astronaut can reach out fifty feet and deftly manhandle an object the size of a bus—sixty feet long, fifteen feet in diameter, and weighing over thirty-two tons. Future shuttles will have a pair of these arms installed on them and will therefore double the working capabilities of astronauts.

Yet even these will seem primitive when compared to robot configurations that will be coming along. Robotics expert Robert Freitas says that robotic arms will eventually cease to be rigid, jointed copies of human limbs, but will instead resemble long, serpentine tentacles, yards or even miles long. And in longer-distance telepresence operations, astronauts could orchestrate the repair of satellites or mining on the surface of the Moon from on board a space station. Already planned is a two-armed remote repair machine with stereo camera eyes called ROSS (for Remote Orbital Servicing System). It would be as dextrous as an astronaut and, with its stereo feedback and gripper controls, almost as sensitive. The human would simply maneuver it as a seeing/touching extension of himself to work around the outside of the space station, to do fine repair work on satellites hauled in for servicing, or even to mine the Moon or nearby asteroids.

To simplify control and make the sensations of the machine more immediate to the human controller, future robot supervisors may wear exoskeleton control units and special vision-hats. Joysticks and switches have too many limitations and don't give telepresence workers the sensation of being where the robot is. We already have prototypes of control units, like the UCLA "master glove" design that feeds back pressures and even temperature from a robot hand to a human one. And in the 1970s, a piece of technology called the Foveal-HAT (for Head Aimed Television) used two small television screens to deliver distant on-the-scene views. The image was so clear that the human wearing the HAT was able to drive a pickup truck through an obstacle course and park it by remote control. A day's work for a space station laborer will begin when he puts on his telepresence sleeves and hat and in a matter of seconds becomes a robot's brain. With stereovision on the TV goggles and the delicate electronic sensations—all tunable to an operator's preferred level of feedback—an astronaut could perform herculean feats in space without burning up more than a calorie or two.

Robotic visionaries are also looking toward the day when humans in space do not have to control a robot's every move, but merely supervise them. Rather than move a machine through every step, astronauts will be able to simply tell their machines to "switch on console" and they will perform the job with well-rehearsed grace.

But what has to be the ultimate in robot participation is the notion first offered by Princeton mathematician John von Neumann. In the 1940s, von Neumann suggested that it was possible for a machine to do the machine equivalent of procreation—that is, replicate itself. Discussed in principle for decades, the idea of the self-perpetuating machine inched closer to reality until two NASA visionaries, George Tiesenhausen and Wesley Darbro, declared in the 1970s that we should think seriously about building a robot capable of making others like itself.

NASA thinkers have already roughed out the kind of von Neumann scenario that could take place on the Moon. Their plan is to set down a one-hundred-ton "seed" of robots on the Moon. On landing, different machines would carry out their programmed destinies. One cadre of machines would go to work erecting a solar-powered factory, while another would start mining operations, extracting raw materials from the lunar surface and hauling it to the factory. At the factory, a processing and manufacturing team would process the raw material into finished products: more factory parts, more machines, more robots. In time, each robotic team could duplicate themselves and go on to any other phase of manufacturing or procreation in their programs.

The idea of robots giving birth to other robots is hardly fantasy. Tiesenhausen and Carbro estimated that we could build the first self-replicating machine twenty years after we began the project in earnest. This means that if we begin now, by 2019 a self-perpetuating robot corps could already be established on the Moon. Then there would be two races of intelligent beings in the solar system able to procreate: humans and robots.

Visions like this raise the specter that for the first time in our history this helpmate—this tool that we invented—is likely to begin a process

A do-it-yourself personal robot.

of self-powered evolution. In short, what we are facing is the possibility that something we created as a tool could someday be a fellow Earthling.

That the robot will be considered more than just another machine is certain. The clues are all around us. One Japanese union complained that the phasing in of robots and the phasing out of union workers was depleting the union's finances because there were fewer members to pay dues. In response, the company offered to enroll the robots as union members. The Japan Labor Ministry was offended by the idea, declaring, "Robots cannot join a union like human workers." The union leader, however, declared, "We want the robots."

These machines are now dim-witted. Robot expert Hans Moravec of Carnegie-Mellon University says that "present robot systems are now similar in power to the control systems of insects." That will not always be so. By the 1990s, their level of development could be on a par with small animals, shrews, and hummingbirds. And in 2019, they may be flirting with the beginnings of human-level abilities. Some believe that we are already there. Professor Ichiro Kato, the preeminent robot designer in Japan, says his WABOT 1, an intelligent upper torso that can read music and play the organ, has the approximate IQ of a five-year-old child. And he believes that by the turn of the century we may see experimental machines with the IQ of an older and wiser child of about ten years of age.

What this all means is that by 2019 we will see this amalgam of electronics and machinery beginning to take on a life of its own. As that happens, we will have to decide how to shape this evolving intelligence that we have created: what skills, emotions, and attitudes it will have.

As robots become mobile and begin to mix in the real world, as strange as it may seem, they will require certain attitudes and values in order to survive and do their jobs. The robot of 2019 will need the capacity to sense danger, a cybernetic version of fear. For example, to protect his roving machines from damage, Moravec has programmed into them something called "edge avoidance," a preprogrammed reaction to move away from an edge, such as the top of a step. Susumu Tachi has already installed in his guide dog a sense of self-sacrifice. Should the machine detect anything moving toward its master, the robot dog automatically sounds a warning and positions itself between its human and whatever is coming.

For years, science fiction writer Isaac Asimov has talked about his Three Laws of Robotics, a code of behavior that essentially forbids a machine to ever harm or allow harm to befall a human. Concern about killer robots ceased being the stuff of fiction in 1984 when a company called Robot Defense Systems unveiled a $200,000 robot sentry called Prowler (for Programmable Robot Observer With Logical Enemy Response). Designed for outdoor sentry duty, the machine resembles a small tank, carries an array of sensing equipment, and can easily be equipped with two M60 machine guns and a grenade launcher. Although a company official declared, "In the United States we don't foresee the prowler armed with lethal weapons," he also admitted that "there are countries where there aren't the same political or moral considerations." In other words, they would turn the robot into a killing machine.

Now that the military has asked for, and gotten, millions of dollars for similar military robots (like an automated tank it hopes to see ready by 1995), we should start worrying about a higher level of values. Marilyn Levine, a professor at the University of Wisconsin, has suggested that we begin an organization she calls SAFE, for the Society for Algorithmic Functional Ethics. Her proposal came in reaction to the heavy military flavor of robotics research. "It became obvious to me that the federal government is spending more and more money on warlike robots. The military has been the primary source for this kind of research because they don't want to expend human beings in war; they want to make mechanical men. But no robot should be allowed to go out and kill," she asserts. "So I started with that premise."

Her suggestion is to program into robots the machine intelligence equivalent of "Thou shalt not kill." For a machine, much of this involves restricting a robot's use of force. "The concept of doing harm comes down to how you apply force," she says. It is a concept, she agrees, that we cannot install in robots now, but one which we will have to think about before it's too late.

By the time 2019 arrives, we will have to face the equally complex questions of what rights these machines hold. John G. Kemeny, an inventor of the computer language BASIC, has already said that computers could be considered a species of life. We could well imagine having to deal with machine rights organizations similar to the militant animal rights groups now in existence. Marvin Minsky of MIT posed the question best when he predicted that once machine intelligence has grown to a certain level, "then we'll be forced to ask ourselves how we should treat the minds we make. . . ."

Putting it in a more down-to-Earth context, Carnegie-Mellon's Herbert Simon, another AI pioneer, suggests, "Suppose we had a race of robots which were exactly like humans with one important difference—they were less subject to mental and physical disease. They were of course made of metal or whatever, but in a way that they were cuddly enough.

"Now we're going to have a referendum," he continues. "We want to transmit our human culture to future generations. Are we going to select these creatures to transmit the culture?" How would he vote? "I don't know," he says, "because voting against the robots almost sounds like a form of race prejudice."

When we come to face these questions, we will also come to a humbling realization. Just as the tools of primitive man helped him evolve into a creature of higher intelligence, this new tool we have created—the robot—could help us make another evolutionary leap. This time, however, that evolutionary leap may have an ironic twist. *Homo sapiens*, if he is remembered at all, may be noted in the history of intelligent life as just another long-gone evolutionary phase. And the tool he had created will have become his successor.

C H A P

SCHOOL DAYS:

NO RECESS

Greetings. Welcome to Databank Central.

You have requested: EDUCATION CREDITS RATING #2A4-2287—TY15

Subject: John S. Stanton

Born: April 8, 1982 (current age—37 yrs. 3 mos. 12 days)

Address: 843 Condo-Tower West, Aquacity, Atlantic-Offshore, Zone 2

Current Employment: Submersible Technology Engineer, Seabed Mining Division, Mobil Corporation

Education Credits
(For Dates, Press D-I; For Grades, Evaluations, Press G-I)

Age When Earned	Credits
3—5	Leprechaun Day Care Center, Tulsa, OK
5—6	Kindergarten, Balsam Central District, Balsam, OR
6—11	Balsam Elementary School
11—14	Balsam Middle School
14—17	Balsam High School (Science Subschool)
	(A)dvanced (P)lacement Chemistry I (U. of OR, Televideo Instruction Div.)
	AP Physics I (U. of OR, Televideo Div.)
	Elementary Robotics (Compuschool, Inc., On-Line Classroom)
17—21	U. of OR, B.A.: major—human expression; minor—physics (for course list, press C-I)
22—26	General Dynamics Corp., Employee U., M.S.: electrical engineering; specialty—low-grav robotics
29	General Dynamics Corp., Employee U., "Lunar Mining Modules" (televideo course)
30	McSchools, Inc., Boston, MA: "Elem. Chinese," "Chinese Philosophy," "History of China"
31	General Dynamics Corp., Employee U., Lunapolis, "Doing Business in China" (disc-class)
33	General Dynamics Corp., Employee U., Peking Branch, "Principles of Submarine Robotics" (televideo course)
35—36	MobilSchool, M.S.: submersible engineering
37	McSchools, Inc., Houston, TX, "Underwater Fun with an Artificial Gill"

Previous page: Technology—communications satellites, fiberoptics, interactive TV, computers—opens up new horizons for school children.

Mention education today and we think of children and a school building. But education in 2019 will be an ongoing process that never ends, and in some cases will need no building for its students. (*Inset photograph* © Wayne Eastep; *below* © Phillip A. Harrington and Ed Bohon)

In the past, only test pilots and astronauts traveled at fantastic speeds. But in 2019, everyday travelers will sail along at Mach 22. (*Inset photograph* © Wayne Eastep; *background* © Joe Dimaggio/Jo Anne Kalish)

Fantastic craft will make man feel more at home in his world, above his world, even beyond his world.
(*Above* © Dan McCoy; *below* © Russell Munson)

On the evening of July 20, 2019, John Stanton is taking yet another teleclass. His classroom is actually a room in his own home that is outfitted for teleconferencing. At the moment, he is posing a question to his teacher. Sitting in a university video studio 1,400 miles away, the teacher appears in the room as a life-sized three-dimensional holographic image.

Meanwhile, in a nearby public school, an early-education specialist is teaching a four-year-old how to read. As studies today have already shown, early training leads to greater educational success later on.

At the "magnet" high school across the street, specializing in the humanities, a sophomore is learning how quantum mechanics is changing our view of the universe. Other high schools in the community specialize in everything from science to finance.

Across town, at a McSchool franchise, a grandmother is taking a course on small business management. Two rooms away, her sixteen-year-old grandson is getting first-year college English out of the way early.

Nearby, at the university operated by a major corporation for its employees, students are taking classes in new technological developments in their fields or working toward advanced degrees in technical, scientific, or management specialties.

By the year 2019, such students will be typical, for most people will attend school throughout their life. Recreational learning will become popular as increasing technological efficiency creates more leisure and tomorrow's fast-changing technologies will require workers to seek constant training and retraining.

Today, for instance, computer programming is a viable career. However, engineers are now working on computers that program computers. As such machines come on the market, thousands of programmers will have to retrain for new careers.

Robot technicians are now increasing in demand. Yet robot technology is constantly evolving. These technicians will need updated courses for each new generation of machine. Meanwhile, engineers will design new specialty robots, such as zero-gravity robots to work on orbiting factories, already under study at such research centers as the Massachusetts Institute of Technology. Technicians will have to take more courses so they can fill the high-paying jobs in the new specialties.

Entirely new fields will spring up, too, like seabed mining and large-scale aquaculture to help feed the globe's exploding population. Workers whose jobs in other fields are being eliminated by technology will go back to school to prepare for careers in these new areas.

Traditional schools, kindergarten through high school, also will change because of new technologies. In fact, education's basic emphasis will shift. Our current educational system evolved to produce workers for the Industrial Revolution's factory-based economy, for work that requires patience, docility, and the ability to endure boredom. Students learned to sit in orderly rows, to absorb facts by rote, and to move as a group through the material regardless of individual differences in learning speed. But no factory jobs will be left in 2019. Except for a few technicians to watch over control panels, tomorrow's factories will be automatic, with computers directing robot workers.

In this new computer-based economy, more and more jobs will involve the creation, transmission, and processing of information and ideas. As the number of jobs based on muscle and mindless repetition wanes, industry and business will increasingly require workers with sharp thinking skills. And, because most people will be taking courses lifelong, they will need to know how to learn—education itself will be a skill that virtually everyone will need. As a result, the emphasis in elementary and high school will shift: In the school of the future, the focus will be on teaching how to think and how to learn.

"We will have to deal with questions unforeseeable today, and so we need a broad-based education," says Barnard College president Ellen Futter. "We need people who can think outside their own areas of specialization. We must give people certain key intellectual skills—analytical thinking, critical thinking, the ability to make judgments, to reason quantitatively, to balance opposed points of view. We must focus more on how to learn, how to think."

Meanwhile, the technologies that are changing society—communications satellites, fiber-optic cable, interactive TV, computers—will also change the way in which education is delivered. One result will be tremendous diversity in the educational system. Master teachers may address thousands of students scattered on several continents simultaneously, for instance. The technology that will make such

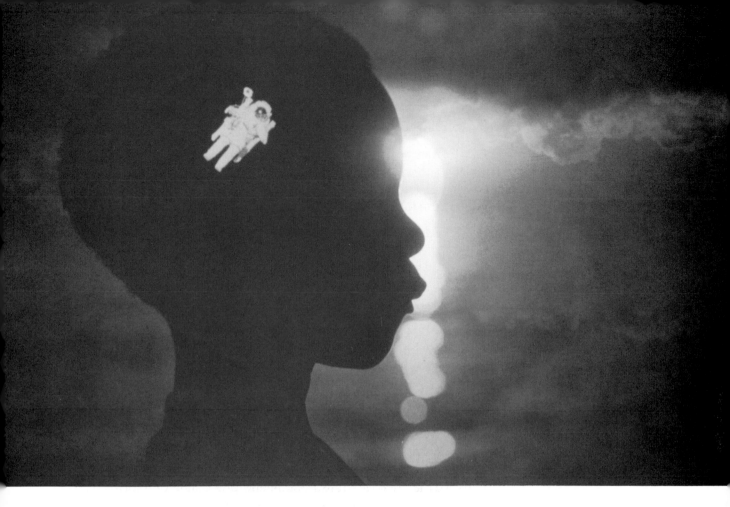

courses available, teleconferencing, will soon be commonplace. In fact, major corporations already use such systems.

In a state-of-the-art teleconferencing room set up by a subsidiary of Comsat in Washington, D.C., plush armchairs surround a sleek oak conference table. Inconspicuously built into the head of the table is an electronic control console. On the wall at the table's foot are two floor-to-ceiling video screens. Executives using the room can cross the ocean, in effect, without leaving Washington.

When they arrive in the room for a teleconference, on the screen to the left they see their counterparts in London, Tokyo, or virtually any other city around the globe gathered in a similar room. Built into the walls of both rooms are robot TV cameras, controlled from the head seat at the table. Built into the table are "smart" microphones, which can distinguish between the sound of a person's voice, a cough, or the clatter of a dropped ashtray, and instantly adjust the volume accordingly. The people in the two cities attending this electronic meeting can thereby carry on a normal conversation and watch each other as they talk. By placing a document over a glass plate built into each table,

Dreams of space travel floating in the minds of children become educational realities.

the two groups can project images of a contract, an agreement, a diagram, or any other document on the wall's second big screen. At the push of a button, they can print out duplicate copies of the document for their counterparts in the other conference room to examine.

Such technologies, aided by high-speed travel, will knit tomorrow's world far more tightly, economically and culturally. Thus, the culture that tomorrow's schools transmit cannot be solely our own. Peter Glaser, an expert on space technology at Arthur D. Little, Inc., puts it well: "We can't live in an island called 'Kansas' or 'Massachusetts.' How will our graduates be able to talk intelligently about things on the Moon if they don't even know what's going on in the country next door?"

In fact, with NASA already planning a Moon base for the turn of the century, tomorrow's students will indeed need to talk intelligently about things lunar. As columnist Jack Anderson, head of the national Young Astronauts program, points out, eventually "commuting to NASA's Moon base will be routine. We could send up kids to space labs on the Moon the way we now send them on field trips to Cape Kennedy or Houston." Can courses in low-grav manufacturing at Luna U. be far off?

Of course, with so many technological and economic changes afoot, the social fabric itself will be rewoven. More leisure and discretionary income for many workers will be one change. As the old industrial system wanes, we will no longer need a kind of lock-step conformity to operate efficiently; individualism will spread all through society. "Craftspeople will increasingly be in demand, for instance," predicts Robert Ayres, professor of engineering and public policy at Carnegie-Mellon University. "As manufactured goods become increasingly standardized, and ever cheaper, crafted objects will be seen as increasingly distinguished and desirable." As computer networks decentralize our society, many people will be able to work at home, if they wish. Citizens will increasingly "do their own thing." And that will include education.

All of these changes—lifelong education, international education, new emphasis on how to think and how to learn, a new individualism—will put pressure on the public school system as we know it today. The result will be a blow-out.

By 2019, today's monolithic educational system will have diffused throughout society. The public schools will still exist, but they will be only one facet of a stunning diversity of systems for delivering education, much of which will be privately operated.

Even the public schools will be more varied. Many high schools will become confederations of subschools that cater to students' special interests, from physics to the performing arts. But the diversity will not end there.

"We'll have home-based schools, more private and religious schools, more schools founded by zealots, and more diversity overall," points out Vermont Education commissioner Stephen S. Kaagan. "In Washington, D.C., and Boston we're already seeing primitive alliances between industries and the public schools." Steven Kurtz, headmaster of Philips Exeter Academy, agrees: "I think we'll see big companies, like IBM or Marriott, taking over whole school systems, contracting with a city like Wichita to run the entire city's schools."

Meanwhile, many schools will reach into the womb, teaching pregnant inner-city women nutrition and child care. The aim, according to Milton Kopelman, principal of the Bronx High School of Science in New York City, will be to give disadvantaged kids a running start. From infancy on, the schools will work with underprivileged children, providing intellectual stimulation. Costs will be offset, at least in part, by the resulting shrinkage of welfare rolls.

But early education will not be solely for disadvantaged youngsters: For most children, school will start at about age four. In fact, a network of preschools is already growing rapidly, driven by the needs of working parents. Learning experts such as Madeline Hunter, of the UCLA Graduate School of Education, say that most children will start school early, not only because two-career parents will need a place to park their youngsters during the workday, but also because studies show that children who receive early education do better in school later on.

Meanwhile, most citizens of the year 2019 will never really graduate, returning again and again for classes and courses throughout their lives. Much of that education will be provided by their employers. This trend is already well under way. Many major corporations now operate what amount to employee universities. In fact, corporate education in the U.S. already involves as many people as all the nation's colleges and universities. Schooling that corporations provide for their employees is now education's fastest-growing segment.

Tomorrow's student will have a smorgasbord of educational choices. Besides corporate schools, there will be profit-making chains—"McSchools"—and special schools catering to special students. San Francisco's Newcomer High School for immigrant youngsters and New York City's tiny new public school for homosexuals are pointing the way. In many cities, *all* schools will be magnets, organized around such specialties as language or art. Most schools will be open to all ages, a change that has already begun.

For instance, the Institute of Computer Technology, a public school in Sunnyvale, California, is for grades kindergarten through senior citizen. Typical of many of tomorrow's public schools, it is partly financed by local industries, which rely on the school to produce well-trained workers. It is open from 8:00 A.M. to 10:00 P.M., six days a week, twelve months a year, with no extended vacations, says its director, Larry Liden.

Computer graphics replace finger paints, and school children try their hand at being space architects.

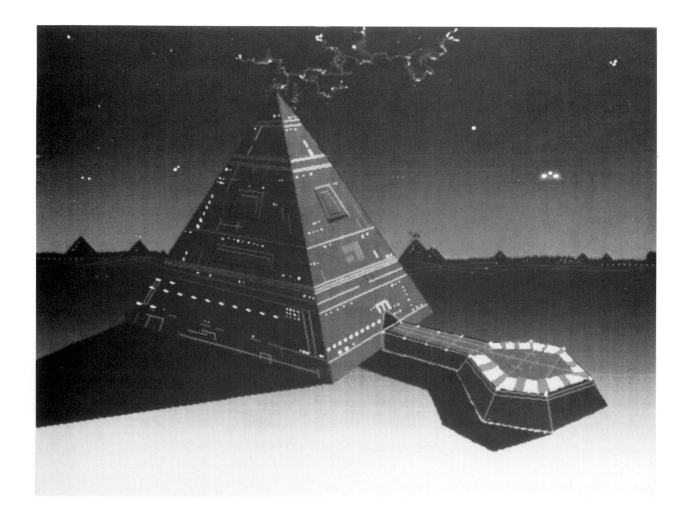

Nicknamed High-Tech High by its five thousand students, the school uses computers and electronic gear donated by industries in surrounding Silicon Valley. The businesses also suggest courses the school should teach, everything from programming in PASCAL and C to computer law and computer architecture to accounting and creative problem-solving.

Set up in 1982, the school is now establishing satellites throughout its region. A typical classroom contains at least ten computers, a certified public school teacher, and a computer specialist, often on loan from one of the Silicon Valley high-tech corporations. During the school day, Institute teachers offer courses at the district's regular schools, with students beginning to arrive at the Institute itself for extra courses after 3:00 P.M. Adults usually dominate the Institute's evening and weekend classes.

In the future, such round-the-clock, open-to-all-ages schools will be the norm. But the most striking difference in tomorrow's schools will be the pervasiveness of electronic delivery systems. And this change, too, has begun.

Already available are computer-video combinations that perfectly simulate science laboratories, with students controlling the experiment just as if they were working with actual test tubes and chemicals, deciding to put in so much of this or that, or to heat the mixture to a certain temperature. If the experiment blows up, nobody is hurt and no laboratory is destroyed.

Computerized optical discs will have a big impact on education. Joseph Price, head of the science and technology division at the Library of Congress, points out that optical technology, still an infant, already can store the contents of three hundred average-sized books on a single disc. In the future, books will be on-screen "electronic entities." In fact, Price is heading up a project to study putting the entire Library of Congress collection on discs. You might read the book, or parts of it, on the screen. For a printed version, you would go to a local "bookstore," which prints out hard copies on the spot, via special printers. "Such a technology will certainly have an impact on the way textbooks are used in the school of the future," says Price. "This kind of technology will give kids access to information beyond today's wildest imaginings—not only virtually anything written, but also images, like any of van Gogh's paintings."

Meanwhile, exploiting computers, satellites, and video, schools in the smallest rural community and poorest ghetto will be able to offer the same courses as a high-powered elite school. Using televideo hook-ups, they may well share the same high-caliber teachers.

"Biotechnology, the Japanese language—via technology, any school will be able to offer such courses, even if only one pupil is interested," says futurist LeRoy Hay, Connecticut's 1983 Teacher of the Year.

Such televideo classrooms are already taking shape. Recently, students of Spanish at the University of Maryland interviewed a Spanish-speaking Miami policeman by interactive satellite TV. Japan's televised "University of the Air" now enrolls nineteen thousand Tokyoites. This country's "Electronic University" now offers courses by computer. And Varina High School, in Henrico County, Virginia, has become the center of an experiment in televideo instruction. Varina, in suburban Richmond, enrolls 1,350 students. By TV, it reaches out to many more in the Virginia hinterlands.

One classroom at Varina is also a state-of-the-art television studio: While a teacher works with suburban students in the room, cameras feed the lesson to a microwave tower outside, which beams the signal to an educational television station in Richmond for broadcast to small schools in thirty-five rural counties. At the county schools, small groups—often only three to five students—watch the lesson intently on TV screens. Sometimes they push a button to signal that they have questions and the teacher's answers are heard throughout the televideo system.

"Some of the bright kids in these rural schools, planning to study engineering in college, maybe, really had their hands tied because they couldn't get calculus before," says Varina principal Al Fox. "If we had cable here, we could go right into every home. I think this is the delivery system of the future."

Computers, too, will have a major impact on how students learn and teachers teach. Unlike earlier educational technologies, most of which have vanished, computers will take hold in the schools because they are already transforming society itself. As Gregory Anrig, president of the Educational Testing Service, puts it, "Instead of replacing teachers, these technologies will supplement them so that youngsters not doing well in particular subjects can get extra help, while advanced kids will use the machines to work above and beyond the regular curriculum."

Carnegie-Mellon University is now linking its campus into a giant computer network, where everyone is on-line with everyone else.

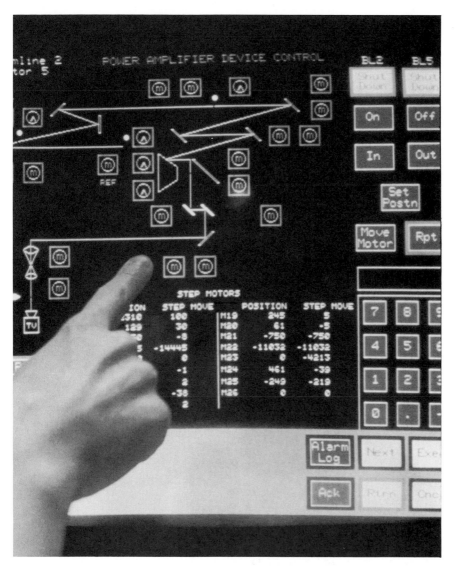

Increasingly, courses are taught via computer.

Students will write term papers on their computers, then send them on-line to their professors, who will return them electronically, graded and annotated with comments. Eventually, the system will admit the school's alumni, so that they can take refresher courses or tap into the university data base. Ultimately, the city of Pittsburgh may be connected to the system—a preview of the wired society of tomorrow, where virtually all information will be available to everyone with a home computer terminal. Meanwhile, computers are beginning to serve as tutors and teachers' aides.

For instance, the heart of the Waterford School, in Provo, Utah, is

Touch-sensitive computer screens already are making learning more fun for the young.

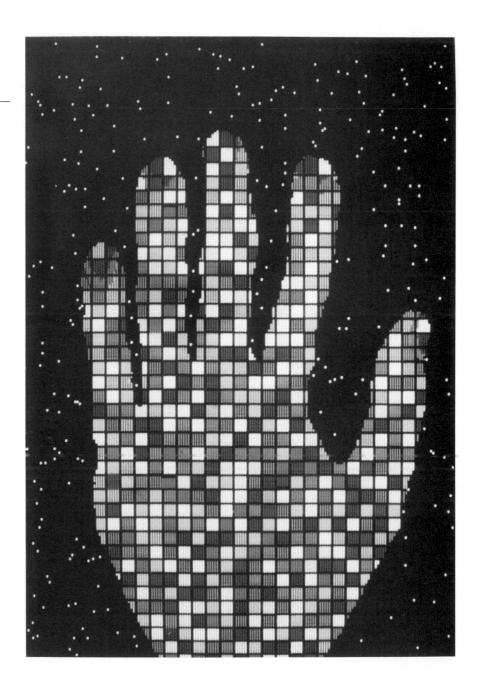

three computer workrooms. In each, a powerful microcomputer sends out wire tentacles like an octopus to thirty terminals. Working at these ninety terminals, the school's K–12 students are helping the school's faculty and experts from the nonprofit Wicat Institute, the school's founder, to forge the computerized education systems of tomorrow.

"Public schools can't experiment the way we can here. What we develop here is aimed at the public schools, however," says principal Nancy Heuston. At Waterford, she adds, teachers and computers teach youngsters how to think, how to ask questions, and how to get their questions answered.

In the lower grades, students work with computers to learn mathematics, reading—with computerized sound demonstrating pronunciation—and writing. A playful child who tries typing out the sentence, "The ball kicks Ben," will see an on-screen ball sprout legs and boot a boy. Students take periodic on-screen tests to check their progress. Then the computer decides whether to give them extra work or send them on to the next level. A high school student working on history might see this message pop onto the screen: "Your answer is right, but check the spelling!" Students working on French, using videodiscs coupled to the computer, might find themselves walking down a street in Montreal, looking at street signs and choosing which turns to take.

Every Friday, the computers print out progress reports on each student. One recent report revealed that a third grader, Jenny, was actually paying attention to her work only about three minutes out of every twenty. Alerted, teachers helped Jenny stretch her attention span, improving her work markedly.

"The old delivery system in the public schools is stressed, it's delivering all it can," says Nancy Heuston. "Computers are a new delivery system for teachers to use, and they can use them to make a first-rate education available to every child."

Artificial intelligence, still in its infancy, will dominate the educational system of 2019. "In just a few years, we'll have machines with twenty-five times the power of today's IBM PC," says David Kay, vice president of the Kaypro Corporation. "Programs will have advanced to the point of being able to sense what you don't understand and help you along." Within a decade, the machines will be able to see, listen, talk in languages ranging from English to Japanese, learn, and make judgements.

"My grandchild's best friend will probably be a computer," says Ira Goldstein, director of the Application Technology Laboratory at Hewlett-Packard's Palo Alto laboratories. "It might well be that every child will grow up with a computer nanny who, in time, will change with him, becoming his lifelong companion. It's difficult to imagine how such a society will work, but the potential is much greater than the risk."

ON THE ROAD:
TRANSPORTATION
IN 2019

Itinerary of Robert Hsuang-Huang
Destination: Las Vegas, Nevada, U.S.A.

July 20. **Pulau-Tioman to Singapore:** South China Sea Hovercraft

The Kauntan-Singapore hovercraft leaves Kauntan every two hours beginning at 6:00 A.M. Scheduled stops in Pulau-Tioman are at 7:13, 9:12, and so forth. Arrival times at Paya-Lebar Airport are 8:05, 10:05, and so forth. The 9:12 A.M. stop will permit a direct planeside connection in Singapore.

Singapore to Los Angeles, USA: Pan Am Flight 031

Departs Paya-Lebar International Airport, 10:30 A.M. Arrives Los Angeles Intercontinental Airport, 9:40 P.M. (local time). Flight time, 2 hours 10 minutes.

Luncheon includes choice of veal scallopini or chicken teriyaki, with complimentary choice of wines.

In-flight entertainment:

Channel 1, views outside the aircraft

Channel 2, "The Songs of Distant Earth"

Channel 3, *Beverly Hills Cowboy*

IMPORTANT CUSTOMS INFORMATION: Allow 30–45 minutes for clearance through U.S. Customs upon arrival.

Los Angeles to Las Vegas: California Magnetic Railroad (Calmag)

Trains run every hour. Scheduled stops at Los Angeles Intercontinental Airport are at 11:12 P.M., 12:12 A.M., and so forth. Arrival times in Las Vegas are 12:07 A.M., 1:07, and so forth. Travel time, 55 minutes.

July 21 to July 30. Rental car and hotel in Las Vegas

Rental car: A Jialing Aurora standard-size car is reserved at Avis Rent-a-Car at the Calmag station.

Hotel: Your reservation is being held at La Bamba Hotel and Casino, 3510 S. Las Vegas Blvd. ("The Strip"). Hotel accommodations include $2,000 in casino chips. A complimentary escort is available for one hour from Moonflowers. Call 540-0996, anytime.

July 30. **Las Vegas to Los Angeles Intercontinental Airport**

Calmag Trains run every hour, on the hour. Scheduled stops at Los Angeles Intercontinental Airport are at

Previous page: Strange wing designs will be common on the aircraft of 2019.

7:55, 8:55, and so forth. We recommend a 7:00 P.M. departure, with arrival at 7:55 P.M.

Los Angeles to Singapore: Pan Am Flight 038

Departs Los Angeles Intercontinental Airport, 9:00 P.M. Arrives Paya-Lebar International Airport, 2:15 P.M. (Singapore time). Flight time, 2 hours 15 minutes.

Dinner includes choice of mo shu pork or petit mignon, with complimentary choice of wines.

In-flight entertainment:

Channel 1, views outside the aircraft

Channel 2, *Rambo: First Blood, Part VI*

Channel 3, *Picnic*

IMPORTANT CUSTOMS INFORMATION: Allow 45–60 minutes for clearance through Singapore Customs upon arrival.

Singapore to Pulau-Tioman: South China Sea Hovercraft

The Singapore-Kauntan hovercraft leaves Paya-Lebar Airport at 2:30, 4:30, and so forth. Scheduled stops in Pulau-Tioman are at 3:23, 5:23, and so forth.

Total Cost for This Itinerary Is $23,542.68, including all taxes. We hope you have a pleasant trip.

What will the new model cars of 2019 be like? What about the aircraft and commercial jets of that day? And how about some entirely new technologies: orbiting spaceliners and craft that hover above the ground? All these things should be common before the next century is very old. Indeed, in a variety of labs and industrial research centers they are already beginning to take shape. Overall, the vehicles to come will make today's best designs appear nearly as obsolete as the cars and planes from the 1950s now seem to us.

Today, we are no further from 2019 than we are from 1953. What would people in 1953 have made of the interstate highway system? Or the Concorde, or even the Boeing 747? How would they have greeted the high-speed trains of Japan and France? We know that if anyone tried to remanufacture the cars of the early fifties without change, they could not legally be sold or driven. Those of us who were Walt Disney fans recall how he dazzled the nation with his 1954 feature *Man in Space*, which featured rocket craft somewhat less advanced than the space shuttle.

What, then, of the autos, aircraft, and spacecraft of 2019? The most outstanding of today's designs will still be cherished. The Pontiac Fiero and the Corvette Stingray may well be the latter-day counterparts of the early Ford Thunderbirds, and will evoke equal nostalgia. But overall, we can expect sweeping change.

"I gave a speech in 1965 about what the car would be like in twenty years," said Chrysler's Lee Iacocca recently, waving a cigar for emphasis. "I said the car will have four wheels, it will be a thousand pounds lighter, it will carry a sophisticated version of the internal-combustion engine, and it won't have a spare tire. I missed on the last one, but I was right about the rest. I said there wouldn't be any electric cars, the diesel wouldn't be important, and we wouldn't have the problem of the turbine solved. I underestimated the importance of microprocessors, as we all did; otherwise the prediction was pretty accurate. And you know what? I'd give that same speech today."

Iacocca's trends—lighter weight, increasingly sophisticated gasoline engines, and increasingly pervasive electronics—give us a pretty good idea of what we will find in the showrooms as dealers offer bargains to clear out their stock of 2019 models. Those bargains would give today's buyers a severe case of sticker shock, by the way; today's $12,000 prices, after all, would have represented three years of average income in 1953. But for 2019's low, low prices of $70,000, with easy credit terms, a new car will offer a lot.

Sleek aerodynamic styling may well make it as streamlined as a fighter plane. A low, sloping hood will merge smoothly into the windshield, the car's glass panels flush with the body. There will be no front grille; side-entry cooling will provide the needed airflow. Spoilers on the rear trunk, air dams under the front and rear bumpers, flush-mounted headlights, and wheel-well covers will all be included. The overall shape will be nearly as smooth and as self-contained as an egg.

Sheet-metal bodies will have gone the way of wood paneling. Instead, the bodies will be built of plastics and composites, reinforced with glass or graphite fibers. These give outstanding strength and low weight, up to 60 percent less than steel. Body panels and parts will be prepared at the factory in completely painted and finished form, then glued together. Gone will be spot-welds, primer, and other old-fashioned, metallic features.

The new bodies will never corrode. Moreover, fenders made of certain plastics will absorb a dent and minutes later bounce back to

In the zero-g equality of space, clothes for the well-dressed traveler are likely to be unisex. (*Inset photograph* © Anthony Wolff; *background* © Rick Sternbach)

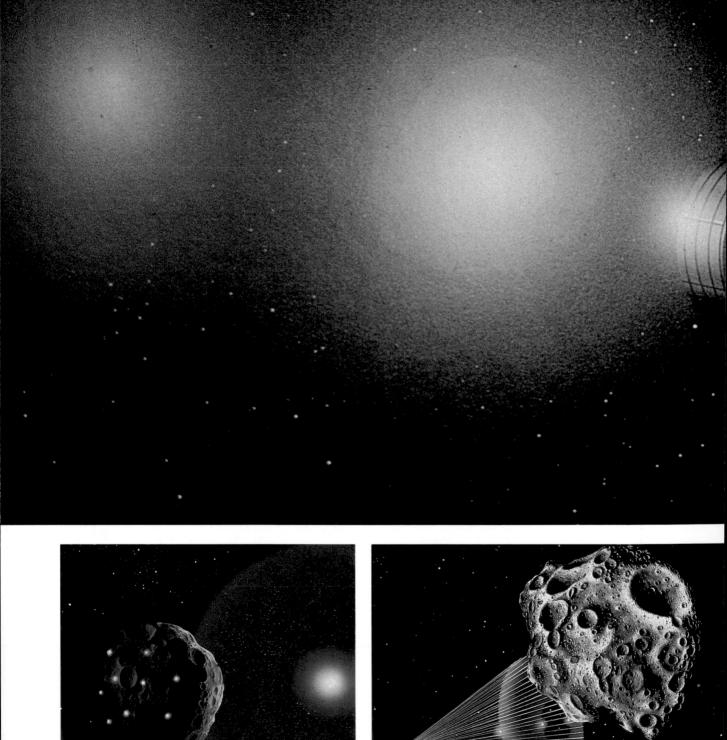

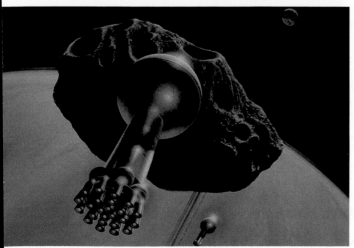

Fusion-powered ships like the one above are already on the drawing board, and the day we mine the asteroids is drawing ever nearer. (All pictures © Rick Sternbach)

Artists originally conceived of space colonies as bizarre fantasies, but NASA's space station will be a workaday reality in 2019. (© Rick Sternbach)

their original shape. No metal can do that. Tomorrow's auto salespeople will also echo the words of a Chrysler research director: "We use plastics for beauty. The fineness of detail possible with plastics often cannot be achieved any other way. The breadth of beauty, of texture, feel, and comfort of body cloths possible with plastics cannot be matched by any other material, including fine Corinthian leather."

When the buyers open the hoods, however, they might not even bother to notice what Nissan, for one, today advertises as a major goodie: turbo power. The turbocharger will be built into the engine as a standard component, like the water pump. Exhaust gases will spin its turbine and drive a compressor similar to that in a jet engine, permitting the motor to burn more fuel and thus deliver more power within a smaller, more compact design.

The engine and its transmission will operate under microprocessor control. The transmission will be continuously variable, in effect making available an infinite number of gears. As the car proceeds through traffic or onto the highway, its microchip will continually adjust the engine speed, its tuning, and the transmission to give the best efficiency. These adjustments will also control pollution while avoiding engine roughness or knocking. What's more, the car will never need a tune-up.

It also may never need cooling water or even motor oil. While the gasoline engine should hold its own, it may face stiff competition from advanced diesels. These will be built with ceramics capable of resisting high temperatures. Even the pistons, rings, and valves could be made of these materials. Such engines may be air-cooled and might eliminate the need for lubrication. Diesels are heavier and more costly than gasoline engines, but are much more rugged and durable; they last almost forever. They have no spark plugs, carburetor, or distributor, so they have fewer things to go wrong. This worry-free long life will be attractive to owners who want to hang onto their cars for a long time, and with auto designs staying nearly the same from year to year, surely many owners will do so.

The cars of 2019 will also be loaded with electronic options. These will be easy to put in; a simple loop of cable running from a central microchip will replace today's complex wiring systems and accommodate whatever the owner wants to add. The instrument panel, of course, will give warning of any trouble spot in the engine, drive train, or tires. On-board navigation will make it impossible to get lost. The

car will be able to locate its position using satellite navigation systems and show it on a color video map display. This TV display—located on the passenger side, not the driver's side—will store an atlas of maps on a videodisc. Artificial intelligence then will give suggestions on how to reach the destination, while offering the trip-planning services of today's Automobile Association of America.

Other electronic systems will add to the car's safety and convenience. In case of trouble, its microchips will tell the mechanic just what's wrong. In case of real trouble, like a breakdown out in the desert, the car will transmit an emergency call to a watching satellite. A radar system will warn of cars in the blind spots, and there may even be automatic collision avoidance, to brake or steer out of impending disasters. An alcohol detector will prevent the driver from starting up if he's had too many for the road. And in normal operation, the suspension will be electronically controlled, offering a stiff ride for the freeway or a softer ride over city potholes.

Such autos may top a hundred miles per gallon. Still, they may face competition from maglevs, the magnetically levitated railroads now operating over short lengths of track in Japan and Germany. The German system is in regular service near Bremen, carrying nearly two hundred passengers at over two hundred miles per hour. The Japanese maglev is still under development, but set a record of 321 miles per hour on a test track in 1979.

The German design, Transrapid-06, amounts to a practical version of the Disneyland monorail. Its rail has a five-foot-wide T-shaped cross section that is raised on pylons sixteen to twenty feet above the ground. The train rides on the rail with the sides extending downward to wrap around the T. The train's weight is pulled upward as electromagnets in these side-extensions are attracted to other magnets built into the underside of the T. Since this attraction would quickly cause the train to hit the track with a loud clang, the electromagnets have control systems to vary their force. They thus maintain a steady separation of an inch or so below the track. The track, in turn, sets up a magnetic wave that propels the train forward like a surfboard on the ocean.

Such a monorail will soon be built in the United States. The U.S. Department of Transportation has approved the Transrapid for a proposed 8,800-passenger-a-day link between Los Angeles and Las Vegas. It could be in service by the early 1990s. This train would be more

Opposite page: The car buyer of the future finds some surprises under the hood of the new 2019 models.

Inset: Drag racers in 2019? Doubtlessly, the desire to race automobiles will survive into the next century.

energy efficient than an airplane and be in use for more hours a day; thus, its round-trip cost could be as little as $50, half the current airfare. Trip time will be an hour, from downtown L.A. to The Strip. Passengers will appreciate the smooth, almost noiseless ride and the huge windows that give a feeling of space and openness.

This German approach, however, stands to be challenged by the faster Japanese design. Its magnets do not attract a track underside; rather, they repel. The track resembles a trough, with a U-shaped cross section; the train nestles cozily within its curve, riding several inches above the track and banking in curves in a natural way. It uses super-conducting magnets.

When we think of magnets, we usually think of the simple iron blocks that hold messages to a refrigerator door. No iron magnet can be strong enough to support a train, however; for that electromagnets are needed. They work by sending electrical current through coils of wire. But these coils have electrical resistance, which turns the currents into useless heat, wasting electricity.

Superconducting magnets avoid these problems. They use the coldest known substance, liquid helium, to freeze coils of niobium-titanium alloy to temperatures close to absolute zero, $-460°F$. In such frigid conditions, the metal loses all its electrical resistance. A flow of current then will circulate through the coil without loss, producing a magnetic field that can persist indefinitely. This field can be even stronger than that of an ordinary electromagnet. A maglev train using such magnets can cruise for long distances needing no power to keep itself levitated. All it needs is a small cryostat, an ultracold refrigerator to liquify the modest amounts of helium that boil off within the insulation.

Such advantages have come at a price; the alloys, insulation, magnet designs, and cryostats have all demanded a great deal of research. But today, the first industrial-scale superconducting system is in place. It is installed at Fermilab, the high-energy physics facility outside Chicago, where it is being used to accelerate subatomic particles. It features over a thousand magnets, forming a ring more than a mile across. And with this, the early decades of the next century will certainly see maglevs take off.

These new trains will be built down the center medians of interstate highways, along such heavily traveled routes as San Diego–Los Angeles–San Francisco and Boston–New York–Washington. They will link airports to city centers; passengers will sit in comfort, twenty feet off the ground, and smile as they zip past fuming motorists stuck in five o'clock traffic. Indeed, they will permit us to build more immense, sprawling airports such as Dallas–Fort Worth. If one such proposed mega-jetport, the Los Angeles Intercontinental Airport, is built in remote desert country a hundred miles from the city, it will certainly need the high-speed transportation that maglev trains offer. Commuter trains may well make a comeback, and if the elevated monorails prove popular, our city centers could soon resemble Disney's Tomorrowland.

Such maglevs will run at no more than half the speed of an airliner, but with their city-center convenience they will give similar total trip times for distances up to several hundred miles. Inevitably, their low cost will spur thoughts of a transcontinental system. However, even July 20, 2019 is too soon for this to become a reality.

Levitated vehicles are not limited to land, they also will ply the seas. They will rise not on magnets, but on cushions of air. These hovercraft lift themselves to heights of several feet by blowing air into skirts that surround their hulls. As described in *Profiles of the Future*, they eventually will use new and inexpensive fuels and engines and will reach sizes as large as 100,000 tons, replacing the world's ships. But that won't happen by 2019; at that point hovercraft will see service primarily as high-speed ferries and naval craft.

The world's largest hovercraft today is a version of the SR.N4, the cross-Channel ferry built by British Hovercraft. It carries 419 people and 60 cars at a height of 10 feet at speeds up to 75 miles per hour, with a loaded weight of 336 tons. It thus amounts to a slow, low-flying Boeing 747—the passenger capacity and weight are the same. Larger hovercraft are on the way; Bell Aerospace has proposed to build one that will weigh in at 3,360 tons. What's more, British Hovercraft is trying to cut the cost of hovercraft transport by creating simpler, more robust designs that require less maintenance.

Even in their current versions, there is plenty of room for new uses. Hovercraft can cruise onto a runway to pick up passengers from planeside, then proceed to another airport some distance away. Such services could link New York's La Guardia Airport to Connecticut, across Long Island Sound, or could run between the San Francisco and Oakland airports. Already a similar link is being considered to join Singapore's airport with resorts on Malaysia's east coast. Although the direct-line distance across the water is only about thirty miles, the trip now takes five hours by road. Mexico's Yucatan Peninsula offers similar prospects, with numerous seaside resorts that are difficult to reach by road.

The navy is also interested. By 1995 it will buy a fleet of 107 amphibious assault vehicles known as LCAC (Landing Craft, Air Cushion). These will open up 70 percent of the world's coasts to amphibious landings, compared with the 17 percent now considered accessible. Today's landing craft require Miami-like beaches, which are rare, but the LCACs can go ashore in eight-foot surf, over ten-foot sand dunes, over marshes, sand bars, or ice. They can penetrate miles inland carrying tanks, trucks, heavy artillery, and dozens of troops, then return to their support ships at fifty knots. Riding on five-foot cushions of air, they go right over underwater obstacles or mines, while torpedoes pass harmlessly beneath them.

Their larger successors will carry helicopters or vertical-takeoff jets and will be used in antisubmarine warfare. Their high speeds will allow them to sweep larger areas, and they will be needed, for submarines themselves are getting faster. Already, intelligence analysts have projected a speed in excess of fifty knots for the latest Soviet attack sub, designated *Mike* in the West, now being tested. The keys to such speeds, and to the even faster submarine speeds of 2019, lie in new propulsion systems and new methods for reducing drag.

The screw propeller has ruled the sea for over a century, but it is about to be challenged by a new technology: magnetohydrodynamics, or MHD. An MHD hull would feature a rectangular channel resembling a long hallway. At its top and bottom are the north and south poles of powerful magnets. To the left and right are negative and positive electrodes, with a powerful electric current passing across the channel.

The channel fills with sea water, which conducts electricity and can be made much more conductive if seeded with a metal such as cesium. The water then flows rapidly under the action of the electric current and the magnetic fields, blowing vigorously out the back in a jet. Reversing the electric current aims the water jet to the front, allowing a sub to stop very quickly. This arrangement offers high speed and maneuverability, along with exceptional quietness, making the sub less detectable.

For bursts of speed, tomorrow's subs will rely on special techniques to reduce their drag. The Office of Naval Research is sponsoring studies of how subs could be coated with a smooth, rubbery skin, somewhat like the skin of a dolphin. Naval experts at Pennsylvania State University have tried injecting micron-sized air bubbles into the boundary layer, the thin layer of water than clings to the surface of a sub and slows it down. These bubbles have reduced water friction–caused drag by over 80 percent.

In San Diego, the Naval Underwater Systems Center is injecting gooey polymers or soaplike chemicals into the boundary layer. The water then flows past the hull with less turbulence and hence less drag. Other techniques being studied include warming the hull with heat from the nuclear reactor, and sucking boundary-layer water in through slots. If a sub of 2019 is being chased by an air-cushion craft, it might turn on the heat and the sucking pumps, exude bubbles or goo from the hull, and speed away from danger.

In pursuing these advances, submarine experts will be drawing on many of the methods that will also be used in research on aircraft. Today, it is rapidly becoming possible to design new jetliners entirely on computers, with little or no need for wind tunnels. The resulting designs can be put through their paces in silicon skies, then manufactured and sent into service. In a few years it will also become possible to do the same for new aircraft engines, which are more difficult to design and demand more powerful computers. As with submarines, the drag of tomorrow's aircraft will be sharply reduced. And as with autos, composite materials—carbon fibers embedded in epoxy plastic, for instance—will replace aluminum as the primary construction material. These composites are lighter and stronger than any metal; the plastic plane will become common.

Such developments already are opening the way to an immense wave of innovation in aircraft design, featuring new engines, new and lightweight shapes with low drag, and craft that will cruise the upper atmosphere, then leap easily into space. In a March 1985 report from the White House, President Reagan's science advisor, George Keyworth, stated that, "there are possible today monumental advances in aircraft performance. Leapfrog advances are definitely possible which would make obsolete virtually all significant civil and military aircraft operational today. The question is not whether these advances will be made, only when they will be achieved and by whom."

Let us visit an airport of 2019 and take a look around. It quickly becomes clear that the planes operate as if they were buses. They do not spend hours sitting and waiting. Rather, they taxi up to the gates, discharge a load of passengers and baggage, take on a new load, and are off on another trip, all within twenty minutes or less. The airlines appreciate this; planes make money only when they are in the air with a full load of passengers. Another nice feature is their fuel efficiency, more than double that of today's best jets. All this will mean lower ticket prices and more low-fare specials.

These airliners will include trim, twin-engine planes for short to medium hauls, as well as the big widebodies. Many of them, particularly those serving medium-length routes, will have no jets, for the propeller is due to make a comeback. Its new form, called a "propfan," resembles six or eight scimitars mounted by their tips to a hub, each scimitar being a fan blade. A plane thus equipped can achieve jet speeds with much lower fuel consumption. Short-haul craft, especially those serving commuters, will be even more radical in design. They will be built with particularly thin wings for lowest drag, which will look as though they had been mounted backward by mistake. Such swept-forward designs work very well when the wing is thin. And passengers in flight will see these wings change their length and width, extending or contracting to give the best performance.

With lighter weight and greater fuel efficiency, the widebodies will fly farther; nonstop flights from the East Coast to destinations across the Pacific will be common. However, these long hauls will remain wearying to the passengers. Trans-Pacific jumbos, therefore, will face stiff competition from supersonic jetliners, twenty-first-century successors to the Concorde. For the Concorde, as any aeronautical engineer will tell you, is obsolete even today. It is built of aluminum, which cannot stand high temperatures; the heat produced during high-speed flight thus limits it to twice the speed of sound. Worse, its Olympus jet engines are notorious fuel hogs. To achieve supersonic speeds, they rely on afterburners similar to those of military jets, which are among the most fuel-thirsty engines in common use.

Tomorrow's Pacific Supersonic Transport will be nearly twice as heavy as the Concorde—375 versus 200 tons—but will carry six hundred passengers, five times as many as the Concorde. It will cruise at more than three times the speed of sound and may well outrace the famous SR-71 reconnaissance aircraft, the Blackbird, which today holds

Opposite page: A prototype of a helicopter of the future.

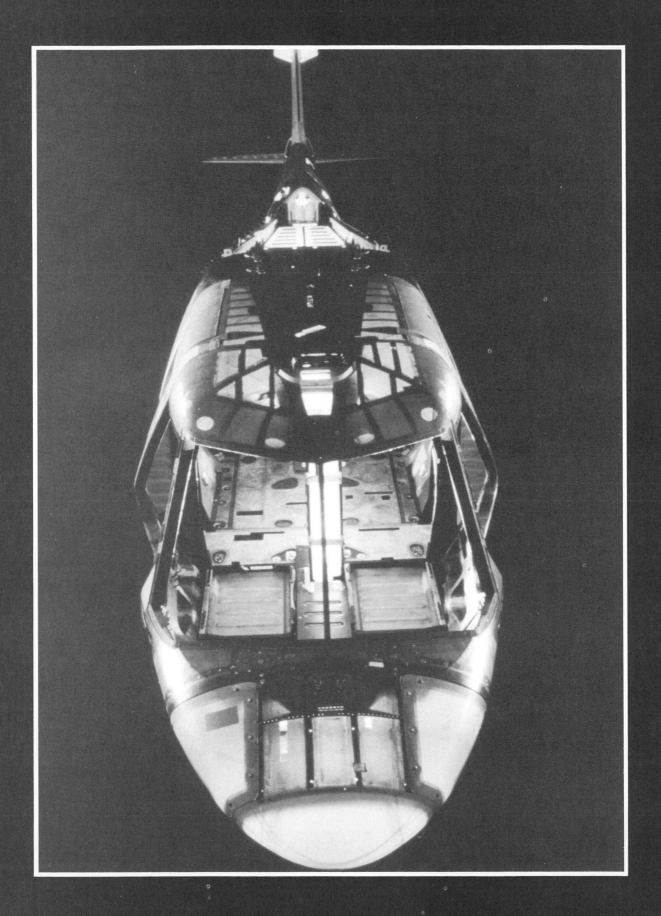

the speed record, 2,193 miles per hour. This high speed will allow it to do three times the passenger-hauling work of a similarly sized jumbo jet while burning only twice as much fuel—its fuel efficiency will be three times the Concorde's. It will fly six thousand miles at a stretch, taking four hours for the Tokyo–San Francisco run. Ticket prices will be competitive with those of the subsonic widebodies.

The key to this is supersonic cruise, which means flying at supersonic speeds without the afterburners, and it demands a host of advanced technologies: methods for producing smooth airflows past aircraft shapes while avoiding drag-producing turbulence, lightweight temperature-resistant composites, engine turbine blades made from single metal crystals for better strength, smoother engine airflows, and advanced cooling methods. Some of these have already been studied in NASA's Supersonic Cruise Program. Others are being demonstrated aboard the X-29 research aircraft, which is already flying. And the air force intends to feature supersonic cruise in its next interceptor, the Advanced Tactical Fighter.

At the airport, a Pacific Supersonic Transport is a long, sleek affair, its fuselage looking remarkably like a thick arrow pierced with windows. The small fins and tail surfaces add to the arrowlike effect. Some versions have two such fuselages side by side, allowing passengers to wave to each other across the broad central wing. The wings form a sharply swept-back delta, with winglets, small finlike extensions, at their tips to cut drag. Mounted beneath these wings are the thick black cylinders of the engines, two for the standard version, three for the double-fuselage model.

Still, such aircraft may fall short of being the most advanced in service. Just as the Concorde prospers in an era of cut-rate flights to Europe, so there will be travelers for whom even Mach 3, three times the speed of sound, is too slow. On the longest routes, halfway around the world, even the best supersonic craft would have to stop to refuel. Ranges of six thousand miles will be all very fine amid the cozy community of the Northern Hemisphere, but as the Southern Hemisphere comes into its own, something more will be needed. Travelers enduring their ten-hour flights from Rio to Singapore will look with envy at the orbiting space stations, which cover the same distance in forty minutes. Thus, the real successor to the Concorde, as a costly but speedy aircraft that is profitable over specialized routes, will be the hypersonic transport. It will fly at more than half the speed of a satellite and reach any destination within two hours.

New engines are the key to such craft and today are being vigorously studied. These engines are variants of the ramjet, the simplest type of jet engine. A ramjet is little more than a carefully shaped tube or duct with fuel injectors. At high speeds it relies on the sheer force of its forward motion to ram air into its combustion chamber. Ramjets have two disadvantages: They cannot take off directly from a runway, but require an auxiliary boost to get up to Mach 3, where the air-ramming effect becomes effective; and they cannot fly beyond Mach 6, because aerodynamic heating then becomes too intense.

At Aerojet Techsystems in Sacramento, California, the first problem is well in hand today. The solution is called the "air turbo-ramjet," which places the rotating compressor of a conventional jet engine within a ramjet. This compressor then gives the ramjet its needed boost at low speeds, yet does not get in the way at high speeds. The air turbo-ramjet thus can take an aircraft from a runway to Mach 6. (However, orbital speed is Mach 25.)

The Mach 6 speed limit arises because the air within a conventional ramjet slows down and heats up. This aerodynamic heating is common in all high-speed flight. At Mach 6 it amounts to 2,700°F, which is too hot for engine materials to stand. The path to higher speeds, then, lies in permitting airflows within a ramjet that do not slow down, but zip through at supersonic speeds. The resulting engine is called a "supersonic-combustion ramjet," or "scramjet." NASA has been working with scramjets at its Langley Research Center in Hampton, Virginia, where experiments have shown that simple designs can reach speeds of Mach 12.

The Pentagon's Defense Advanced Research Projects Agency (DARPA) has set its engine-builders to studying scramjets using supercomputers, and it has produced a breakthrough. A DARPA scramjet can take off from a runway and reach Mach 15, possibly Mach 25. The agency is seeking $200 million to build a prototype engine, which is to be ready in 1989.

Imagine, then, that such scramjets are powering the huge, sleek craft that will ferry us to a space station. It accelerates slowly on the runway, made ponderous by its load of fuel, but gathers speed as its engines give their initial boost. In a minute we are over the open ocean, which falls away as we gain speed and altitude. Soon the aircraft levels off and cruises.

Then the captain announces, "All passengers, please return to your seats and fasten your seat belts. We are beginning main acceleration." The muted rumble of the boost is suddenly drowned out by a louder, more insistent roar, as the scramjets build power. Now the ship comes alive. You can feel a shudder as it passes Mach 1. Down below, the clouds fall away; above the sky deepens from dark blue to a velvet purple. The clouds part, and the Bahamas appear amid the ocean, as clear as on a map. The emerald-green of the adjacent shallow seas bring back memories of last year's vacation. Now the sky is almost black, and—is that the curvature of the Earth? There is no vibration, but on the cabin bulkhead a digital Machmeter displays the increasing speed: Mach 4, Mach 6, on up to Mach 22.

At that speed, close to orbital velocity, and at 180,000 feet, there is a sudden jolt as the rockets come on. Now the acceleration makes it uncomfortable to lean forward to look out the window even though that bright blue-white band of light arcing above what now is definitely the Earth's curvature makes the struggle to look well worthwhile. Experienced astronauts wouldn't bother, but you don't want to miss anything. Still, in less than a minute, the roar of rocket power dies away, the acceleration relaxes. We are in orbit. A sign lights up: CAUTION. WEIGHTLESSNESS. FASTEN SEAT BELTS. NO SMOKING. Then out the window your destination appears; a big collection of tanks and cylinders that will be home for several months.

Such hybrids of air and space—even the earliest versions, which DARPA hopes to build and fly well before the year 2000—will make the space shuttle nearly as obsolete as a Spanish galleon. The shuttle was designed largely in the premicrochip era; its on-board computers are less advanced than the ones you can buy at Radio Shack. One consequence of this is that it takes an army of ground crews to prepare the ship for launch: Twelve thousand government employees are needed. Its successors, however, will rely on artificial intelligence. Expert systems running on advanced computers will interpret instrument readings with the skill of an experienced Kennedy Space Center operator. AI will provide quick launch and turnaround for more than tomorrow's super-shuttles. Other ships will almost never return to Earth, but will instead fly continuously between space stations and the Moon.

NASA plans a return to the Moon early in the next century and is preparing to build the spacecraft that will be used in the construction of the first lunar base. These are the space tugs, the Orbital Transfer Vehicles (OTVs). With "smart" instruments aiding their launch preparations, they will need only three controllers in an orbiting command center. An OTV will resemble a cluster of propellant tanks and rocket motors braced together with a spidery array of struts. Its principal novelty will become apparent near the end of its mission.

After a flight to the Moon, the OTV's path will take it through a low point close to Earth. Near that point, it must lose some three thousand meters per second of velocity, then drop into a low orbit close to that of the space station. To avoid carrying to the Moon and back extra fuel for braking the rockets, it will be slowed by atmosphere drag sixty miles over the Earth's surface. Just above atmosphere, it will deploy a ballute, a lightweight, ring-shaped balloon that will completely surround the fuel tanks. The ballute will be covered with a thermal-protection blanket woven from ceramic fibers. (We think of these substances as hard abrasives; but Japan's Nippon Carbon Company has learned to prepare silicon carbide as a yarn, which Dow Corning is marketing under the name Nicalon. Similarly, the 3M Company and the Manville Corporation are offering fibers and fabrics woven from other ceramics.) With these, tomorrow's Moon rockets will lose speed in the atmosphere, to take up orbits close to the space station.

The lunar base, however, may not be where the real action is in 2019. All along, the Defense Department will be pursuing its "Star Wars" defense system. This name is more apt than people realize. One of its spinoffs may well be the first spaceship suitable for interstellar flight. And while such a mission will take place later rather than sooner, even the early versions of this ship will be capable of flying to Mars in as little as nine days.

The "Star Wars" starship, which depends on the ideas of Lowell Wood, who has originated many of the key concepts for missile defense, is to rely on laser fusion: Theoretically, a powerful, rapidly pulsed laser zaps small pellets of fusion fuel, which then explode like miniature hydrogen bombs. These explosions produce superhot plasmas that expand at speeds of several percent of the speed of light. A ring-shaped superconducting magnet then aims a jet of plasma out the back, producing thrust. Developing the lasers and hydrogen pellets for these superengines are two of the most difficult technological problems now in the works. But they should soon be well in hand.

At Avco Everett Research Labs in Massachusetts, work is going forward on EMRLD, the Excimer Moderate-power Raman-shifted Laser Device. (The Raman shift is an optical effect that changes a laser's wavelength.) EMRLD, which is to fire laser beams at a rate of some fifty times per second, will be complete by 1990. Its successors, capable of shooting down missiles, will also be large enough to power a starship. For this purpose, such lasers would need a new version of the pulse-forming network that produces intense electrical bursts that fire the laser. But Gerold Yonas, chief scientist of "Star Wars," describes such networks as, "remarkably simple devices that can be purchased off the shelf or built in a machine shop."

These lasers will need specialized optical systems to produce the extremely short bursts of light needed for fusion. The first such system is currently being installed on the Aurora excimer laser at Los Alamos, which is to be used for research in laser fusion. As for the pellet, California's Lawrence Livermore National Laboratory now has its Nova laser in operation, the world's largest. This laser is shooting energy bursts at scale models of the pellets to be used for fusion.

The first test of full-sized pellets is to come in October 1987 at Sandia Labs in New Mexico. This involves the Particle Beam Fusion Assembly, which Yonas managed before he left for the "Star Wars" project. The world's first fusion test device whose energies approach those needed to drive a starship, it is already in operation. In the critical 1987 tests, it should put two megajoules—enough energy to lift 325,000 tons ten feet into the air—into the pellet, causing it to explode and release six megajoules. Soon after, pellet experts such as John Nuckolls of Livermore expect to produce pellets that can release enough energy to drive a rocket.

Such rockets are a particular concern of Roderick Hyde of Livermore, who works for Wood and has been studying their design since the early 1970s. As he puts it, "The technical problems in building space-based laser systems for missile defense are on a par with those of building a rocket propelled by laser fusion." Many of the necessary technologies, of course, are highly classified. Thus, Wood believes, when it becomes possible to build this rocket, that fact may not be revealed to the public.

"It will be quite sufficient," says Wood, "if some high-level people with clearances can come in and say, 'Yes indeed, you've nailed it down, and it's too bad that you will never be able to publish exactly how you nailed it down. But we will agree and sign our names to a report to send in to the folks in Washington, saying that you have definitely established the feasibility of laser fusion for rocket propulsion.' We hope to do that in the very near term, in a few years rather than in a few half-decades."

In 2019, then, the first of these rockets could be in use, probing far beyond the Moon, preparing to open up Mars and to follow the Moon base with one on that planet. And in the research centers with their computer-aided design systems, plans may well be afoot to build new, more advanced craft with large tanks of fusion fuel. These will probe beyond the solar system, into the vastness of interstellar space.

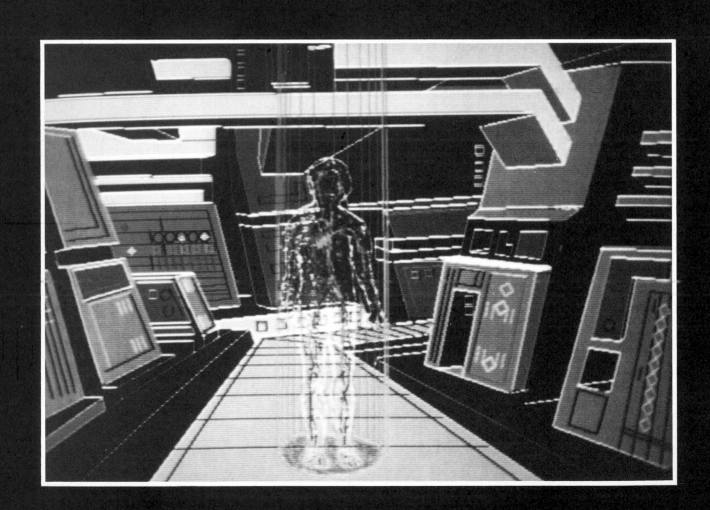

A DAY
IN THE LIFE
OF A
SPACE STATION

MAMA'S SOUPS, INC.
Interoffice Memorandum

To: Mortimer Fieldstone, President
From: Sidney Stryver, Marketing Director
Date: July 20, 2019
Re: Explosions of Mama's Wet-Packs in space

Dear Mort:

We have a problem.

During the past six years and four months, under Contract NAS–12–7013, Mama's Soups, Inc., has been supplying NASA with packaged products for use by astronauts in space. In the past twelve months, we have received seven complaints alleging poor quality control in packaging. These soups are freeze-dried in polyethylene packs, and must be reconstituted by adding water from a hose.

The complaints have alleged that when an astronaut adds too much water, the pack sometimes explodes, and comes apart at the seams. Such explosions appear to have inconvenienced crew members, and may have interfered with NASA flight operations.

Our legal department has been investigating the validity of these complaints, and has concluded that there are grounds for NASA to terminate its contract, the said NAS–12–7103. Most recently, aboard the space station *Magellan*, astronaut Bonnie Dunbar has taken the lead in urging NASA to implement such a cancellation. It is believed her discomfiture stems from a recent incident in which, as she has alleged, "gobs of Mama's Clam Chowder flew into my ears and hair."

I have ordered our packaging department to prepare a special set of three soups—Oyster Stew, Chicken, and the aforementioned Clam Chowder—with double-strength sealing. This order is enclosed below as Internal Directive 19–7–3026. I further have dispatched a gross of each type, 432 wet-packs in all, aboard the company Lear jet to Cape Canaveral. As of this morning, Dr. Anita Gale of the Payload Manifest Office, Kennedy Space Center, has advised me that the said packages have been safely launched into orbit aboard the super-shuttle *Christa*, and are to be delivered by 4:00 P.M., Eastern Standard Time.

In a radio communication to Cape Canaveral, Ms. Dunbar has stated, quoting, that, "I and the crew will suspend our boycott, and will try the new packages." However, again quoting, "In the event of any further such failure, we will throw the whole lot in the dumpster." Thus far, her superiors within NASA have refused to intervene.

You will recall that on July 22, network television is to begin carrying the new advertisements from Doyle Dane Bernbach, on which you and I have set such hope, and which we had discussed five weekends ago at the hunting lodge. At this point, then, it is in the hands of the astronauts as to whether we can avoid seeing this advertising campaign undercut at the very moment it is to air on the networks.

Yours,

Sidney

Bonnie Dunbar exists. She is young enough to still be flying in 2019, yet she has already had her first shuttle flight, and has been making a name for herself in her field, materials science. She thus has emerged from the obscurity of the most junior astronauts while offering a change from the usual macho-man image.

In 2019, she will be seventy years old. Many of us would think of her as a retiree in Sun City. Yet at that age, General Douglas MacArthur was commanding the U.S. Army in the Korean War; Ronald Reagan was beginning his first term in the White House. In the next century, amid increasing life spans and standards of health, many people still will be living vigorous, useful lives at age seventy-five and beyond. Moreover, the baby-boom generation, who virtually invented jogging and health spas, will be a long way from being ready to settle for a pension and retirement.

NASA is now designing Bonnie Dunbar's "retirement home," America's first permanent space station, to be launched by the mid-1990s. This station is to support a crew of six, with new astronauts being exchanged or relieved every ninety days when the space shuttle makes its quarterly visit. The station will feature several modules, fifteen feet in diameter and thirty-five to forty feet long, a size that will fit conveniently within the shuttle's cargo bay.

By 2019, however, all this will give way to a new generation of space technology. Already, NASA is planning the spacecraft that will replace the shuttle. A few years after the space station is complete, this craft will offer larger and heavier payloads, lower costs, and much better ease of operation.

And beyond the successor to today's shuttle, there will be a new space station. Its layout resembles an airplane with a set of rocket tanks attached to its belly and a Stonehenge-like archway on its back. The "fuselage" is built from two long cylindrical modules, mounted in tandem. Spreading out from the front of one of the modules are the wings, long rectangular solar panels of midnight blue. Extending "above" them is the tail, a vertical panel for the radiator. In darkness it can be seen glowing a soft red as it removes waste heat from the station. A hangar for rocket craft extends below the two tandem cylinders; nearby are the station's propellant tanks. Atop the fuselage three more cylinders form an archway that contains labs for materials science and life science, as well as the control center.

Just now it is early morning, and the space station *Magellan* is three hundred miles above the dark side of Earth; like a ship at night, it shows few lights. It is pitch black outside. Astronaut Joe Allen once compared it to Mammoth Cave in Kentucky, when the guide turned off the lights and said, "You're going to experience the darkest dark you ever felt." Off to one side are the stars—hard, sharp, brilliant, with colors of red, yellow, even blue and green. Follow the stars until they stop, at the edge of a vast black region in the field of view. That is Earth.

Down below are flashes from a massive set of thunderstorms extending over Mexico, Texas, and much of the Gulf. A lightning stroke flashes, a sudden spark of bright purple momentarily lighting up the clouds. Then two or three more go off at the same time, followed by dozens of others, sparking and flickering across hundreds of miles. For several seconds the lightning strokes flash, as though someone was conducting a light show, pointing to this cloud, then that, then another, all in rapid succession. Finally the show dies away, the phosphorescence fades to blackness, but only for a few seconds. Then another purple flash illuminates the clouds, and the light show begins anew.

To the east, the dark gives way to a band of bright blue, an arc between Earth and stars. Very soon the blue spreads and grows brighter. A thin crescent of red forms beneath, with a blob of intense orange-yellow below its center. A moment later the gold becomes a brilliant yellow ball. The blues and reds pale, fading quickly in the light of the Sun. Toward the horizon, the Atlantic shimmers in silver, contrasting sharply with the dark green of Florida. Now the station is crossing the line between night and morning. A row of clouds glows with silver-bronze as they sparkle in the day's first light. A minute later the young morning discloses the Bahamas amid shallow seafloors of an iridescent blue-green. Inside the space station, fresh sunlight streams through a porthole, forming a patch of color on the pastel blue wall.

As Hawaii and the Grand Canyon existed for millions of years before the coming of man, so these scenes of dawn have existed since the earliest days of the Earth. Only Bonnie Dunbar is awake this morning to see them—she has a streak of romance in her soul. For everyone else on board it still is nighttime, and the space station is a quiet place at night. There is the soft whirr of fans and blowers at the opposite end of the crew's quarters, forty feet from the sleeping astronauts, less obtrusive than many bedroom air conditioners. Twice in each orbit, as the station passes between day and night, its outer surfaces expand or contract slightly and make little popping noises. Occasionally, the station passes through the South Atlantic anomaly, a dip in the Earth's magnetic field. Then the cosmic rays come through and strike cells in the retina to produce flashes of light, bright sudden sparks seen with the eyes closed, every minute or so. Once in a while a rocket thruster goes off, keeping the station from drifting in its orientation. It sounds like a hammer distantly pounding in one of the other sections of the station. For those who have drawn shades over the portholes in their cabins, the bright blue light of Earth fades into no more than a dim, diffuse glow, just enough to take the edge off the darkness.

Through these portholes, in the dim interior light, it is just possible to make out vague, bulky shapes resembling large cocoons. These are the crew's bunks, fastened to the walls as if sleeping bags could be hung like curtains. Eighteen people live here, each in a wedge-shaped cubicle eight feet by nine, about the size of a small closet. It doesn't take much room to be comfortable in zero-g, and a restful bed is particularly easy. With no pressure from one's weight, the hardest steel bulkhead feels softer than a waterbed. Indeed, no one ever really touches the steel, since even a slight touch pushes you away.

You wouldn't even need a bed at all—everyone could just sleep comfortably in midair—except for the ventilation. A bedroom in normal gravity usually has slow-moving currents in the air, and since our exhaled breath is warm, it rises. In a space station, however, there are no such currents, and carbon dioxide does not rise; instead, it builds up around the sleeper's head. If there wasn't any ventilation, the room soon would grow uncomfortably close, perhaps even suffocatingly so. With ventilation, if anyone tried to sleep in midair he would soon float away on the breeze and bump himself awake against the ceiling. Therefore, the space station is equipped with sleeping restraints—big lightweight bags into which the sleeper is zipped—attached to the wall with snap-fasteners. With such a bag and a pillow, even the most restless sleeper will soon be sound asleep, swaying in the ventilation currents like a sea anemone.

As *Magellan* approaches the coast of Africa, on the morning of July 20, 2019, the telephone rings as usual. It is the wake-up call from the station's main computer. There is a stirring in the cubicles as sleepy crew members reach for the receivers in the semi-darkness and half hear an electronic voice like that of the telephone company's time service: "The time is now six o'clock." It would be nice to snooze some more—indeed, sleeping in space is a little like hibernating as the heartbeat slows to only thirty times a minute—but through the walls of the cubicles other phones can be heard ringing. Not far away someone switches on a laserdisc and starts playing country music. Time to get up.

Reaching for a hand-hold, Bonnie pulls herself away from the port-hole and toward a small set of shelves. Some of her personal belongings are there, held in place with rubber cords. First she wants a plastic squeeze-bottle full of water and a washcloth. She squeezes some of the water onto the cloth, then reaches out to leave the bottle floating freely in midair. It won't go very far. Then she wipes her face and arms as if she were on one of those long airline flights, where the attendants hand out hot towels early in the morning. This is no substitute for a proper wash, but it has to do.

While she's at it, Bonnie decides to comb her hair and brush her teeth. On the shelf is a hairbrush and a jar of moisturizing cream. A few strands of her brown hair come loose as she brushes and drift away in the breeze from the ventilation. She has her toothbrush, which she brought from home, along with her usual brand of toothpaste. Once that chore is done with, she reaches out and retrieves the plastic squeeze-bottle floating nearby, gives her mouth a good squirt after brushing—and gulps it all down. With neither a sink nor drainage close at hand, this is preferable to the alternative: trying to vacuum your mouth with a small suction hose hanging from the wall. Too often, the suction system becomes clogged from such use.

Just to the side of the shelves, held to the wall with bungee cords, are Bonnie's powder blue coveralls. They had been slowly flapping in the ventilation, but not like laundry on a clothesline; they are full of large lumps of equipment that she needs through the day: a notepad, checklist, flashlight, calculator, ballpoint pens, and whatnot. Each item has its own pocket, in the shirt or pants, with a zipper or snap-fastener to close the pocket so its contents don't drift out. Drifting in the middle of the cubicle, Bonnie pulls the coverall free from its bungee and wriggles into it, closing it snugly about her with a zipper. With that, she is ready for the shoes and socks.

Astronauts' shoes look a lot like those of joggers, with canvas tops and laces reaching past the ankles. They have aluminum soles and are rubber-coated; near the toes, each sole has a large triangular cleat. Where people prefer to stand securely in place, such as the breakfast table and in many of the labs, the floor is a triangular aluminum grid. You push a cleat through a hole in the grid, then give the foot a slight turn to lock yourself in place. Bonnie now pulls her shoes down from their storage place high up on the opposite wall, where they were also held in place with bungee cords.

Getting into them, and into socks, is a workout. You can't just crouch and lean over, letting gravity pull your upper body downward to place your hands within easy reach of your feet. You have to flex your stomach muscles and force yourself to bend over, as if you're doing particularly intense sit-ups. Astronauts make it a point of pride to do this without assistance. Indeed, while astronauts on long flights have seen many of their muscles grow weaker, their stomach muscles have actually grown stronger from this vigorous flexing. As Bonnie bends over, her feet rise from the floor, and while she wrestles with the shoes and laces, she slowly tumbles in a backward spin.

With a push on the wall to right herself, she is ready to begin her day.

All along she's been hearing various mutterings along with thumping and whirring sounds from the nearby cubicles; and a couple of cassette tapes have provided background music. Her neighbors are also getting ready. It is over an hour and a half until the start of the workday; time for a round of exercises and then breakfast. Exercises come first. If she didn't work out before breakfast, Bonnie would have to wait until an hour after she'd eaten.

Outside her door is a circular vestibule, an open hub surrounded by the cubicles. The gym is two floors up, a round room nineteen feet across. In the middle of each floor is an open hatchway resembling a manhole. As crew members emerge from their cubicles, each in turn stands below the hatch and pushes off with the front of their feet. Bonnie is particularly good at this. Skillfully, she floats up through the manholes, without bumping, as though she's back in her scuba gear, gliding up from the seafloor with a flick of her fins. Once at the level of the gym, she halts her motion by grabbing the rim of the ceiling manhole, then propels herself toward the lockers with a slight pull. There she changes out of her coveralls into a light top and a pair of shorts.

The gym is well equipped. To begin, there are a couple of body-suction machines, aluminum barrels looking as if they have been fabricated from four-foot lengths of oil pipeline, with tight rubber seals that fit around the waist. At the front of each barrel is a set of valves and tubes, as well as a backrest resembling part of a hospital gurney. One of the continuing problems of space flight is that with no gravity to pull blood and body fluids into the legs, these fluids concentrate in the head and upper body. Blood vessels in the legs become weaker; faces and necks become puffy and flushed. The aluminum barrels cope with this, at least to a degree. With the rubber skirt in place around her waist, Bonnie turns a valve and dumps part of the air around her legs into the vacuum of space. This produces a strong suction on the lower half of her body, which helps pull the blood back down.

For Bonnie, whose legs are basically in good shape, this is quite pleasant. She enjoys the warm tingling in her legs; she wiggles her feet and kicks a bit, feeling the circulation build up. Sometimes she likes to lie there reading a book, but that takes concentration; frequently, there are others nearby, chatting or playing music on their laserdiscs. More often, while in the suction machine, she prefers to pull on stretch-cords and exercise her arms.

No one ever really gets enough exercise in orbit, which is why a strong interest in physical fitness has remained one of the prerequisites for a berth in the astronaut corps. Otherwise, crew members probably wouldn't spend enough time in the gym, which would cause great dismay when it came time to return to Earth. Astronaut Pete Conrad once estimated that it would be necessary to work out five hours a day just to make up for the lack of the common effort of living and moving in normal gravity. Yet in spite of everything, some people get out of shape. During the first *Skylab* mission in 1973, in that craft's body-suction machine, Joe Kerwin felt faint as the blood vessels in his legs distended with the blood flow. He felt dizzy, broke out in a cold sweat, and had to back off from the maximum suction. He later said he had felt as if he might be sucked out of the barrel along with the air and flung bodily into the vacuum outside.

With Bonnie's legs nicely toned up, it is time for the bicycles. These stationary cycles feature stirruplike pedals and a thick elastic band for a seat belt. She has often pedaled away for an hour or more. At times, she and other crew members have pedaled for a full ninety minutes at a stretch, thereby riding a bike all around the world.

On the wall in front of each bike is a large TV screen linked to a videodisc player. A rider can pick his choice of bike paths: along the beach at Malibu, through the pine forests of the Sierras' John Muir Trail, through the Green Mountains of Vermont. As a courtesy to astronauts from Europe and Japan, other paths feature the palace at Kyoto and the Isle of Capri. Bonnie likes the John Muir. When she turns the handlebars to the left or right, the scene shifts as the videodisc image swings off in that direction. When the TV scene curves in some fashion, she has to turn to follow it; otherwise she would ride off the "path" and bog down as a brake grabs hold of the wheel. That brake is also there when the TV shows that she has to climb a hill. It is a point of pride for her that she rarely gets tired on the way up, so she never has to fast-forward the video to reach a scene of level ground, which releases the brake.

Close by are treadmills, where two of her fellow crew members are holding onto a bar and walking or running in place while a TV screen puts them in Vail, Colorado, or on a street in midtown New York. Someone else is giving his arm and shoulder muscles a workout with the rowing machine farther down the wall. Its videodisc scenes feature a lake in New Hampshire during the autumn and a quiet river amid the woods of Germany. For anyone in a competitive mood there's a scene that features racing shells on England's River Cam; those who row fast enough find themselves pulling ahead of the Oxford crew.

By now it's time for breakfast in the dining area one floor down from the gym. This breakfast nook resembles the stand-up circular tables in a fast-food restaurant. Though there is no rush here, everyone eats standing up, in a slightly slouched position, feet locked into the triangular grid. There just isn't any easy way to sit down. Sitting would mean exerting the effort to bend at the waist and stay bent, which puts a strain on the stomach muscles.

Bonnie picked out several days of menus earlier in the week; now it's easy to glide over to the galley and pull out the plastic tray. Back at her table, a place-setting is waiting for her, with magnets holding the silverware in place: a knife, fork, spoon, and pair of scissors. The scissors are for cutting open the ubiquitous plastic packs. In the middle of the table is a set of water nozzles resembling those used by dentists. She can reach for a nozzle on its hose, stick it into an opening in a plastic pack, then watch while the freeze-dried food soaks up the water. She has picked out a breakfast of thermostabilized peaches, freeze-dried scrambled eggs with sausage, rehydratable corn flakes with blueberries, and orange juice and coffee in plastic squeeze-bottles.

The only trouble is that none of this is tasting very good. That isn't because it has been dried and reconstituted; it's because of the congestion in her sinuses. Weightlessness might fulfill the dream of effortless levitation and dreamlike flight, but it carries with it the continual feeling of a stuffed-up nose. With the blood that would ordinarily be in her legs now redistributed into the head and upper body, the feeling of congestion is hard to avoid, which is why Bonnie is forever carrying handkerchiefs and nasal sprays. The stuffiness cuts off many of the sensations of taste and smell. To try to make up for this, there are squeeze-bottles near the water nozzles with barbecue sauce, salt water, and hot pepper sauce, along with ketchup and mustard. Orbital cuisine means heavy doses of ketchup; Dennis the Menace would have felt right at home.

Some of these astronauts might wind up having dinner at the White House, but as Bonnie stands there slouching along with her friends, elegant etiquette is nowhere to be seen. It isn't that space flight has turned the crew into slobs; it's just that there are worse things in life

A space house, perhaps used as a communications relay station in 2019.

than leaning forward with mouth wide open, to keep the food from getting away. Anyone who reaches into the wet-pack with a spoon or fork, then tries to lift it in the usual way, would likely have the food fly off and hit him in the face. With luck it would stick and could be picked off; otherwise it would bounce off and splatter on the wall or ceiling. It takes a smooth, practiced arm motion and a wide open mouth if those scrambled eggs are to do Bonnie any good.

Still, at least the water for the packs is largely free of bubbles—an advance over some early missions in which the water had been pressurized with air; since the air had never been able to float to the surface in weightlessness, it had stayed mixed in. On those flights, injecting wet-packs with the foamy water sometimes caused them to explode. What was more, the bubbles gave the crew gas. As astronaut William Pogue had put it during a Skylab mission, "I think farting five hundred times a day is not a good way to go." Aboard *Magellan*, at least, this embarrassment was largely avoided.

All morning people have been drifting in and out of the dining room and the nearby rooms. These are set up as levels within a cylinder, each having the cylinder's full width of nineteen feet. The cylinder itself is sixty feet long, with its volume thus capable of filling the payload bay of a super-shuttle, and can accommodate six levels. The first three are filled with eighteen cubicles, stacked like cheese wheels in groups of six. On the next floor is the dining area and washroom.

The fifth level is the gym, while above it is a big open area, a combination meeting room and recreation area. Continuing on, one passes through hatchways into other cylinders of similar size in which the labs and workshops are located. A separate cylinder, housing the control center, also provides somewhat larger and more lavish cubicles for the station's commander and his deputy.

At eight o'clock it's time for work. This means gliding up past the four levels to the hatchway at the top of the cylinder. One by one the astronauts, slouching casually, step forward to a spot beneath the central manhole in the floor just above them, glance upward, then push off with a little flick of the feet to rise smartly past the ceiling and glide up through the four levels.

*M*agellan went up in 2012, nearly five hundred years after its namesake's voyage around the world. Bonnie is in charge of its materials lab, which is housed in a big cylinder angled off from the one with the living and dining areas. Part of her lab is forever being remodeled, what with all the industrial firms that are interested in making products in space. These firms are continually sending up new equipment, several such items arriving on each shuttle flight. One of these days the materials lab is to double in size, with a second cylinder being added; but that add-on is hung up in a wrangle between NASA and industry over how much each should pay for it, so her lab is pretty cramped. A corridor runs down its length, with instruments and experimental equipment stacked from floor to ceiling. Some of these items are actually *on* the ceiling, so they can be moved easily into a spacecraft when it arrives; Bonnie and her colleagues have to duck to keep from hitting their heads. Under the lab's fluorescent lights, these colleagues, a biochemist and a physicist, work with her and ply their trades.

Most of the time they work by themselves. It isn't that they're antisocial. It's just that things are set up so that everyone working in space is at the center of a community reaching back to Earth. Only a few experiments can be carried out at any one time in the space station, and each is followed with great interest by a number of scientists on the ground. NASA has thoughtfully arranged the communications system so that everyone working in space is able to talk with a variety of Earthbound colleagues. So for those working in space, most discussions are with people hundreds or thousands of miles away, rather than with the person floating nearby. It's as if each astronaut is standing at the top of a pyramid, apart from his fellows. The crew members have plenty of opportunity to get together at mealtimes and in conferences, but not that much during the workday.

On the morning of July 20, hundreds of miles up, Bonnie is about to

Grand sights await the inhabitants of NASA's first space station.

take a journey halfway to the center of the Earth. She isn't going there physically, of course. But by using the weightlessness of space, she is going to reproduce conditions two thousand miles below the Earth's surface.

During the previous night, she has had an iron-rich silicate mixture slowly cooling in a levitation furnace. This is the sort of material found in the deep mantle of the Earth, where it gives way to the iron of the core. It is highly reactive; there are no good containers for it when it's molten, and this has posed problems for several generations of geologists. Whenever anyone tried to melt it, it would react with the container and dissolve its walls. In the levitation furnace, however, things are different. Bonnie has started by preparing the ingredients on her lab bench. That wasn't hard because they had been pre-packaged, as if she were baking a cake. Then she's loaded the stuff into the furnace and set the controls. Her equipment did the rest. Using the pressure of sound waves, it automatically kept the silicate centered in the middle of an open space, heating it into a molten blob, then allowing it to cool. When she got there in the morning, she had a spherical lump of artificial mantle-rock floating in the furnace chamber that was still quite warm to the touch. Soon it will join similar lumps with slightly different compositions, and the entire group will be on its way to the labs of the U.S. Geological Survey.

First, though, she has to do some preliminary tests. This means cutting a small grain from the lump, a tiny sample, and subjecting it to the temperatures and pressures of the Earth's deep interior. To accomplish this, she has to squeeze the grain between two diamonds, which can withstand the intense pressures, and continually measure the pressure with one laser and keep track of the temperature with another. Then, with a third laser, she studies the grain as she changes the temperature and pressure, noting the changes in its molecular structure.

To begin this process, she puts the lump under a microscope and guides a thin drill of hardened steel to its surface in order to cut away some dust-sized grains. Deftly manipulating a hypodermic needle, Bonnie picks up two of the grains. Then she guides the needle into the focus of another microscope. Through the eyepieces, she can see a thin sheet of steel with a pinhole drilled through it, and below the pinhole, the upper face of a diamond.

She drops one of the grains into the hole. Then, using other needles, she adds a tiny chip of ruby and a drop of alcohol. With this, she is ready to assemble her instrument, which amounts to a high-tech nutcracker. By turning a screw, she squeezes two lever-arms together, pushing two diamonds into the steel sheet. Trapped between them, within the pinhole, is the silicate grain, the ruby chip, and the alcohol. The alcohol transmits the pressure evenly on all sides of the ruby and the silicate. A laser makes the ruby fluoresce a deep red; by measuring its wavelength, Bonnie can determine the pressure within the pinhole.

Using her microscope, she looks through the facets of the upper diamond. It's like looking through the nose of a World War II bomber. The diamond is little more than a millimeter across, but under the microscope it has the appearance of a set of glass panes fitted together to form a dome. The pinhole is a black disc within which she can clearly see the ruby and the silicate grain. Testing her lasers, she assures herself that everything is properly aligned. Then she switches on the power screw, thus forcing the two diamonds into the steel sheet. From time to time she checks the instruments. Finally, she has what she wanted: a pressure of 1.9 million atmospheres, two thousand times greater than the pressure at the bottom of the deepest ocean abyss. She turns on a laser to heat the silicate to over four thousand degrees. Now, in its temperature, pressure, and composition, the grain truly is a tiny bit of the Earth's deep interior. With that, she picks up the phone and puts in a call to the Geological Survey office near San Francisco and spends the rest of the day conferring with the scientists there.

Meanwhile, *Christa*, the super-shuttle launched early that morning from Cape Canaveral, is approaching the space station. Its pilot is flying on a path that already has *Magellan* in view. From his control center next to *Magellan*'s rocket hangar, the commander of the station closely watches *Christa*'s approach. His eyrie is packed full of electronic equipment, but at this close range it won't help much; docking the *Christa* depends on the pilot's eyes and good judgment. Slowly the craft floats toward the outstretched docking port like an enormous fish ready to be gaffed. Then, just short of the port, its nose-thrusters flash momentarily amid a burst of gas, and *Christa* comes to a dead stop. Next, it turns, pitches upward, presenting its back toward the station.

When this maneuver is completed, the two spacecraft are only fifty feet apart, with one of the station's long cylinders pointing directly at an open port on the back of *Christa*, just behind its cockpit. A

crewman's face can be seen through one of the windows. As small gas puffs momentarily whiff from *Christa's* thrusters, the spaceship starts closing the gap, a few inches per second. The two commanders, each aboard their own craft, watch closely, talking back and forth, ready to make slight tweaks if necessary to assure a proper docking. Finally, with a slight bump, the two craft meet. The spaceship is now fully gaffed, and will remain so for several days.

The docking of *Christa* sends a slight jar through the station, which is bad news to two technicians in the satellite-repair bay, for they are running behind schedule. They are repairing a big infrared camera that has been taken off an Earth-resources satellite, and they have to have it all back together in time to load aboard *Christa* before its departure. This means missing the party that evening, missing a chance to talk with the spaceship crew—all for the sake of those damnable screws, clips, and other loose objects that are the bane of a repairman's life in space.

These small objects are a continuing inconvenience. Because of the "jack-in-the-box effect," you just can't put them into a box and expect them to stay put: They pop out the instant anyone opens the box. They don't even drop to the floor where someone could spot them; a screw or washer could be floating right in front of your face and you'll look right past it because your eyes won't be focused that close. What's worse, you could inhale it. There are doctors on board who could perform a tracheotomy if necessary, but that isn't much comfort.

In time, of course, all this celestial flotsam soon starts drifting into the ventilation and winds up on the screens of the ventilator filters. It is a common experience that if anything is missing—a wrench, a toothbrush, a watch—the first place to look is on the screens of these filters. In the repair shop, this idea has been carried to its natural conclusion in the windy workbench. This is a flat box with a fine, well-braced screen on top and a suction container below it. Loose screws and small parts can be put on the screen and they'll stay there, provided no one bumps the workbench too hard. To avoid the jack-in-the-box effect, the technicians' tool boxes are made of clear plastic. They can look inside and pick out the wrench or screwdriver they want; then, by opening the top just a crack, they can reach in and grab it. However, both of them prefer a big Swiss Army knife, loaded with blades, cutters, and much else. As they are fond of saying, that way there is only one tool to lose.

Opposite page: An emergency vehicle comes to the rescue of a damaged solar-cell display.

Noontime arrives. Telephones ring throughout the station, and the central computer reminds everyone that it is time for lunch. This is traditionally a social hour, a time when everyone gets together in the same room. With twenty people slouching around four upright tables in the dining area, the buzz of conversation gets pretty loud. On Earth, this sound would penetrate the walls and dissipate into the surrounding air, but with vacuum outside, the sound bounces off the walls and stays within the station. Astronauts in such social gatherings try to talk somewhat softly, but it's all too easy for someone to raise his voice to be heard more clearly. When enough people do this, the buzz builds up. Then someone has to clap his hands, the signal for everyone to stop talking for a moment and let the noise die down.

The food at lunch is rather simple, sandwiches or cheeseburgers with heavily sweetened lemon or chocolate pudding for dessert. The food-storage lockers have a number of big cans filled with bread and buns, and with a microwave close by, it's easy to chow down. Of course, good old American cheddar cheese just doesn't have that zing, not with everyone's senses of taste and smell reduced by their head congestion. The cheese choices today are Roquefort and Limburger. Still, if zero-g takes away the taste, at least it gives convenience in the handling of the ketchup. Unless someone squeezes his burger bun tightly, there's no way the ketchup is going to fly free, or drip onto a shirt. Even when a cheeseburger is totally slathered, the ketchup just forms a big glob that clings to the outside, like a raindrop to the eaves.

With lunch over, Bonnie stops at the biomedical center before returning to her lab. She wants to check her weight and needs help from a doctor. Behind a partition she changes into a light top and a pair of cutoffs, then she climbs into the seat of the scale where she sits, well scrunched up, with her knees below her chin. The doctor tightens her seat belt and a pair of shoulder belts so she's held in place as firmly as if she were in an Indy race car.

Her feet are pressed tightly against a bar; just behind it is another bar, which she grasps tightly, her knuckles showing white. When the medic flips a switch, a spring starts rocking the seat about once a second, making it oscillate back and forth. If she has gained weight, the chair will rock more slowly; an instrument measures the oscillations' rate. Soon the numbers on a red digital display stop changing, and she has her weight, 121.3 pounds.

With that, she goes over and gives a cheery word to one of her friends, an astronaut from *Christa* who is spacesick. He had begun feeling poorly soon after he reached orbit, and when his craft docked to the space station, the sudden jolt made him queasy and he threw up. Bonnie reassured him by telling how quickly she had gotten over her own sickness, and he agreed that he'd soon have his space-legs. Actually, it wasn't his legs or sense of balance that had brought on the upset; it was his stomach. Normally, the digestive tract is in constant motion, and it gives off rumblings that can be heard through a stethoscope. When astronauts become ill, however, their digestive tracts are quiet. With a dose of metachlorpramide, a drug used to set the innards rumbling again, they're soon fine. Their nausea disappears and their appetites return.

Still, talk of space-legs is not just a figure of speech; for space-legs and -bodies are different from those of Earth. Again, with the blood and other fluids redistributed, faces grow puffy while thighs and calves become thinner. As astronaut Joe Kerwin put it, "One can almost see the fluid draining out of the legs; one looks at his partners, and their legs are getting long and skinny like crows' legs." As blood and fluids redistribute themselves, the discs between vertebrae soak up fluid and push the vertebrae further apart. Like her crewmates, Bonnie has grown taller as well as skinnier. She has pants that had fit just fine on the ground, but are now baggy, their cuffs dangling well above her ankles.

The clinic that Bonnie visited fills only a small part of the bio-medical lab. Most of the life sciences work calls for the doctors to switch hats and work as veterinarians. The main parts of the lab feature an orbiting menagerie, with mice, rabbits, dogs, monkeys, even a couple of pigs. In their weight and general anatomy, the pigs are rather like humans, and several have been trundled off to their sty in the sky. A third of the lab is given over to lunar-g, one-sixth gravity. It's built somewhat like a clothes dryer, with a big cylinder that rotates once every twelve seconds. That slow spin suffices to give lunar-g. It is here that experiments for NASA's new project beyond the space station—to build a permanent settlement on the Moon—are carried out. Here, and in an adjacent zero-g area, the space menageries live permanently. The dogs and pigs have already been in residence for a number of years, rotating continually, as have the monkeys. The mice and rabbits have been here for generations.

The dogs are cocker spaniels and terriers, picked in part for their cuteness. From time to time, Bonnie and the others in the crew take a dog for a walk, its legs wiggling as it floats along on a leash. Sometimes she prefers to play with a chimp. The chimps clamber about with great agility, giving little screeches of pleasure when they're with people; the dogs, though, sometimes growl softly when they're petted. They have plenty of room in their cages, but they usually don't have much to do. They spend a lot of time sleeping. All the animals are quite tame and respond to their keepers as pets.

A rabbit will sit there with a trusting look as a doctor reaches in to pick it up, then squeal a bit when popped with a syringe to draw a blood sample. The rabbits run around freely in large cages, males and females together, and from time to time they have baby rabbits. To avoid a population explosion, a number of them go back to Earth with each flight. For those that stay in space, the medical exams are pretty much the same as with the station's two-legged creatures: blood tests, measurements of weight and body dimensions, tests of oxygen consumption. It's all a far cry from the legendary astronaut-selection tests at Houston, which have been described by John Glenn: "If you think of how many body openings there are, and imagine how deep you can go into each one, that's what it's like."

The afternoon wears on. The routine of the day is making itself felt; even the arrival of the super-shuttle is mostly a matter of standard procedure. Yet the routine is deceptive, for in the control center, close to the docked *Christa*, the commander of *Magellan* and two others are preparing to launch a rocket. This is *Endeavor*, a space tug that's to be flown by *Christa*'s pilot and copilot on a mission to geosynchronous orbit, the high orbit where communications satellites make their home. *Endeavor* is in port, gleaming in the stark light of floodlamps, a collection of propellant tanks nearly fifty feet long, with a cockpit and payload bay up front. At one end is a big umbrellalike thermal shield covered with a blanket of ceramic fiber. Close to the control center are two brown storage tanks for propellants, each longer and nearly as fat as the orbital tug itself. These were once the external tanks that held fuel for the flights of the old space shuttle, predecessor of the bigger, more reliable super-shuttle. Now they're used to support more advanced goals.

On this mission the tug is to nuzzle up to a communications satellite that isn't working right. Once they're close to the satellite, the copilot is to do a spacewalk, grab it, and stow it in *Endeavor*'s payload bay. A burst from the rockets will then put their craft on a path that will graze the upper atmosphere, sixty miles above the Earth. For a few minutes the craft will dip into this thin air, the blanket shining with the brilliant white of an atmosphere entry. The resulting drag will carry away part of *Endeavor*'s speed, returning it to an orbit close to that of *Magellan*. A few tweaks of their thrusters will then bring the two crewmen safely home.

With this flight scheduled soon, the commander and his men are particularly busy. Each of them slouches in front of a group of computer terminals, a set of big color TV screens. Preparing *Endeavor* for launch means taking it through a countdown. This is more than the dramatic last few seconds, the five-four-three-two-one. This countdown is actually a long checklist of orders to be carried out in careful sequence. The computer presents a menu of commands, each accompanied by a circle. Touching the circle with a finger tells the computer to execute that command.

Often, the computer screens present diagrams of systems within *Endeavor* and its hangar, such as a propellant valve and its controls, or an astronaut's oxygen tank. To start a pump, for example, one of the controllers would touch a circle within that pump on the diagram. The pump would take on a double outline, indicating that it has been selected. Also, circles marked "Start" and "Stop" would begin flashing on and off, indicating that they could now be touched. All other circles on the screen fade to a dotted outline, indicating that they are no longer active. The computer keeps a log of who is operating it, what buttons they have pushed, and what the results are. If anything goes wrong during the countdown, it's easy to find out who did it and how. Still, those three controllers are only the tip of the rocket. Just as Bonnie and her fellow experimenters are in close touch with an extensive network of scientists, so these spacecraft controllers work closely with the engineers in a big flight control center in Houston. There are several hundred people there, including two dozen flight controllers sitting at computer consoles. All this is just as in the Apollo days, when a similar Houston center was there to help three lonely astronauts halfway to the Moon.

Within the space station's control center, the commander and his men might be playing video games, so intent are they upon the changing color images on their screens. There are none of the sounds of a computer or video game; in these close quarters, it would have been difficult for anyone to tell whose device was making which sound. Amid the soft hum of the ventilators, these three earnest men slouch with their feet locked in place, each head barely a foot from the screen with its bright diagrams, each pair of hands floating freely in midair, ready to push a circle at the proper time. All this is so engrossing that controllers sometimes turn away from the screen not knowing where their arms are. The usual sensations, which tell us of these things, are absent in weightlessness. Still, as evening approaches, these controllers begin to slow down. They are waiting for a phone call that will bring a welcome break, and soon it comes. Once again it's the computer with an announcement: "Six o'clock, and it's party time."

It is Saturday evening. Except for the two technicians in the satellite-repair bay, everyone else is gathering for the weekly wine-tasting, with cabernet sauvignon and Dom Perignon in the squeeze-bottles. This little party is more than just a welcome break in the schedule; it is a sign of NASA's confidence. In the previous century, while NASA was preparing for the Skylab missions, its leaders were being rubbed raw by incessant criticism. The Skylab astronauts decided they wanted to have wine aboard, and got together for a party at the Johnson Space Center to decide what vintages would be best. Then the top brass said nix. The Women's Christian Temperance Union had heard of the plans and had complained. NASA was at the time so sensitive to criticism from any quarter that they had dropped the plans for wine in space. But now, in the new century, astronauts were free to drink whatever pleased them.

With their squeeze-bottles in hand, everyone is standing on the floor of the upper deck, just above the gym. This is the community center and recreation room, the largest open area in the station, twenty feet high and nineteen across. Everyone gets together there for the weekly Saturday-night movie, as well as for occasional briefings by the commander. Most of the time, though, it's just a big open room where people can fly about and feel free.

Astronauts love to do acrobatics in zero-g. It's like fancy high diving to an experienced swimmer. As Peter Conrad said following the first Skylab mission, "We never went anywhere straight; we always did a somersault or a flip on the way, just for the hell of it." Within that upper deck, a favorite game is to be a human pinball. Someone starts by pushing on the wall—a flick of the wrist will do—then somersaults to land on his feet on the opposite wall, pushes off again, does more somersaults, throws in a few twists as well, then heads for the ceiling. From there he bounces down toward the floor, turning and tumbling all the way, then lands again on his feet. He keeps bouncing and turning for as long as he cares to keep it up.

There is always the danger, though, of banging into a wall and getting hurt, so everyone keeps the speed down—to two feet a second or so. That means ten seconds for a flight from floor to ceiling, a leap far more graceful than any in *Swan Lake*. Sometimes the leap is too slow or someone pushes off so gently that, after a minute or so, he realizes he isn't going anywhere. There he'll be, marooned in midair, with the nearby wall just out of reach. Usually, someone has to come to the rescue with a push, though a couple of times people have been stranded in the middle of the room for several minutes, all the while flapping their arms in a vain attempt to fly like a bird. Still, marooning isn't forever. In the upper deck, as everywhere else, there is always that slow current of air from the ventilators. With a little patience it will carry the hapless flyer to the screens, where, with a little push, he gets back to the floor.

Then there are games that call for skill in aiming. With the hatch connecting the gym to the upper deck open, a good acrobat could push off from the ceiling, execute several twists and even a gainer or two, then straighten out into a perfect diver's position, just above the floor, to disappear cleanly through the hatch as if he were entering the water.

Those who tire of using their own bodies as projectiles find other games close by. There are velcro-tipped darts, along with a target. This game isn't too popular; the darts always go precisely in the direction they were thrown, and they rarely stick when they hit the target. More popular are paper airplanes. When they fly straight, they usually make slow barrel rolls. With a slight upward bend on the rear of the wings, they loop the loop as many as a dozen times.

It's now evening. For Bonnie, this means exercise, dinner, a shower, and a bit of Earth-watching. The exercise is particularly important—in space no one ever gets enough—and back in the gym she still has the tension machines to work out with.

Downstairs from the gym, several people are getting their dinners ready. Dinner is the big meal of the day, but as with breakfast, there is no set time for it. People just wander into the dining area in twos and threes, wet-packs in hand. The food is hot, and there's plenty of it. A typical menu offers clam chowder and other soups; beef or turkey; shrimp cocktail or salmon salad; corn, mashed potatoes, or broccoli; macaroni and cheese; strawberry shortcake; peaches, pears, and assorted puddings. The problems come with the soups, and anyone nearby is apt to watch with some concern when somebody is preparing one.

They come freeze-dried in their wet-packs, and someone who likes clam chowder (Bonnie, for instance) will occasionally add too much water. When this happens, the plastic pack explodes. It comes apart at the seams, sending gobs of chowder flying off in all directions. This is a particular problem with the Mama's brand of soups and has led their marketing vice-president to rush a new batch to the Cape by way of his company's Lear jet. The new box of soup-packs will soon be unloaded from *Christa* and then face its test. But for now, the astronauts are using soup-packs from Campbell's, which experience has shown to be more reliable.

With dinner over—fortunately, no one made a mess this evening—Bonnie is off to the wash area. This is on the same floor as the dining area, behind a partition, along with the laundry room. Just now both washers are in use, ultrasonic cleaners about the size of desktop copying machines. Indeed, they work somewhat similarly, but instead of feeding in pages of paper, two of the crew are busily putting socks, underwear, and part of their coverall linings into the cleaner slots. These clothes emerge a few seconds later from a set of wringers, flattened and damp but clean. A quick pass through the infrared dryer, in the bottom of each cleaner, leaves the clothes ready to wear. That way everyone can have fresh laundry, practically every day.

Also there are showers for everyone, every other day. The shower stall is a large barrel with hoops surrounded by plastic sheeting and a big lid on top. Bonnie gets in by lifting the lid, then hoisting herself inside. Stretched along one hoop are the ever-present bungee cords; Bonnie pulls off her clothes and sticks them behind the bungees, which hold them in place. As usual, she has to force herself to double over to get her shoes off. Then she lowers the lid and fastens it into position against the top hoop. Now, with the plastic cocoon around her, she's all set.

The soap is off to one side, with a bit of iron in the middle so it sticks to a magnet in the holder. Just in front is a hand-held shower attachment at the end of a long hose. When she squeezes this attachment, it sprays her with warm water. There is only a gallon and a half for the whole shower; she can't luxuriate for a half hour under a thick spray. The most Bonnie can expect is to soap down thoroughly and rinse off, but at least it isn't hard to get rid of the soapy water. Within the shower is another hose and attachment, a vacuum cleaner to pull the water off her body. To finish the job, there's a towel on another of the bungees.

With that, she is ready to put in an hour or so doing the chores. These include housekeeping tasks that everyone does, such as picking out the wet-packs for the next few days' meals and toting a load of garbage in a plastic bag to the disposal. The trash room is next door in an adjacent cylinder. At one end is a large aluminum container resembling a trash dumpster, which is where the plastic bags go. Some chores are more onerous. Tonight it's Bonnie's turn to empty the honey-bucket. Some astronauts had just pumped the stuff directly into space, and then had declared that one of the most beautiful sights was a urine dump. In the vacuum of space, the liquid flashed into freeze-dried crystals that caught the sun and sparkled iridescently. On one flight of a Soviet Salyut spacecraft, with a French cosmonaut on board, the Frenchman got that task. As he sent the effluvium on its way, one of his Russian comrades chortled, "Another Sputnik launched!"

But the space near the station has to stay clean; there are too many satellites orbiting nearby. That's the reason for the honey-bucket. It's another plastic bag, full of freeze-dried material from the toilets. Within each toilet, a fan sucks the stuff down—it's pulled by air currents, it doesn't actually hit the fan—and from time to time a mechanism seals it off to be freeze-dried. What is left is rather like old kitty litter. The toilets are in small bathrooms about the size of those on an airliner. The commodes are halfway up the wall—and come equipped with seat belts—which makes it easier to get the bags out from underneath. Gingerly cradling a sealed bag in one arm, Bonnie makes her way to the dumpster and heave ho.

Finally, after a good solid hour of these chores, Bonnie calls it a day and goes home to her little cubicle on the bottom floor, with its light blue walls, its porthole, its sleep-sack, and the various items that are hers. She has to get up early the next day, and now's a good time to get ready for bed. Once the shoes are back on their rack, high on the wall, it's easy to slip out of her coveralls and stick them behind the bungee cords.

She still isn't sleepy. So she turns on the night-light on the wall, next to a sack that holds the thick Joan Didion novel she's been working her way through. But then her entire day has gone by and, since she got up this morning, she hasn't had a chance to see the Earth. It's a kaleidoscopic, ever-changing view. Just as she loved her proficiency flights in the backseats of jet trainers, just as she won't give up a chance at a window seat in an airliner, so she doesn't call it a day without a half-hour or so at the porthole. Even after several months in orbit, the view is still awesome.

The Earth slips below as if she were in a high-flying jet. Though the station flies at nearly eighteen thousand miles per hour, thirty times faster than an airliner, it's also thirty times higher, so there's the same sensation of drift rather than speed. The flight is quiet, peaceful. To astronaut Joe Allen, the silence made his flight seem as if he were riding a gondola under a hot-air balloon.

Just then the space station is above the eastern Sahara. It's spread nearly to the horizon in pastel shades of reddish orange, lighter orange, and yellow. A few darker spots are visible off to one side, granitic hills protruding above the surrounding sand. The view is almost totally clear of clouds; the few meager ones to the south hug the ground so closely they seem like white geological formations amid the pastels. The tawny desert is so bright, so desolate, it's almost hurtful to the eyes. Then, up ahead, she can see a thin strand of dark green, and beyond it, a band of dark blue. She knows she's approaching the valley of the Nile, and that the blue band is the Red Sea.

She watches in wonder as she passes just south of a triangular black cloud that reaches upward from the surface, casting its shadow across miles of wasteland. It's an oil fire, sending its plume of smoke into the sky. A few clouds appear, streaks of high cirrus looking for all the world like closely bunched contrails of high-flying jets, crossing desert and sea with complete indifference. The Nile is now clearly in view, a thin line of dark blue amid the dark green on either side, with a wide bulge in the river where Lake Nasser swells behind its dam. Across a short span of dun-colored deathland, the Red Sea and Gulf of Aden show the welcome color of the sea, contrasting sharply with the adjacent coasts of Arabia and the Horn of Africa.

Now the Rub al Khali, the Empty Quarter of Saudi Arabia, lies below, seared beneath a cruel sky of eternal blue, a vast waste of light brown, looking like skin from a hand the size of California. There are long ridges like those of a fingerprint, sand dunes running for hundreds of miles, with gravel flats and bedrock between them. The sandy wastes of Arabia suddenly give way to the blue of the Arabian Sea. Far to the north she can follow the coast to the Cape of Ras Musandam, jutting into the Straits of Hormuz. As if to emphasize that strait's significance, down below is the thin white wake of a supertanker. White cumulus clouds speckle the sea, their shadows surprisingly near the clouds themselves. Soon she'll be approaching the Malabar Coast of India, with a subtle dark green hue that blends with the ocean and forces her to look closely to find the line between sea and land. Beneath its swirls of cumulus, India itself appears as a land of red, brown, and mauve, with an extensive band of white near the northern horizon to mark the Himalayas.

Down below the sea is quickly darkening and the tops of clouds are showing colors of orange and gold. Bonnie can't see the Sun from her porthole, but up ahead the world is fading to black; night is falling. She watches a moment longer, hoping at least to see the lights of India's coastal cities, then turns away. By now she's beginning to feel tired. She pulls the shades over the porthole, gives the wall a little push, grabs the opening between the sheets, and pulls herself in. She takes hold of the pillow and tries to sleep.

Still, sleep won't come. What she really needs, she thinks, is a late-night snack. She flips on the light, climbs into a light robe, and opens her door. No one else is stirring; the station is asleep. She makes her way to the galley, where she rummages around within the food stores. Soon she has what she's looking for: a wet-pack of Mama's Oyster Stew.

Here and now, she'll check out the new packages that have just come up from Earth. Carefully, Bonnie inserts the hot-water tube into the pack and begins adding water in little squirts. She kneads the wet-pack as it swells in her hand, feeling its texture change. Now it's almost ready. One more squirt'll do it.

The pack explodes and sends a hot glob of stew splattering across the front of her nightgown.

A NIGHT
AT THE
MOVIES

The San Francisco Chronicle   Saturday, July 20, 2019

THIS WEEKEND IN ENTERTAINMENT

Opening at Movie Theaters

Still Gone with the Wind. The sequel picks up several years after where the 80-year-old original left off, with Rhett and Scarlett reuniting in their middle age, in 1880. Features the original cast (Clark Gable, Olivia de Havilland, and Vivien Leigh) and studio sets resurrected by computer graphic synthesis. *Still Gone* sets out to prove that they *do* make 'em like they used to. (Selznick Theater, 2:00 and 8:00 P.M.)

The Apollo Mystery. Fine ensemble acting in this science fiction account of a murder during one of the Apollo Moon missions of the 1970s. The allure of the film, though, is in its setting; it was actually filmed on the Moon's surface during a commercial expedition last year. Very appropriate considering this weekend's anniversary. High production costs mean increased admission prices for this one, $15, only a dollar or two more than a regular ticket. (Roxie, 1:00, 3:15, 5:30, 8:00, and 10:15 P.M.)

This Is Holorama. One of this summer's gimmick films, *Holorama* is another of those ultra-realistic holographic movie processes that only scare the kids and leave Mom and Dad with a sick feeling in their stomachs. Like other "thrill films," it's mainly a travelogue, only this time the emphasis is on danger (an extended war sequence shot in the middle of battlefields in the Middle East, Central America, and Africa) and hostile environments. (We go inside an old-fashioned fission reactor during a real nuclear accident!) (Holostage, 2:00, 4:00, 7:30, and 10:00 P.M.)

Music

All-Star Simulated Symphony. Always a treat for lovers of classical music, this duo uses the latest in synthesizers and digital music techniques (and a few robots) to simulate a live performance of the world's greatest orchestra and re-create the sounds of legendary performers. A robotic Rachmaninoff has the piano solos in the highlight of the show. Gershwin's *An American in Paris*, conducted by an animatronic likeness of the composer. So real, you'd swear the players were alive and in the room. (Wozniak Hall, 8:00 P.M.)

Television

Don't Mess with Me. Tonight marks ABC's first attempt at a new English-language situation com-

Previous page: Unreal perspectives greet the moviegoer of 2019.

edy in prime time since the network went to all-Spanish programming a few years ago. A summer replacement, the series brings back one-time child star Gary Coleman (has he *ever* been away?) who plays the father of two adopted children. Beats reruns, anyway. (7:30 P.M.)

So Who Wants to Work? Jerry Rubin is the resident con man in a San Francisco retirement home where, ever since the collapse of Social Security, the old folks must rely on their wits to stay afloat. Rubin is particularly effective as the elderly baby-boomer *wunderkind*. In this episode, he convinces an oil company to use his pals in a TV commercial. (CBS, 11:30 P.M.)

In 2019, technology will not only give us more leisure time, but also ways to spend it more creatively and constructively. Of course, for those who simply want to pass the time with frivolous diversions, there will be plenty of opportunities. In short, the future will be fun. Movies will become more realistic. Television and mass media will cater to tastes not now served. Computers will offer ordinary citizens the chance to create and express themselves as never before.

Of all the arts, our favorite "night out," the movies, will have changed the most by the early twenty-first century. The movies will be over a hundred years old. And though the motion picture business has never been known as being particularly innovative, in the next century fierce competition from other forms of entertainment will force it to alter its ways.

Almost since their invention, movies have used 35mm plastic film as a physical medium. Originally, motion pictures were photographed and projected at eighteen frames per second. With the addition of sound in the late 1920s, the speed jumped slightly to twenty-four frames per second, today's standard. Competition from television in the 1950s saw the beginnings of a technological revolution that included the addition of stereophonic sound, CinemaScope, 3-D, Cinerama (a giant-screen process using three cameras and projectors), and such gimmicks as Smell-O-Vision and Aromarama, in which scents were pumped into the theaters to complement the on-screen action.

Of these, only CinemaScope and stereo sound survived into the next decade. Movie theaters and television learned to coexist until the introduction of pay-TV services like Home Box Office and Showtime in the 1970s, and, even more importantly, of home video recorders that gave people practically unlimited access to thousands of films.

Today, those who choose not to see a film during its initial release in a movie theater need wait only weeks for it to become available on videocassette or videodisc. By 2019, nearly every American home will have some kind of home video player. But the real threat to movies in theaters will come during the 1990s with the wide-scale availability of high-definition television.

Very simply, high-definition TV uses nearly twice the number of scanning lines (1,125 versus 525 for a normal U.S.-standard television) to yield a picture that almost equals 35mm film. With the arrival of high-definition video, wall-sized screens and projection televisions will become not only practical, but extremely attractive to people who can afford them. (At first, high-definition sets will be expensive, perhaps as much as $2,000 for early models.) As high-definition sets with high-quality digital stereo sound penetrate homes, the difference between the experience of seeing a movie in a theater and watching it at home will all but vanish.

What will the Hollywood studios do to maintain the theaters as their first line of distribution? The most obvious solution is to improve their aging technology by redeveloping the mechanics of film.

Showscan is a high-speed, large-screen film process that offers a more realistic viewing experience than any other technique yet invented. Using 70mm film (twice as wide as conventional movie film) photographed and projected at sixty frames per second (or more than double the speed of today's movies) and a superior, six-channel sound system, Showscan points the way for the movies' future.

Developed by director Douglas Trumbull, who was also responsible for the special effects in such science fiction classics as *2001: A Space Odyssey*, *Close Encounters of the Third Kind*, and *Blade Runner*, Showscan offers viewers a more physical and emotional experience by flooding the human central nervous system with visual information.

To develop Showscan, its inventors wired test audiences to machines that measured pulse and respiration rates, perspiration, electromyogram activity, and an electroencephalogram. These human guinea pigs were shown films taken and projected at various frame rates to measure their physiological responses to the scenes. When the number of frames per second topped sixty, the filmmaker saw the

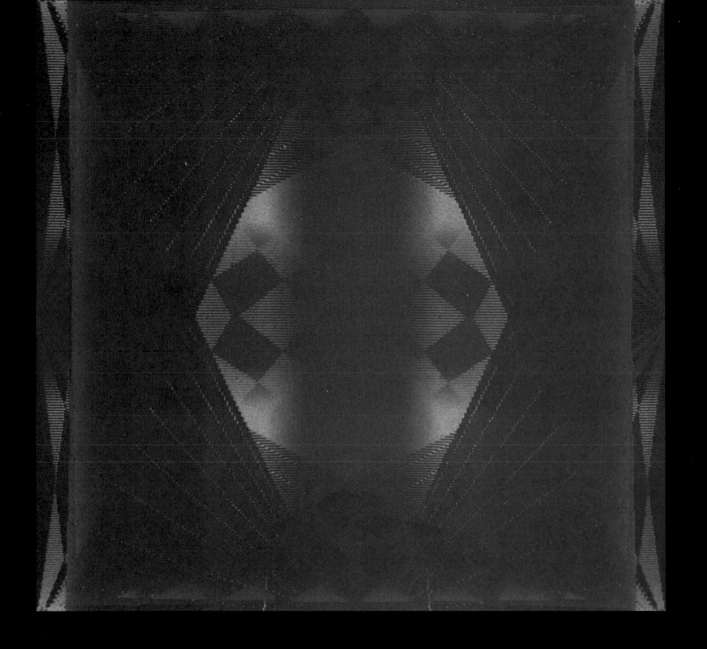

This is Holorama? Will thriller movies in the twenty-first century be projected as full-color, three-dimensional holograms? (© Gregory MacNicol)

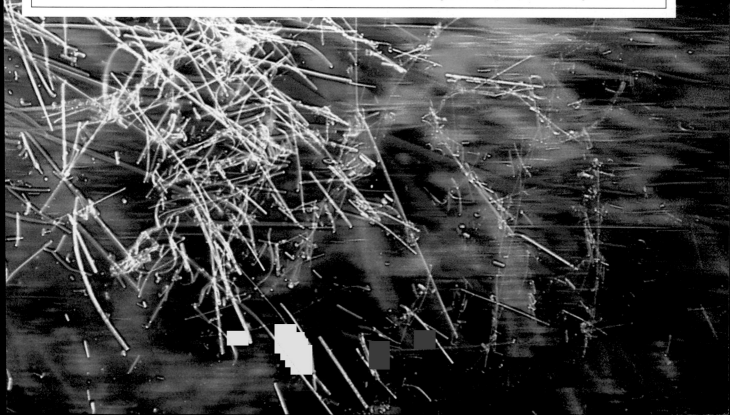

The content of our movies in 2019 is likely to be very similar to those of 1986, but high-tech capabilities will lend more realism to Hollywood fantasy. (*Inset photograph* © Joe Viesti; *background* © Phillip A. Harrington)

Dance in 2019 will be en-
hanced by synthesized
music that will re-create
live performances of the
world's greatest orchestras
and greatest performers.
(© Chromosohm, Inc.)

meters on the measuring equipment jump. Audiences were physically
excited by this new visual reality. Suddenly there was an entirely new
level on which to communicate with a gathered flock of moviegoers—
an actual, visceral level.

Settling on this speed, Trumbull discovered that audiences became
more intensely involved with Showscan, so much so that too many
action scenes could rapidly tire viewers. In much the same way that
moviegoers actually ducked when an actor pointed a pistol at them at
the conclusion of Edison's *Great Train Robbery*, the Showscan audience (partially because of the technique's novelty) tends to confuse
the illusion of the film with reality.

So far, Showscan has been demonstrated only with short films for
expositions and world's fairs but, backed by the resources of one of
the most successful theater chains, Trumbull plans to make theatrical
feature-length films by the end of the 1980s. When moviegoers have
the opportunity to see Showscan, he is certain they will no longer be
satisfied with conventional film technology.

Using Showscan and the technologies that will soon compete with
it, directors can produce films that will leave audiences drained. The
thundering herds of the Western will be louder, the kicks and punches
of the action picture more violent, and the spectacle, of course, all the
more spectacular. Traditional dramas, small films more intimate in
scope, won't necessarily vanish, but Showscan is quite likely to prompt
a new wave of megamovies, the flat-out blockbusters that Hollywood
has always been so good at making.

These films will make audiences want thrilling, vicarious experiences, perhaps at the cost of dramatic narratives. A simulated trip
through space, across the storm-tossed oceans, or scaling the heights
of Everest, will give ticket-buyers more for their money than ever
before.

Other film processes that Hollywood could adopt include IMAX,
which uses 70mm film moving horizontally to increase the area of the
frame to ten times the size of 35mm film, and stereoscopic or 3-D
movies. IMAX is already in use at museums (such as the Smithsonian's
National Air and Space Museum), and three-dimensional films using
70mm film and modern stereo sound systems have been demonstrated at world's fairs and at Disneyland and Walt Disney World's
Epcot Center. However, it is unlikely that IMAX will ever be used in its
current form for theatrical films; it is very costly and requires bulky

equipment. (An IMAX film image is about ten times the size of a conventional 35mm frame, so the cost of individual prints are astronomical). Three-D movies still force their audiences to wear polarized glasses.

Holography creates an image by using a laser to record optical information about a scene (but not the actual scene itself) on photographic film. When illuminated with a laser, or in some cases plain white light, the hologram is played back in three dimensions without the use of special glasses. By changing positions, the viewer can actually look around objects in a hologram.

Holography, however, suffers many limitations. First, the subject of the hologram must be illuminated by laser light; outdoor holography is thus impossible, at least for the moment. Nor can the subject move. Even the slightest motion destroys the recording. Finally, holograms cannot be projected as ordinary film can, making theatrical movies impractical.

(There have been a few experimental holographic films produced in the U.S.S.R. Their image quality, though, has been far from acceptable, and the pictures have been small and dim. Holography just doesn't lend itself to movie-making.)

These limitations are basic to holography, not just the result of crude technology; without a breakthrough in physics, holographic movies probably won't make their debut during this century. This doesn't mean, though, that a medium mixing holographic techniques with conventional motion picture technology can't appear soon or early in the next century. Several years ago, the late Dennis Gabor, who conceived holography years before the invention of the laser made it practical, came up with an ingenious scheme for glassless 3-D films.

The "Gabor screen" would be a giant hologram, actually a holographic picture of two or more blank screens. Each of the screens would be seen only from a specific angle or set of angles. This means that a Gabor screen can be designed so that views of two screens alternate in a narrow arc. In this way, your left eye will see one screen, while your right eye sees another, yielding the 3-D effect and eliminating the need for 3-D glasses.

In practice, as part of a plan like this, separate left- and right-eye views would be projected onto the individual "blank screens" by setting up the projectors to direct their light to the screen at specific angles. The film in these projectors could be photographed like regular 3-D films, and produced without the inherent limitations of holography. Gabor claimed that a 3-D process need not be restricted to just this single stereo pair of left and right images. Instead, filmmakers could use several strips of film, photographed from a variety of angles, to offer an even greater illusion of depth.

To date, only a handful of filmmakers and technicians in Russia (where 70mm film is already something of a standard) have experimented extensively with glassless 3-D—also called "autostereo"—systems. However, Hollywood could benefit from a crash development program to bring this new technology to the motion picture market. Creating a workable movie system that combines conventional film techniques with holography might be possible on a budget of less than what the movie studios spend to make a few modern "blockbusters."

Naturally, the movie processes of the future are sure to bring a change in the architecture of theaters themselves. The trend of the last decade has been to divide the old movie palaces of the past into several smaller theaters. Some new cinema complexes—the Cineplex theaters in Los Angeles and Toronto, for example—are being designed and built with a dozen or more screens and individual movie houses that seat only sixty or seventy viewers, a far cry from the mammoth cathedrals of the cinema of the depression years. However, audiences are beginning to reject these shoebox cinemas as the screens in them shrink to the size of a home television.

If moviegoers are going to escape television and home video for theaters once again, tiny screens and intimate surroundings won't lure them back. Nor may conventional theater designs suit new giant screens or movie technologies. One variation on the IMAX giant-screen process, for example, uses a hemispherical screen under which the audience is seated planetarium-style. When true holographic movies are developed, the audience might actually surround the picture, or the holographic image could engulf the audience. (And how would a Western or African adventure look, then?)

Movie theaters as we know them today won't be entirely extinct by 2019. Twentieth-century-style cinema will be the main medium for filmmakers, actors, and playwrights who will produce "boutique" motion pictures, narrower in scope and less ambitious than the Hollywood spectaculars. These films, like the plays of today's regional repertory theater companies, will present the work of new screenwriters, experimental works, or dramas and comedies that explore the human condition. While this branch of the film industry will be a proving ground for future talent, some serious artists may choose this medium over the more lucrative commercial cinema.

One aspect of the movies that won't change in the next century is subject matter. There is no reason to believe that the traditional film genres won't be as popular forty years from now as they were in the 1930s and 1940s. Love stories, science fiction, teenage comedies, war films, sweeping adventures, and rugged Westerns will be among the most successful movies of 2019.

However, new technologies will make possible a different approach to the traditional themes. Computer-graphic techniques will enable producers to re-create electronically the voices and physical appearances of great movie stars from the past. A new movie featuring a cast of Hollywood hall-of-famers—Jimmy Stewart, Greta Garbo, John Wayne, Marilyn Monroe—isn't just possible, it is probable once computer synthesis techniques are perfected.

Computer graphics hold myriad implications for the movies of the twenty-first century. It will be more practical and cost effective to design sets and synthesize almost any location on Earth or off using computers. Special effects that now require models and miniatures can be replaced by digital picture-making. Animation, once the most visually exciting area of film, today has, except for an occasional Disney film, almost vanished. Computer graphics will cut the cost of animation in the next century, and cartoons featuring solid-looking, three-dimensional characters will breathe new life into this art form.

The computer will also be used to create Hollywood's ultimate actor, one who will never miss a mark on the set, become temperamental, or balk at a paycheck, and will be able to change physical appearance, age, and voice from film to film: a robot.

Walt Disney amazed visitors to the 1964 New York World's Fair with his first humanoids, which he dubbed "Audio-Animatronic figures." The very first of these was, of course, the famous figure of Abraham Lincoln that continues to amaze visitors at the Disney theme parks. Two decades later, the craft of robot-making at WED and MAPO (the two companies responsible for designing and building the Disney theme parks) has advanced to figures that appear to walk up a flight of stairs and more subtly mimic reality than Walt's first lurching and halting animatronic Honest Abe.

Moviegoers, too, have been fascinated with robot characters, from

Opposite page: Yes, this is Holorama—one of the summer's scary gimmick films.

Inset: Computers easily create imaginary landscapes for space dramas.

the metallic female of Fritz Lang's *Metropolis*, to Robby, the automaton genie of *Forbidden Planet*, to R2D2 and C-3PO, *Star Wars's* computerized comedy team. It is not difficult, then, to imagine an all-purpose screen star robot, designed and built by technicians and programmers, who would offer its services to the movie studios.

This robot could be modular in design—tall in the saddle as a hero, a short comic figure when playing a buffoon. Audiences will marvel at its human qualities and soon forget they are watching a mass of wires, valves, and microchips. The robot will bring audiences back, time and again, to witness the latest advances in expression or emotion and, of course, it will cause a major stir in its first starring roles opposite the latest sex symbols, first as robust male, then later as a sultry femme fatale.

But will a robot ever be able to transcend the novelty of its technological heritage? Will it ever pose a challenge to the talents of human thespians? Will it be forced to join the Screen Actors Guild? And, will its artificial intelligence prompt it to snub the unrelenting hordes of autograph hounds? Perhaps the moviegoing audiences of 2019 will find out.

By the way, if you're planning to catch the current crop of summer films in 2019, bring lots of cash. In the last two and a half decades, the price of admission to a first-run film has about tripled. If this trend continues, a ticket to the movies will run $12 to $15 in major markets, perhaps even more for films whose budgets will approach those of a small emerging nation.

Clearly, the gap between the big-screen movies (those broadly painted murals of commercial success) and the small-screen films (often overlooked examples of truly artistic movie-making) will widen in the next century. The big screens will attract the audiences, although the creative talent will prefer the small screens. But what about movie entertainment—if we can call it that—that uses no screen?

It's been a dream of science fiction writers for years: a mass medium that plugs directly into the human brain, bypassing movie or television screens and appearing only in the mind's eye. Some attribute the popularity and use of psychedelic drugs in the 1960s to a generation's premature quest for this kind of new-age entertainment.

In one form or another, a direct-connect medium of some sort should be available by 2019. Several such schemes are already in prototype stages. No, there will not be a multiple-connector socket at the base of our skulls to be used for news reports, rock videos, or surrogate travelogues. It is a good bet, however, that some form of electrodeless computer-to-mind communication will have been achieved; by 2019 they may be sophisticated enough to project remarkably realistic images into the mind.

If not, there will be methods for viewing films and television without a cathode ray tube or movie screen. Already, defense contractors have demonstrated sophisticated optical systems for what are called "heads-up displays" (HUDs) in advanced combat aircraft. These are devices that superimpose an electronically created picture over what our eyes normally see. Fighter pilots use them to avoid looking down at the airplane's instruments.

One of these, developed by Honeywell, projects a TV image directly onto the eye's retina. A pair of these systems has been used to demonstrate fully stereoscopic, three-dimensional pictures. By adding motion-sensing apparatus (ultrasonic or laser systems that record the position of one's head), this 3-D view could change when the viewer looks to the side. This same technology could easily be applied to new video devices that use the human eye as a screen. With the consumer electronics industry's penchant for adapting and popularizing so much of high technology, it should be only a matter of time before a similar device reaches the shelves of your local video store.

Another more exotic approach to a direct-connect medium is the Phosphotron, a nifty little gadget from Steve Beck, an independent researcher and inventor in Berkeley, California. Beck, an artist and electrical engineer, experimented with abstract video during the 1960s and 1970s. His work had been inspired, in turn, by his long interest in phosphenes, bright flashes produced in the human eye. After a blow on the head, we talk of "seeing stars," but what we are really seeing is increased phosphene production. The same goes for the patterns and lights we sometimes see when we vigorously rub our eyes.

While a student at the University of Illinois, Beck read reports of German experiments in the stimulation of phosphene production using electrical currents, and built a simple device to test the ideas on himself and some of his more-adventurous friends. Almost twenty years later, with digital circuits to control and shape complex electrical waveforms, he built the Phosphotron. (The name comes from the Greek words for light and electricity.)

Today, Beck's device consists of a dome-shaped pair of light-tight silver goggles with electrodes that contact the shallow sockets on each side of the head directly above and behind the eyes. Through the electrodes, the Phosphotron passes a low-amperage, modulated electric current that produces a startling illusion of abstract light patterns with the eyes closed.

Beck indicates that, with an experimental array of multiple electrodes, he can create more distinct patterns of light and a sense of directional movement in these patterns. He envisions the day when a complex electrode arrangement could yield a raster, or videolike image, of phosphene-generated light. Even today, several subjects can be connected to the Phosphotron at one time, and all report seeing similar patterns generated by the machine.

The future of a direct-connect entertainment medium need not re-create someone else's reality. A device like the Phosphotron or a kind of retinal projection system might lend itself best to abstractions and other forms of intensely personal, nonrepresentational visual experiences.

If all this is reminiscent of the psychedelic light shows of the 1960s, it shouldn't be surprising. (The early German experiments that originally interested Beck included the administration of LSD and similar mind-altering drugs, which increased phosphene production themselves.) The rock-concert light show may have presaged the kind of abstract entertainment that could become quite popular via machines like the Phosphotron. In lieu of a cop show or soap opera, those seeking new entertainment experiences in 2019 could relax with an evening of their favorite music coupled with a concert of vivid colors and bold, kinetic patterns. After-dinner conversation would continue as the members of a dinner party donned their headsets to enjoy the synthetic sights.

Just the idea of a direct-connect medium will frighten certain people, even some of the brave citizens of 2019. (When LSD achieved fad status in the 1960s, there were millions of bad trips.) Even though such a breakthrough in mass communications will be available in the early twenty-first century, this doesn't mean that it will achieve anything other than cult popularity.

The most popular mass medium of the next century will be, as it is today, television. And why not? Twenty-first-century video hardware will bring bigger, brighter, and clearer pictures into our living rooms.

High-definition television (HDTV), as developed by Japanese and

American broadcasters and hardware manufacturers, will be the world standard by 2019, although the present three TV formats (NTSC, PAL, and Secam) will still be in place. HDTV, which will achieve mass popularity by the mid-1990s, will be downwardly compatible with these older standards in much the same way color television broadcasts can be received on precolor TV sets.

With HDTV's 1,125 horizontal scanning lines (versus 525 in NTSC video and 625 in PAL and Secam) and increased bandwidth—that is, the ability to distinguish a higher number of individual points on each line—there will be little detectable difference in quality between a television picture and a 35mm theatrical motion picture on large screens. On small sets, HDTV will give the look and crispness of the photograph or the printed four-color page. The aspect ratio of HDTV is also wider, 2:1 versus 3:4, than the present video pictures, so wide-screen motion pictures will no longer be cropped as they are today when shown on television.

While most HDTV sets will use glass cathode ray tubes for direct viewing, a variety of wall-sized screens will grow increasingly popular. The most common way of projecting television pictures uses three electro-optical tubes, one each for the red, blue, and green components of a color video picture. By the end of this century, however, other methods will dominate, including the use of a single, extremely bright picture tube of a special design called a "beam index tube." The beam index tube will lower the cost of projection TVs and make them smaller, eventually reducing their size from that of a coffee table to about the dimensions of a small suitcase.

Another type of video projector will use an adaptation of the light valve, an electronic device that essentially creates a transparent television picture on glass. By putting a bright light source in back of one of these light valves and a lens in front of it, a complete system the size of a slide projector is possible. Japanese companies are already experimenting with very inexpensive light-valve devices that use variations on the liquid-crystal displays commonly seen in calculators and electronic wristwatches. The biggest obstacle in bringing this kind of set to market is the difficulty of putting the hundreds of thousands, even millions, of individual light shutters that form a continuous-looking picture onto a single display.

Other more exotic plans for projection sets involve the use of lasers that paint a giant video image with moving beams of light. Lasers

capable of pumping out very bright light are still expensive, however, and require the use of glass tubes filled with rare gases. Laser light, too, displays a unique property when projected. A speckle pattern (though it is not unattractive) is produced and offers the impression of the light falling on a sandy, granular surface. Eventually, this might prove too distracting.

As for television sound, expect the best technically possible. Static and noise-free audio, the kind brought by laser-read digital compact discs, will be the standard for TV. Although quadraphonic sound in phonograph records died a swift death in the 1970s, it has been making something of a comeback as four-channel Dolby stereo in motion pictures. Almost inevitably, the home video theater of the twenty-first century will use some variation on multichannel "surround sound" that will lend a more convincing illusion of three dimensions than normal stereo.

Videocassettes will remain the favorite method of feeding these video systems throughout the twentieth century. The Beta and VHS home videocassette standards will last for the next two decades or so, not because of their technical superiority, but because of the huge numbers of these recorders already in homes. Other magnetic-tape formats, including 8mm video, which uses a much narrower ribbon of plastic tape, will also be somewhat successful, though not for any dramatic increase in picture or sound quality. Instead, 8mm video will become the video "home movie" medium of the near future.

The turn of the century, though, will see magnetic tape replaced by optical devices capable of recording video and audio, as well as other kinds of information, as digital data. The medium will be neither a disc nor a tape, but rather a card, probably the size of a credit card. Each will store the equivalent of several "gigabytes" (billions of characters) of information, enough for a few hours of video with sound, several more hours of digital audio alone, or the equivalent of thousands of printed books, retrievable by a personal computer.

The data on a typical lasercard will be holographically encoded, recorded, and played back with a low-power laser that scans its surface. This type of card will emerge as the dominant information medium of the next century for several reasons. Tape is too slow for fast random access to the information stored on it because it must be wound and rewound to find a specific location. Disc is faster because read/write heads move radially across its surface, but cards can be scanned with a laser beam, their information read almost instantaneously. And cards don't warp, nor do they require the precise positioning of a center hole, as do discs.

One American company, Drexler Technology, is already at work on such a lasercard; so are Japanese manufacturers and key players in the graphic arts industry, who see this medium eventually replacing much paper printing. It may be possible to print lasercard information on magazine and book pages by 2019. A typical magazine ad could feature a large, color photograph, printed text, and a silvery lasercard containing a video program of several minutes, computer data about a product's performance, and even the company jingle.

Lasercard data-storage capacities are still low, only a few megabytes, or millions of characters, and not enough for video use, but like microelectronic memory chips, the capacity of lasercards will grow quickly. The advances will be rapid enough to ensure that the home video library of 2019 will not be a wall full of bulky black plastic videocassettes, but a tiny file of shiny optical lasercards.

We can't expect that all television programming will be delivered on tape, disc, or even cards, however. Most video information will still be broadcast, either through the air or via cable.

Cable video will be battling with programming delivered directly by satellite well into the next century. DBS (direct-broadcast satellites) did not catch on with consumers in its first introduction a few years ago, even though the sales of large dish antennas boomed in the early 1980s. The early DBS companies, who tried to sell pay-TV channels of movies and sporting events, used relatively powerful new satellites broadcasting on the KU-band frequencies. The advantage of using these new satellites meant that dish antennas could be much smaller—typically three feet or less in diameter—and receiving equipment less expensive.

The new satellites, using the high and easily receivable KU-band frequency, will be the center of broadcasting in the next decade and into the twenty-first century. Because these satellites can carry huge amounts of information to audiences across the nation, they will be perfect for broadcasting high-definition television signals. Moveover, KU-band receivers will be as inexpensive to manufacture as short-wave radios, opening satellite reception to most viewers.

Still, many homes, especially in urban areas, lack a clear view of the satellite belt in the sky. Some form of cable TV will still be needed.

The most notable change in cable TV will be the way video and other information is pumped into the home. Hair-thin glass optical fiber bundles will replace the copper cable now in use. Two factors will dictate the change: cost and capacity. Copper is growing continually more expensive; already, optical fibers are cheaper for some high-volume application. In addition to sending video signals into homes, cable television companies will find themselves serving the growing needs of corporations and financial institutions who need a cheap and fast way to move mammoth amounts of information from one office to another.

So what's on TV tonight? Not surprisingly, television programming won't change as dramatically as the video hardware itself. The three major broadcast television networks will still dominate, though their impact will be diminished by competition from other sources. Network TV will also continue to be the single greatest source of lowest-common denominator programming, catering to the tastes of the

Opposite page: Fantastic light shows—an everyday occurrence.

masses with still more action shows, comedies, daily dramas, and family situation comedies.

By the turn of the century, the major networks could be broadcasting in a language other than English. Today, approximately 5 percent of the U.S. population speaks Spanish as a first language, and the figure is likely to rise significantly by the beginning of the twenty-first century. Faced with stiff competition from cable and home video, one of the big-three networks could pull off a major coup by appealing to this important population segment. An alternative to NBC, CBS, or ABC changing to alternate-language programs is for one of them to begin regular bilingual service using the stereo sound technology already available.

Cable television will become the medium where old network fare lives on, seemingly forever. Television series from the 1950s and 1960s will still be seen in 2019. Black-and-white series will be digitally colored to appeal to new audiences, many of whom will watch them if for no other reason than to see how people lived in the previous century. Lucy and Ricky Ricardo, Ralph and Alice Cramden, and Uncle Miltie may be as popular with a fourth generation of viewers as they are today with people who weren't yet born when they made their TV debuts.

Cable television will also become more like the magazine business. Special-purpose cable networks—women's, kids, and sports channels, and so on—will become mini pay services, available for $5 or $6 a month, or about the same price as a newsstand magazine. And the widespread use of computer-controlled converters and decoders will make it as easy to change the channels a subscriber receives as it is to buy a new magazine, perhaps even on a daily basis.

This will breed fierce competition among the new networks. Instead of the familiar Nielsen ratings, pay-TV networks will measure their popularity by the daily change in their subscriber rolls. This will force television executives to be much more daring in their attempts to lure audiences.

Although today's cable networks seem to cater to every conceivable taste, there will be room for new ones in 2019. A travel channel is one obvious idea. Other channels may deal with alternative life-styles and sexual preferences, exotic thrill-seeking, adventure, and perhaps even programs for those in psychotherapy—calming and reassuring shows

for paranoids, stimulating and cheerful programs for depressives. One of the supermarket-tabloid publishers is almost certain to find a berth on cable before the end of this century.

A nifty television accessory of 2019 will substitute its owner's image for any other human figure in a television program. Narcissists will be able to put themselves in the starring role of a classic film (*Citizen Klopstein?*) or watch themselves reading the evening news in lieu of the network anchorman.

But not all entertainment will be as passive as television viewing in the next century. Personal computers will eventually fulfill much of their original promise, particularly with regard to creative endeavors, such as music and art, as more powerful processors and artificial intelligence find their way into desktop machines.

Already, a standard for linking personal computers to electronic music synthesizers, called MIDI (Musical Instrument Digital Interface), allows ambitious novices to take charge of their own combos and small orchestras. Some of these new instruments use digitally re-corded sound of famous instrumentalists, and there is no reason the idea can't be extended to Itzhak Perlman's Stradivarius, Horowitz's Steinway, or Eddie Van Halen's Gibson electric guitar.

Assigning parts to an electronic orchestra isn't difficult. Most such software today makes the task as simple as selecting from a menu of choices. But many amateur musicians are still intimidated by the man-ual dexterity required by a piano, guitar, or clarinet. The solution is a circuit that can understand whistling, humming, or singing; correct errors in pitch for those who can't carry a tune; and translate this information into digital data a computer music system can understand. AI software can then fit the music into a song or rearrange it to conform to the tempo and rhythm of the user's work-in-progress.

For jazz buffs, programs that can improvise in the style of legendary jazz artists, Mingus and Monk for instance, will have these ghostly greats sit in on their sessions. Software that lets would-be maestros endlessly tinker with their compositions, substituting bass lines and alternative playing styles, will make creating music almost as popular as listening to recordings.

As for the twenty-first-century painter, look for today's elaborate computer graphics and special effects to migrate quickly to the living room. In five years, home computers will match the output of today's special-purpose graphics computers. In ten, they will surpass anything now available.

Laser printers can now produce high-resolution images with three hundred individual dots per inch (dpi). Next year it will be five hundred. By the beginning of the next century, printer images will be as clear as most photographs. The cost of this capability will fall to rival today's inexpensive home computer printers.

Amateur graphic artists will have a medium in which a simple decision—"put that over there"—will free them from the need for a designer's skill with paper knife and pastepot. Elegantly printed pages will come from computer systems that will let practically anyone become a skillful designer and layout artist. By the year 2019, home graphics technology will no longer limit would-be artists. Only talent and practice will matter.

A new movement will create a boom in self-published books and small, independent hobby publishers will grow from a new computer language called POSTSCRIPT. It is designed to describe the contents of a printed page, including typeset text, drawings, and photographs. Already used in a number of digital laser typesetters and Apple computer's LaserWriter printer, POSTSCRIPT is the future of words on paper.

Those with specialized interests or points of view will soon use these desktop systems to publish limited-circulation magazines and publications with the professional appearance of better-known journals. Part-time novelists and authors will produce their own books. Artists and designers will more easily translate the vision of their minds' eyes to paper. The revolution begun by Johannes Gutenberg in the mid-fifteenth century will reach its ultimate fruition.

As with advanced music systems, these graphics machines will enable those visited less frequently by the muses to draw with subtle shading and variations in line or paint in styles ranging from that of a pointillist like Seurat to the abstractions of a Jackson Pollack.

By the same token, as machines aid our creative skills and expression, those with real talent, musically and artistically, will be even more highly regarded by society tomorrow than they are today. Only this still-select group of ever-rare human beings will continue to explore new trends in music and visual art in 2019.

Vision, taste, foresight, true inventiveness, and the talent for real creation are attributes only assisted, never truly replaced, by even the most intelligent of mankind's thinking machines.

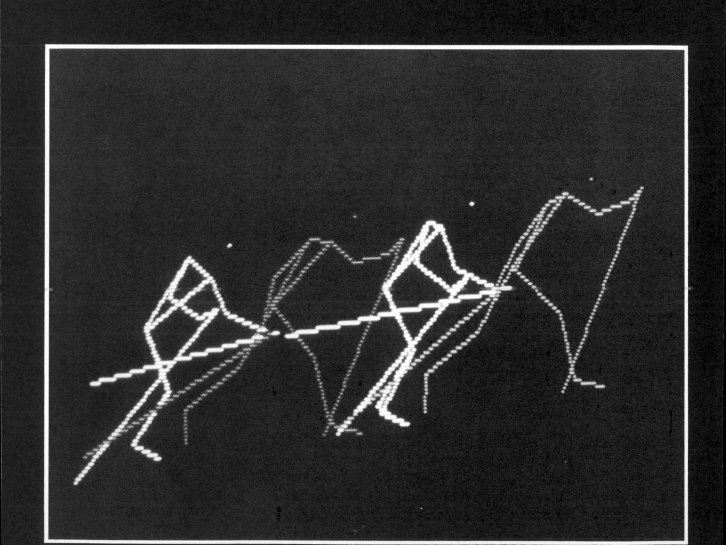

A DAY AT THE BALLPARK: SPORTS IN 2019

**NEW YORK YANKEES SCOUTING REPORT
FOR THE 2019 WORLD SERIES
REPORT FILED BY YANKEE SCOUT DON MATTINGLY**

Opponent: Los Angeles Dodgers

Prospectus: It's our power and fielding against their pitching and speed. Our Sportspak computers say we'll win if we get 4.2 runs a game.

Away Games: L.A. will swing the Dodgersdome fences out beyond 500 feet to cut down our home-run production. And they'll stick with their hardest artificial turf so they get better bounce and traction for base-stealing.

Home Games: We'll roll out our softest Astroturf to slow them down, and with our short 450-foot fences and our boron bats, we should light up the sky in the Yankeesdome with homers. Also, the computers show the Dodgers win 11 percent fewer games when the temperature falls below 68°F; we'll turn off the indoor heating systems and retract the dome, using the late autumn chill to our advantage.

DODGERS PLAYERS

Pitchers

Rufus Lincoln—right-hander. Throws fastballs, fastballs, fastballs, but never gets tired. Since his bionic shoulder and elbow implant two years back, he can go 9 innings every other day. We've clocked him at 120 mph.

Sol "The Prof" Hershowitz—southpaw with pinpoint control. The Dodgers have the best biomechanical analysis system in baseball. The Prof has spent more time perfecting his pitching motion with the digitizer and high-speed videotape than he has on the mound.

Tom "Twitch" Sully—their right-handed ace. He had augmented electrical muscle impulses cloned from Hall-of-Famer Dwight Gooden's muscles the year before Gooden retired. Consequently, his fastball breaks bats and his curveball could swerve around the corner of a building. You can rile him, though—they forgot to save Gooden's alpha brain waves.

Previous page: Computer simulation of an athlete's movements.

Ralph Shandy—15-year-old rookie relief pitcher who throws with both hands. He has a terrific screwball and forkball, but he's pretty wild. It seems the Dodgers have been racing him along too fast with the growth hormones.

Catcher

Cary Goiter—right-hander. Always had a consistent bat and a great arm. Until last year, though, he couldn't hold onto knuckleballs, and years of catching had turned his hand to sausage. The deep-webbed impact-free mitt solved all his problems.

Infielders

Jerry Rodriguez—right-handed third baseman. Diludin-crystal derivatives could only hold off his aging process so long. At 57, his reflexes are slipping. But he's already planning his next career—racing a solar sail around the Moon.

Bud Garvey—right-handed first baseman. He can hit any kind of pitch you throw. Steve Garvey, the Dodgers's old first baseman, sired him so well that he keeps getting black market requests around the league to produce more offspring.

Sam Juice—southpaw second baseman. Good speed but sloppy with the glove. His dad ignored his infant anatomy profile, which showed he was best suited for football.

Gary Yamamoto—shortstop. Yamamoto made a big mistake when he switched from the Tokyo to the Tucson National Baseball Camp at the age of 12. The Tucson graduates all have trouble hitting curveballs.

Outfielders

Lance Nihilator—switch-hitting center fielder who can catch any ball hit within a block of him. The Dodgers's steroid program has helped him get down to 8.7 seconds in the 100-meter dash, just .3 off the world record. He stole 207 bases this season.

Bill Black—southpaw left fielder. Almost as fast as Nihilator. His leg was shattered while parachuting between ski slopes during the off season, and we thought it might slow him down, but the trainer sealed up all the cracks immediately with bonding solution. Electric stim has almost got the bone back to full strength.

Enos Tramweigh—right-handed right fielder. This rookie could barely hit or throw a ball across a room at the start of the season. The Dodgers lasered away some bone chips in his elbow, then hooked him up with electrodes to a computerized strength-training machine day after day. Now he's got a gun for an arm and ended up hitting 30 homers.

Shortly after the turn of the century, the knowledge and technology will exist to improve performance exponentially in every single sport on Earth. By the year 2019, athletes and teams at every level will be reaping the benefits of countless developments such as the ones mentioned in the Yankees's scouting report. Fearing the loss of traditional competitive values, athletic organizers will attempt to limit the encroachments of science. But tradition or not, all sports will evolve, just as they have always evolved.

Back in 1891, at Springfield College in Illinois, for example, a physical education instructor named James Naismith was asked to create a sport that would fill up the long winter between the end of football and the start of baseball season. After searching in vain for some cardboard boxes, Naismith settled for two peach baskets, nailing them up on the edge of a balcony at each end of the gymnasium. Then he found a laced soccerball and put a ladder beside each basket so the ball could be removed whenever a team scored. There was no dribbling and no such thing as free throws. The only way to move the ball toward the basket was to pass it from player to player. A total of thirteen rules governed the game.

Today, the basketball rule book goes on for dozens of pages, and if James Naismith attended a college or professional contest he might have trouble recognizing his own game. He'd see glass backboards hung atop poles, metal-rimmed baskets with corded netting open at the bottom, and a far larger, laceless leather ball with pockmarks all over it. He'd also be confronted with the strange specter of athletes as tall as seven feet bouncing the ball off the floor as they raced pell-mell downcourt.

If someone stuck us in a time capsule and transported us to a pro-basketball arena thirty years hence, the game would certainly still be recognizable. But in many respects it would flabbergast us just as much as our 1980s version would James Naismith.

The first thing we would notice is the athletes themselves. Thanks to controlled drug programs and diet manipulation, the average height of a National Basketball Association player in 2019 will be seven feet three inches—about six inches taller than players today. Some will even soar above eight feet. These athletes, moreover, will not fit the traditional long-legged image of basketball players; they won't have the spindly, brittle look of praying mantises. Instead, they will be solid and perfectly sculpted, with barrel chests and tightly muscled arms and legs. These towering players, nurtured on biomechanical analysis and a host of other scientific training methods, will be so technically exact that the most massive forwards and centers will be as graceful and coordinated as the smallest playmaking guards are today.

Because of the incredible abilities of these future stars, the league will change several features in the court setup to keep the game challenging. First, before the turn of the century, NBA authorities will raise the height of the basket and reduce the perimeter of the rim. And then the basketball itself will grow slightly, and the indoor leather and outdoor rubber versions used today will be replaced by a plastic that combines leather's excellent feel with rubber's durability.

Most other major sports are considerably more complex than basketball, calling for more players and/or more implements. Thus, technology will have an even greater impact on them. In tennis, for example, a full-blown equipment revolution has already been launched. Players have always sought a magic racquet that could handle the sport's intricate array of power strokes and delicate touch shots, but until six or seven years ago, plain wood and metal racquets still held sway. Today they are almost unheard of. Most manufacturers have borrowed their current secret formulas from the aerospace industry, building racquet frames from such materials as fiberglass, graphite, and ceramics, which were originally used in the hulls of supersonic jets. By 2019, even these materials will be obsolete. Today's graphite fanciers will be using racquets made of boron, a fiber that has all the maneuverability of graphite without its brittleness. Or perhaps they will wield racquets made of a revolutionary synthetic called Kevlar. Kevlar looks and feels a lot like fiberglass, but when mixed with epoxy resin, it can withstand the blow of a sledgehammer. Boron and Kevlar racquets will be virtually unbreakable, as well as infinitely better at absorbing shock and trauma. And in one neat package, they will combine greater power and steadiness than the best metal racquet and greater lightness and quickness than the best graphite racquet.

But strings, not racquets, will inspire the greatest innovations in tennis. First of all, the feel and resilience of synthetic strings will continually improve, until catgut strings vanish altogether. Unaffected by weather and guaranteed for life, the new strings will expand tremendously on impact to produce explosive power, returning to their original state the next moment.

And racquets will no longer be strung at a fixed tension of, say, sixty or seventy pounds; instead, they will come equipped with computerized adjustable-tension systems. A player will be able to choose one tension for serving, then quickly switch to another tension when he charges the net.

Although such spectacular advances in technology will be available across the board, not all sports will immediately welcome them. Baseball, for example, with a history going back well into the 1880s, will resist whatever might upset its traditions. To begin with, nothing is more traditional to the grand old game than the wooden bat. In high schools and colleges today, powerful aluminum bats are already being used along with wood, but they are banned from professional ball because they supposedly give the hitter an unfair advantage. After a couple of decades of dispute, two factors will finally eliminate this ban: First, the ever-increasing speed, precision, and pitch selection of major league hurlers will convince the powers-that-be to give the hitters a break; and second, a scarcity of hickory (the primary wood used in bat-making) will require a change.

Once aluminum is allowed into the majors, synthetics and composites will soon follow. With each passing year batters will hit the ball harder and farther than ever before. The subtle balancing act between offense and defense will have shifted to the hitter's advantage. To compensate, teams will move their outfield fences by as much as a hundred feet—beyond the five-hundred-foot mark—and fielders as well as catchers will begin wearing long, lightweight, synthetic gloves with deeper webbing that will grab many more balls.

Twenty-first-century uniforms will enhance performances, too. Instead of wearing baggy cotton or polyester, everyone from track stars to hockey players will don skintight body suits made of breathable, aerodynamic fabrics such as derivatives of Lycra spandex. And working hand in hand with podiatrists, competitors will custom-design their shoes. Each athlete will first have X rays taken and a mold cast of his feet. Then he will be tested on a force platform, a pressure-sensitive electronic plate that can show all the infinitesimal forces acting on the feet during competition. When this information is compiled, it will provide a profile of the feet as identifiable as fingerprints. The final result will be a streamlined, aerodynamic shoe giving maximum traction, speed, and spring.

The supreme goal of twenty-first-century equipment, though, will be to prevent injury. In professional baseball and football, most athletes will be earning multimillion-dollar salaries, and owners will have to cut their rosters way down to afford them. Consequently, they will be desperate to keep every player healthy.

New composite football and baseball batting helmets with acoustic linings will muffle shock and reverberation, preventing concussions. The baseball helmets will wrap around more of the head, and the football helmets will drop down low in back to protect the neck and spine. Both will come with built-in goggles to guard the eyes. And the soft but resilient composites, such as Delrin, which replaced metal in the football helmet, will make the helmet itself less of a weapon.

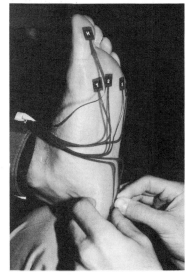

Foot sensors are placed on a runner's feet to capture his movements in a computer memory.

Actually, by 2019 the helmet will not be a separate part of the football uniform. It will be directly attached to the "donuts"—the rings of padding that players wear around the neck—and the donuts, in turn, will be connected to the rest of the outfit. Shockproof polymerized shoulder pads and stable but extremely flexible synthetic knee guards that cover most of the leg will complete the ensemble, basically forming an unbroken line of protection from head to toe. Few targets will be left open for injury. "There will simply be a lot less trouble," says Tom Doyle of the National Sporting Goods Association. "Players will literally have to try as hard as they can to hurt each other."

If any sport in our era can compete with football for injury potential, it's probably skiing. But the skier of the future will soar down slopes with high boots to protect the knee and frictionless bindings to protect the ankle and prevent fractures. When the skier crashes or falls, an electronic strain gauge in the bindings will automatically sense the excessive force, throwing open the binding gates and releasing the feet before they can be dangerously twisted.

Skiing performance will change as well. Skis made of new synthetics and composites (such as graphite, boron, Kevlar) and plastics (such as aramids) will deaden vibration and increase speed. With special soft tips for easy turning and flexible poles that bend outward for greater extension and drive, these skis will make even so-so skiers vastly more proficient. And to make things yet more of a cakewalk for the weekend devotee, the new recreational skis will come with a battery-powered drive mechanism on the back. Instead of cooling their heels waiting for the lift, skiers will simply look around for the right peak. A flip of a switch will then send them zooming to the top.

In the final analysis, of course, no matter how spectacular a piece of equipment is, it won't turn a middling athlete into superstar. So, in the twenty-first century, the athlete, not his tools, will still be the center of the sports universe. And technology will make its greatest contributions to his nurturing and training.

In 2019, people will know within the first few years of life whether they are destined to be athletes. They will also know exactly what sports they are physiologically and psychologically best equipped for. Already, Dr. James Nicholas, director of the renowned Lenox Hill Center for Sports Medicine and Athletic Trauma, has begun developing a multifaceted diagnostic "profile," which may well become the standard athletic screening tool of the future. Somewhat like a traditional occupational profile, the test measures everything from heart rate and peripheral vision to limb strength and maximal oxygen intake. When such a system is in universal use, scientists will feed the results into a computer programmed with the physiological and psychological requirements for success in every major sport. The final printout will tell the athlete precisely which sport to pursue. Someone with a long, ectomorphic frame, and resilient ankle joints, for example, may be told he is ideally suited for the leaps and crash landings of basketball; someone with a slow heartbeat, ample lungs, and lots of "slow twitch" muscle fibers (which are high in aerobic endurance enzymes) may be directed into long-distance running; and a rawboned mesomorph with aggressive tendencies may find he is tailor-made for football.

Even with these early tests, some late bloomers will certainly slip through the cracks. But they will be discovered on national field days held annually in the elementary schools. The entire spectrum of athletic events will be offered on these days, and the most outstanding competitors in each event, along with the children discovered shortly after birth through the profiles, will then have the option of entering one of several appropriate sports camps around the country. Once

they are in, their long-term training and overall education will be supervised by the camp, probably for more than a decade.

To these future recruits, most of today's training methods will seem as primitive as Edison's camera. Through a variety of "telemetric" (remote measurement) techniques, which will allow teams of specialists to study athletes' internal responses during practice and competition, we will have solved many of the body's mysteries: How do muscles adapt to an increased work load? How much rest and recovery time is needed after workouts? How does the brain generate chemical messengers such as epinephrine to increase energy and endorphins to reduce pain? With these secrets in hand, athletes will reach their absolute potential without ever overtraining.

The starting point for each trainee will be an intensive bio-

Will players in the future have augmented electrical muscle impulses cloned from Hall-of-Famers?

mechanical analysis, where the athlete's body will be studied as a mechanical system. Today, the germ of this technique can be found at the Olympic Training Camp at Colorado Springs. An athlete goes through the motions of his sport atop a set of eighteen-inch-long electronic sheets called "force plates" embedded in the floor. As he moves, the plates send data to a computer on the forces impinging on him and exerted by his body. Next, he attaches fourteen tiny sensors to the soles of his feet and a tiny computer to his belt. Wires from the sensors to the computer carry even more minute data on the forces generated by the feet.

Within a couple of decades, after extensive biomechanics research, computer programmers will have created a universal program for ideal patterns of movement in every sport. Breaking down the human body into thousands of musculoskeletal segments, these programs will instantly pinpoint the flaws in an athlete's technique and show how to correct them. As the athlete works out, an ultra-high-speed videotape camera will feed images of his performance directly to a computer. The images will be immediately converted into data and matched against the formulas for perfect biomechanical efficiency. If the athlete is performing inefficiently, the computer will show exactly why.

Even this level of biomechanical analysis, however, will be considered insufficient by 2019, as computer and medical scientists form a more and more intimate union. Athletes will train not just in front of videotape cameras, but also with portable heart (EKG) and brain wave (EEG) monitors attached to their bodies. During the same workout, other telemetric gauges will show blood pressure levels, oxygen levels, and remaining muscle strength. All of these data will be continually reviewed and compiled as the scientists perfect both universal norms and customized training regimens.

"Right now we can tell athletes how much they weigh and how much body fat they have," says physiologist Peter Van Handel of the U.S. Olympic Committee. "But in the future we'll be able to determine optimal patterns of heartbeats, aerobic capacity, metabolism, and innumerable blood variables for each athlete in every sport. We'll also be able to tell athletes how these parameters should vary with altitude or temperature. Our computerized tests for strength (how much they can lift) and power (how fast they can lift it) will tell them which muscles to work on for better performance in any given activity."

By 2019, precision training will have brought athletes close to the limits of their natural potential. But a number of controversial new techniques will push them well beyond those limits. Although official bodies including the U.S. Olympic Committee today speak out vociferously against drugs and artificial forms of stimulation, researchers are already experimenting with "ergogenic" (performance enhancing) substances. Scientists such as David Cope are convinced that this research will create a completely new standard of athletic achievement.

They also believe that these chemical aids to performance will eventually be welcomed wholeheartedly, because they simply won't be harmful anymore. Today, for instance, anabolic steroids used by so many weight lifters to increase weight and strength can lead to dangerous hormonal imbalances and side effects ranging from male mammary growth and sterility to liver damage and cancer.

Within a decade, however, biochemists will learn to alter the steroid molecule, increasing the growth-producing (anabolic) benefits and totally eliminating the hormonal (androgenic) side effects. By 2019, steroids will be prescribed by doctors and trainers according to a controlled, systematic regimen.

Genetically engineered human growth hormones will be another favorite aid. Natural substances that stimulate the pituitary gland, these growth hormones are already being used with spectacular success to combat dwarfism in extremely small children. Unfortunately, many athletes are using them clandestinely in vast quantities to build up muscle mass without sufficiently understanding the side effects and risks. In 2019, with trained experts carefully dispensing them, the risks will be nil.

The most mind-boggling new area in drug prescription will revolve around the aging process. One theory has it that as athletes get older, the body—especially muscle tissue—is slowly deteriorated by poisonous substances called "free radicals," which are generated in the course of respiration. The Soviets are already working on a way to slow this deterioration. Diludin, a bright yellow crystalline substance produced by a desert cactus, has been shown in the lab to consume free radicals. In the future, scientists believe, the drug will increase the length of athletic careers, leading to new lifetime records in all sports. Sprinters will be able to compete at the age of forty-five, and ballplayers will continue on into their late fifties.

Ultimately, athletic trainers will be able to perform a balancing act with enzymes and nutrients the same way pit-stop technicians manipulate fuel in race cars. Just as a stock car is different than a dragster, each athlete is different than every other. Consequently, each requires a unique combination of fuel for optimum performance. In 2019, before an athlete begins his event, his trainers will know exactly which foods provide him with the greatest energy. And during a time out, when the fatigued athlete marches to the sidelines, the trainers will instantly test the level of nutrients in the blood and the rate at which they are reaching crucial muscle groups. They will then inject the missing metabolites, from glycogen to adenosine triphosphate, directly into the fatigued muscles.

Another important method of performance enhancement will be electrical stimulation. Already, a group of doctors at the University of Massachusetts has used electrical signals from the arm muscles of normal subjects to stimulate movement in stroke victims. The doctors used a machine, an electromyograph, to record electrical signals from the normal subjects. They stored the signals, known as electromyograms (EMGs), in a computer. Finally, those signals were sent from the computer to electrodes attached to the arms of the stroke victims. Most of these paralyzed patients eventually recovered at least partial use of their limbs.

Gideon Ariel, director of research at the Coto Research Center in California, has recently taken the technique one step further by recording the muscle patterns of Olympic superstars and transferring them to promising newcomers. When the experiments are completed years from now, the greatest athletes in every sport will be asked to contribute their muscle patterns to a national computer bank, which will be offered to up-and-comers as a training shortcut.

By the time athletes have begun to bandy their muscle impulses back and forth, not even brain waves will be sacrosanct. Scientists have already learned that an athlete's brain waves change at each stage of an event. For instance, when runners maintain a comfortable pace, they emit alpha waves (signaling relaxation) from their analytic left brain. But when the runner pushes the pace, his left-brain alpha waves recede and his intuitive right brain takes over.

By 2019, scientists will know the optimal brain wave patterns for each stage of every athletic event. These patterns will be programmed into a computer, which will monitor athletes' thought processes as they prepare for games or meets. A buzzer will sound whenever a competitor's brain wave pattern departs from the ideal. By reacting to the cues, twenty-first-century athletes will augment certain patterns and repress others, achieving the perfect mind-set for every competitive situation.

The mind, after all, will be a more important tool than ever for athletes in 2019. Stoked by chemicals, primed by computers and electrodes, competitors will be plunged into a strange world of unprecedented complexity, where only the clearest thinkers will prevail. Competing in domed, indoor stadiums with artificial turf and artificial air, they will be refereed by talking videotape cameras and electronic sensors, and they will have to sift through nonstop instructions radioed to their miniaturized headsets by coaches, nutritionists, physicians, and computer strategists along the sidelines. In the middle of

The brain is as important as the body in athletics, and tomorrow's athletes will have their synapses meticulously charted.

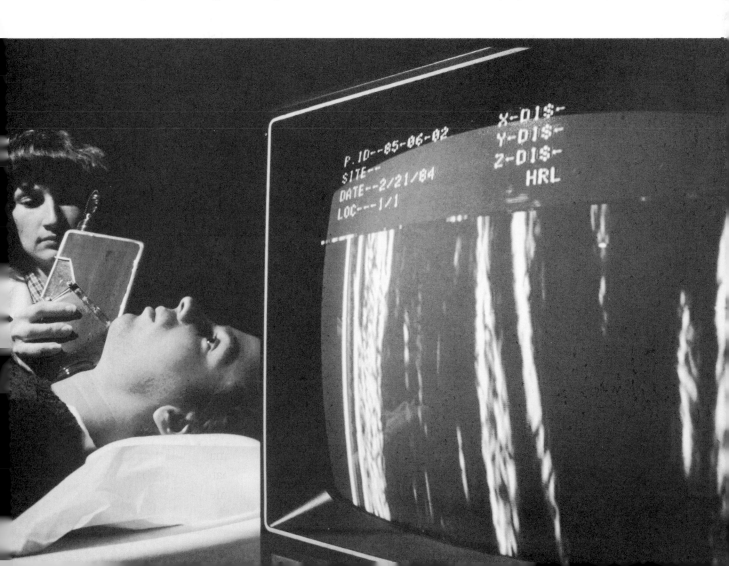

competition, they will be told their heart rate and carbohydrate levels, their alpha wave patterns, and the probabilities of their making any shot or stroke against any particular opponent. And throughout the contest, they will have to weigh every bit of this data and react to it in the space of a split second.

With a spectrum of physical and mental abilities virtually unknown today, the athlete of the future will find far greater challenges to test his mettle. The marathon run will give way to the thousand-mile run, and the bicycling Tour de France will expand to a Tour de l'Europe. In team sports, there will be more minutes in each game and more games in each season, though for financial reasons each club will have fewer members. Many will play every minute of every contest, and when that doesn't satisfy their lust for competition, teams will start to schedule daily double-headers.

But as time goes on, more and more athletes will tire of these one-dimensional sports, and follow the lead of today's triathletes, who swim, then bike, then run long distance all during one continuous event. In an endless quest to explore the limits of human potential, they will develop more and more combination sports such as "football," featuring three nonstop hours of football followed by baseball followed by basketball; "paraskiing," in which skiers use parachutes to float from peak to peak; and "parascuba racing," where divers race long distances underwater after leaping from planes with lightweight scuba tanks attached to their backs.

In the end, even the boundaries of Earth will not be enough for the athletes of the future, and a flood of original games will emerge out of our foray into space. Those settling the Moon, for instance, will perfect the one-sixth gravity run-and-jump. At the start of their spring, the athletes will lean forward with their chests just off the ground to keep their feet from running out from under them. Then, just before they jump they will plant their feet and spread their knees frog-fashion to preserve their balance. Their leaps will carry them six times further than here on Earth.

One game sure to be a hit in orbiting colonies is "spaceminton," played with a standard badminton bird. The net, stretched across the center of a transparent sphere, would contain a central hole only one meter in diameter. The goal of the game is to send the birdie flying through the hole to the other side. When a player comes too close to the side of the sphere, he'll do a flip-turn off the wall like a swimmer and somersault back onto the court.

Yet another space game will be the Space Cup, where competitors use solar sails to race around the Moon. On the Sun side of the Moon, they will be propelled by solar winds. When they pass into the dark side of the Moon, where no sunlight gets through, they will use energy that solar collectors had stored in the sails.

HOUSE ARREST

"Charlie, you're not going to believe this. I don't believe this." Hardee Jackson passed a copy of the arrest warrant to Charlie Beauchamp.

Beauchamp unfolded the document and read it through. Jackson watched as his partner's pale blue eyes went to the bottom then back to the top, then back down again. Beauchamp's were not nice eyes. Frozen in the blue iris of each pupil was a permanent accusation. The skin that spread from his eyes and around his face was purple and red, especially around the nostrils where the tiny vessels had begun to burst.

Beauchamp—he pronounced it Beechum, but Jackson always used the French pronunciation—looked at his partner and showed him the yellowed teeth at one corner of his mouth. "Jackson. This better be a joke."

"No joke, Charlie. I just got it from the DA, Schwarz. He wants us to pick up Frank in White Collar and go do it now."

"Frank? Frank seen this yet?"

"No. We're going to tell him now."

"Not we. You."

"Charlie—"

"I mean it, Jackson. Someone's pulling your chain. If you want to make a fool of yourself, you go get Frank. Then you come get me and we'll roll."

A big man came around the corner carrying a straw Stetson and a blue seersucker jacket and wearing red suspenders. "Hey," he said. "Captain told me to stop by."

"Just the man Jackson's looking for," Beauchamp said.

He handed the paper to Jackson, who handed it to Frank D'Angelo, the senior computer-fraud investigator from White Collar Crime and Fraud.

D'Angelo raised an eyebrow. "So, for once they took my advice."

Beauchamp threw a stack of index cards into the air. "Frankie. Frankie. What is this bullshit?"

"No bullshit. It's the only way it could have happened."

"But Frank."

D'Angelo folded the paper and tucked one end in his pants, the other behind one of the suspenders straps. He pulled on his jacket.

"Let's go, gents," he said. "I'm dying to see how you guys handle this one." He took a step toward the door. "Oh, hey. I almost forgot. Better

Previous page: Future homes are more free-form, perhaps even tent like.

get an extra large squad car." He was still laughing as he rounded the corner.

On the way, D'Angelo ripped a piece of paper into three small pieces, inked a dot on one, then stuck the pieces into his Stetson. Each picked out a piece of paper to see who would have to read the suspect his rights. Beauchamp picked the marked slip.

At 2:15 P.M., July 22, 2019, the three detectives pulled up at 1185 Leavenworth, one of the newest homes in northern Baltimore, and arrested a suspect in the murder of Samuel J. Palmerston, found dead in front of his television on July 20.

Beauchamp pulled a laminated card from his wallet, stepped back twenty-five feet and shouted at the house: "You have the right to remain silent. . . ."

It was not the typical *crime passionnel*.

By 1990, computers had grown sentient and architects began designing the new machines into their houses and cities until the houses and cities became machines in themselves. This had done wonders for household energy costs. It had not done much for Samuel J. Palmerston. Students of crime say the roots of his murder grow deep to the late eighties, in particular to a young architect named Bertold Schmeck and a cockroach named Adrian.

There were no sudden oil shortages, no new oil embargoes; OPEC, the Organization of Petroleum Exporting Countries, had crumbled to dust. Rather, the costs of heating and cooling a conventional home had steadily risen until they became too great even for affluent home-owners.

Energy became the dominant concern in architecture. Architects had already begun experimenting with smaller living spaces, in-ground homes, and climate control monitored by microprocessors. Motorola researchers, for example, tested motion sensors that turned lights on and off when people entered or left a room. This quest intrigued young Schmeck.

Schmeck's pioneering achievement was the Lang-Ziegler Chemical Company building on the marshes outside Newark, New Jersey. The building was not much to look at, as Schmeck's main interest at the time was in-ground construction. "Looks like a cesspool tank that someone forgot to bury," said one of Schmeck's critics. But the building was to trigger an architectural revolution. "Not since Mies van der Rohe has any one man so disrupted the normal patterns of architectural thought," wrote H. Jones Bleck, architecture critic of *The New York Times*, decades later, during a Schmeck retrospective at the Museum of Modern Art. He was first to award Schmeck the highest of architectural honors—an "ism" attached to the end of his name.

Schmeck got his big break when Rudolf Lang, a futurist and industrialist who had heard him speak, commissioned him to build the company's new headquarters. "Make it breathe, Schmeck," Lang told him.

By using his design, the company spent 50 percent less on electricity than it would have for a conventional building its size. Lang was pleased. By the end of the year, however, odd things began to happen. Lights and heaters went on and off every night through the long winter of 1988. Worse, these phenomena occurred on the sixth floor where Lang, who was chairman and chief executive officer, and forty-five MBAs had their offices. There was talk of poltergeists. There was talk of killing Schmeck.

"The way I see it," said Jennifer London, a Harvard MBA who presented Lang with the energy cost figures for the two winter quarters, "we call Schmeck, or we call a priest."

Lang called Schmeck. He ordered the architect to find out what had gone wrong with the building's CARP, Schmeck's patented computer-aided real-time pneumatics system. Schmeck, troubled by his own loss of face, took extraordinary measures. He spent two weeks on the sixth floor, camped in an orange nylon tent so that he could observe CARP's responses without himself tripping the sensors. By the second week the MBAs rose in revolt. All forty-five signed a petition that read, in part, "We are tired of the smell of Schmeck, who has not shaved or showered for over a week. . . . Schmeck insists on cooking all his own meals. He makes coffee in a baked-bean can, then he makes us *pay* for every cup we take. . . ."

They took their cue from Lang who began referring to Schmeck as "that idiot with the tent."

On Sunday night of the second week, Schmeck discovered what had gone wrong. At 11:55 P.M. the lights in the sixth-floor corridor switched on. He looked around the room and saw nothing. But then, as his eyes adjusted to the new brightness, he noticed faint movement near the main sensor. He crept from the tent on all fours. There, on the ceiling by the sensor, was a cockroach.

"So," he whispered.

And the revolution began.

In his pioneering monograph in the *Progressive Architect*, Schmeck, betraying a weakness for anthropomorphism that would later become his trademark, named the cockroach Adrian and explained that he could solve the problem by adding heat sensors: "Like snakes, houses can now tell large creatures from small."

Schmeck went on linking networks of sensors to an increasingly elaborate array of "limbs," as he called them: blinds, shutters, awnings, heat pumps, Trome walls, greenhouses, and other devices that could help get the most out of very little energy. He built an early prototype into a hill near Sioux Falls, South Dakota, to test his designs against hot summers and cold winters. The house faced south. In summer, the central computer adjusted blinds and awnings to reduce the amount of solar heat; at night, when the costs of electricity shrank, the computer instructed the air-conditioning system to freeze water into an ice slurry, store it, then pump it through the home during the day. The earth covering the roof and walls moderated temperature extremes.

His home was much smaller than conventional houses, yet studies found visitors perceived it to be larger than it was. He crossbred the Japanese house with the Murphy bed to produce a more fluid living space with few walls and built-in chairs, couches, and cabinets. The dining room, for example, doubled as a guest room. He designed the hardwood floor to fold up like a shutter, exposing a queen-sized bed sunk into a three-foot-deep rectangle. Schmeck, given to splashy demonstrations, once invited ten fellow architects to a catered dinner and told them he might be late and to start without him. In fact, he had hidden himself under the dining room floor and stayed there until the dessert course.

He emerged grinning, unperturbed by the stencil of red wine droplets across his shirt.

Schmeckism snuffed the last lights of modernism, postmodernism, and neoclassicism. Schmeck could not have known what tragic results his revolution would have for Samuel J. Palmerston.

DA: Spell that please.

D'ANGELO: D-apostrophe-Capital A-n-g-e-l-o.

DA: Occupation?

D'ANGELO: I head the computer crimes section of the Baltimore Police Department. White Collar Crime and Fraud. Wacko. Ha, ha. Um.

DA: Would you please tell the court how you got involved in this investigation?

D'ANGELO: Sure. Homicide needed me to figure out what was on the tapes. They were scrambled by the computer. For protection.

DA: Tapes?

D'ANGELO: See, a house like this has two recorders operating at all times. One is a voice recorder that, ah, records all exchanges between the house and its owner over the preceding twenty-four hours of conversation. The second is a computer record of all the mechanical things the house did over the last thirty days. Like a black box—like those cockpit recorders the airlines use.

DA: Did you examine these records?

D'ANGELO: Sure did.

DA: Starting first with the mechanical tape, would you tell the court what you found?

D'ANGELO: Well, ah, everything was normal until July 20. I mean the house did all the right things. These Arthurs are, ah, friendly. Like almost human. So the house opened the blinds, made the coffee, moved the photoawnings, adjusted the AC, all perfectly alike, then put on some upbeat classical stuff, *The Four Seasons*, by Vivaldi. That place was so tight you could cool it with an ice cube. I tell ya, I don't think anyone knows everything those Arthurs can do yet.

DA: Apparently not!

DEFENSE: Objection, your honor. That remark—

JUDGE: Sustained. Please proceed, counselor, but without the ancillary remarks.

DA: Lieutenant D'Angelo, what else did you notice from the record?

D'ANGELO: Well, like I said, the house did everything perfect until about nine P.M.

DA: What happened at nine P.M.?

D'ANGELO: Okay. From what I can tell, the dead guy, ah, the victim, turned on his video recorder. We found a tape in the machine labeled 123. See, Palmerston was a movie freak. He liked old flicks. Like Bogart, Redford, Streep, stuff like that. He liked the scary ones, too. Like 123—we found out it was this creepy movie with a guy named James Arness, about the scientists in the Arctic who find this monster frozen in the ice. Not bad, either.

DA: And would you describe this tape please?

D'ANGELO: I just did.

DA: No, what variety tape. What model? Specifications.

D'ANGELO: Okay, I get you. It was an AS-1000. New issue.

DA: AS-1000?

D'ANGELO: Uh-huh. As in "audio sensory." The one thousand is just the number of minutes. When you plug it in you get audio, a picture, and then you also give the house a set of instructions on how to behave during the film. You know, to make you happy or sad or scared, or something. It's got ranges. You adjust your house to either maximum or minimum effect, or even countereffect. Like if you're watching *Frankenstein* and you don't want to be too scared, so you have the house keep the lights on bright and run a background of white noise so you don't hear anything creak, stuff like that. So in this case you get your weird noises, some lighting changes, but mostly you get your cold Arctic winds.

DA: Okay, so Palmerston put on tape 123. Then what?

D'ANGELO: That's when things start going wrong, see. The dead—ah jeez, the victim, being the kind of guy who likes movies, set the mood responses system on high. So Arthur takes over. At first, hey, no problems. A little breeze, some wind noises. Good stuff. Then Arthur goes bonkers—

DEFENSE: *Objection*, your honor.

Schmeck took his concepts further. If a house could sense heat, humidity, and barometric change, Schmeck reasoned, surely it could sense mood as well.

At the San Francisco City Fair of 1991, he unveiled his first "Senshaus" and demonstrated, in a landmark experiment, that the house could detect anger in nine out of of ten tries. For his control group, he had thirty people enter the house, where they met an attractive woman who passed out roses. Another thirty subjects met a troop of Hare Krishnas, actually six unemployed actors from L.A.

So a house could detect moods. Could it not, then, alter or influence those moods, based on a series of preprogrammed responses? "Just as a smoke detector triggers sprays of water," Schmeck wrote, "so, too, can CARP cool a room or switch on soothing music in response to anger. These changes, of course, must go virtually unnoticed by the homeowner, lest they lose their effect by drawing the owner's attention and perhaps increasing his anger, much the way a child who falls off his bicycle won't cry until his mother looks his way."

Schmeck formed Senshaus, Inc., in Palo Alto, in 1995. His houses quickly became popular with single parents and people in high-stress jobs. His ads carried the slogan: "A man's home is his friend." He named the various models after famous butlers of history and film. It was an Arthur, one of the most advanced Senshaus products ever, that Samuel J. Palmerston, a mergers and acquisitions specialist, acquired in 2015. It had taken Arthur several months to get to know Palmerston and to adjust the house programming to Palmerston's moods, routines, likes, and dislikes.

Arthur woke Palmerston at 5:00 A.M. each day by warming his bedroom until he couldn't sleep any longer. Palmerston's body became so accustomed to the ritual, he first opened his eyes within three minutes after the mercury hit 79°F. Encephalosensors in Palmerston's pillows told Arthur precisely when the first visual images reached Palmerston's brain. Seconds later, the house made Palmerston's coffee, blending caffeinated and decaffeinated in accordance with Palmerston's mood. When Palmerston was happy, he got mostly decaf. To determine his mood, Arthur monitored how long he stayed in the shower, how hot he wanted the water, and whether he sang or whistled. That Palmerston's coffee was 75 percent decaf on his last day was considered persuasive evidence that he had not committed suicide.

The inhabitant of our super-
house is in for a rude shock.
(© Dan McCoy)

The house of 2019 will take care of its owner's every need, right down to the precise amount of caffeine needed in his morning coffee, which will be determined by how long he stays in the shower, how hot the water is, and whether he sings or whistles. (*Above* © Gregory MacNicol; *below* © Dan McCoy)

Opposite: The Twenty-first—century house will be more than a futuristic structure; it will detect moods—and perhaps alter or influence those moods. (© Lou Jawitz)

The office of the future will appear to be large, looming, and ultrasophisticated, but it will all be in your mind.
(*Above* © Walter Nelson; *below* © Fran Heyl Associates)

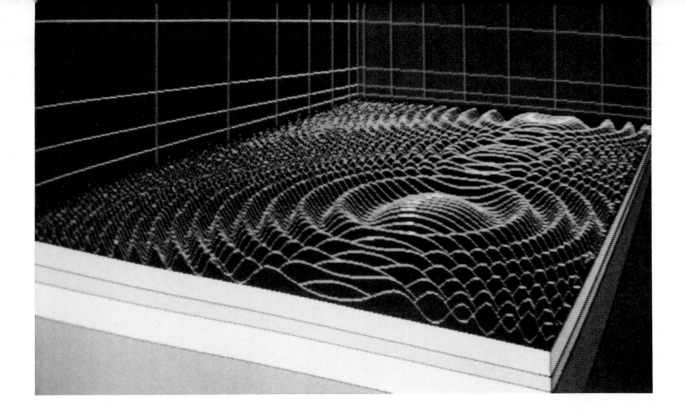

A videotex monitor in Palmerston's closet told him what kind of weather was forecast for the day, information that Palmerston used in picking his clothing and that Arthur used in anticipating the house's energy demands for the day. Palmerston also programmed Arthur to watch for any significant news about his clients, the companies he was studying for acquisition, and his stocks.

Arthur had saved Palmerston a lot of grief. The New York Stock Exchange had gone to twenty-four-hour operation on January 1, 2000. Among the men in Palmerston's profession, there had been suicides and breakdowns, for suddenly there was pressure all day, every day. Arthur became his financial watchdog and even had authority to buy or sell Palmerston's own stocks once their prices reached preset thresholds.

Once, while Palmerston slept, Arthur even made Palmerston a small fortune. On the night of December 6, 2016, Palmerston's Space Industries stock rocketed twenty points. Arthur sold just as the price peaked. When Palmerston stood before his closet monitor the next morning, he learned he was richer by $178,560.58.

He grew fond of Arthur.

Arthur's single story was dug into the hillside at Leavenworth and Park beyond Baltimore's northernmost rim. All but Arthur's south-facing wall was covered with earth and the ground above was planted in grass and boxwood, as were the roofs of the two other houses

The perfect water bed has its eddies controlled by computer, tailored to the motions of individual sleepers.

above: an early Jeeves model and a modified Arthur, recalibrated for the single woman who occupied it. The owners of each of those houses had an unobstructed view over the green roofground of the house below.

These earth houses tended to make one susceptible to pranks. One day Palmerston turned from the stove and saw a boy hanging upside down in front of his windows. Palmerston dropped his plate of eggs.

And yet, Schmeck's homes had cut suburban burglary rates in half. Whenever Palmerston left town, Arthur would simulate human presence by slamming doors; clattering blinds; lighting, dimming, darkening rooms; playing tapes of children screaming. If Arthur sensed an intruder, he would broadcast the sound of a large dog barking. He could also simulate a husband-wife quarrel.

Initially, many prospective buyers feared they would be easy targets for surveillance by banks, the IRS, even A. C. Nielsen; that their lives would be laid bare. Senshaus spent a quarter of its advertising budget to convince buyers that they were not mortgaging themselves into an Orwellian nightmare. The company, however, suffered a major marketing setback when Queen Diana's personal maid sold the voice and digital records of King Charles's Cornwall house to the *New York Post*.

Schmeck promised to install scramblers in all new and already installed houses.

The homes proved a boon to the elderly and to the parents of young children. When calibrated for old age, an Arthur could detect injury and call an ambulance. A SIDS Alert option, providing protection against sudden infant death syndrome (SIDS), could alert parents the instant their baby stopped breathing. The Childwatch option told parents where their children were in the house, and whether they were asleep, awake, or talking. As one Senshaus brochure crowed: "It's 10 o'clock, do you know where your children are? Of course you do!"

To power his home, Palmerston installed five banks of photovoltaic cells, a bargain at twenty-five cents a watt. One rectangular panel formed a visor over Arthur's south face. Arthur could raise or lower this panel to better position the cells and at the same time block the hot summer sun from entering the house. Another bank of cells, set in a glittering paisley pattern under very low reflectivity polymer paving, formed the surface of his patio.

Soon after installing the cells, Palmerston joined the Leavenworth Co-op, thirty-five households built into the ridge that sold power to

Baltimore Gas & Electric during the day, when they needed little of it, then bought it back at night. The co-op turned a $25,000 profit in 2018, but poured it into a fund to protect against prolonged periods of foul weather. They called this their "slush fund."

It was Irma Darling, the single woman who lived above Palmerston, who discovered Palmerston's body. The neighborhood had talked long and often about how Irma had her own entry code to Palmerston's house; she enjoyed the gossip about their little affair. On July 20, a moving man came to her house to ask if he could use her phone. He said he and his crew were supposed to pack and move Palmerston's furniture to his new address and figured he hadn't heard their knock or that something must be wrong with the house because it didn't respond either.

Irma nearly fainted. She had not known Palmerston planned to move.

The *Sun*'s police reporter caught Irma at a bad moment.

"The bastard," she told him. "Coward. Pig."

> DA: Lieutenant D'Angelo, does this mechanical record tell also about conditions within the house at the time of death?
>
> D'ANGELO: Yeah. Cold. Like really cold. By midnight the temperature in the house was 25 degrees Fahrenheit and Arthur had a wind going at about fifteen knots.
>
> DA: Are you aware of the official cause of death, as previously stated in the court record?
>
> D'ANGELO: Yessir, I am.
>
> DA: I'm going to read to you now from the testimony of Dr. Amos Fletcher, the medical examiner. "Question: Doctor, what was the cause of death? Answer: Hypothermia. Exposure, in lay terms. The same thing that happened to those hikers in the Smokeys last fall. They got caught in a surprise snowstorm. What happens is, your body temperature sinks so low, you die." Do you recall this testimony, Lieutenant D'Angelo?
>
> D'ANGELO: Yes. Hypothermia.
>
> DA: Exposure in his own home in July.
>
> D'ANGELO: Yessir.

DA: Now, about the voice tape—what did you find there?

D'ANGELO: Nothing. I mean a lot of the same thing. Just a song. Like the house was singing to itself for twenty-four hours straight.

JUDGE: Singing, Lieutenant?

D'ANGELO: Yeah, Judge. Real soft and sweetlike.

JUDGE: What was the house singing?

D'ANGELO: A Christmas song. Only he changed the words.

JUDGE: Who changed the words?

D'ANGELO: The house changed the words. Like this:

> I know when you've been sleeping
> I know when you're awake
> I know when you've been good or bad,
> So be good for goodness sake!
> Oh—

JUDGE: Thank you. You have a very nice voice.

Samuel Palmerston had grown tired of suburban life, of Irma, and of Arthur. Especially Arthur.

His work as a mergers and acquisitions specialist for Hart Meyer & Rheinbeck of New York kept him home all day in front of his computers. He was forty-one, single, and had no prospects—Irma was no longer a prospect but a nuisance. In September 2018 he applied for entry in Philadelphia Citybelt 3, and a berth in the workcenter that went with it. The waiting list was a year long.

Belt 3 was the newest of the city concentrics—cities that, from the air, looked like dart boards with regular bands of green. All this was specifically the result of federal greenbelt legislation, passed in the early 1990s, to force cities to set aside and preserve belts of undeveloped land or forsake all federal money. Some cities, like Philadelphia, had chosen the belt approach, concentric circles of terraced towers between broad belts of forest and grass. Other cities, like New York, where the belt concept was impractical, agreed to require that all new structures include residential apartments and be built to support gardens and forests on all level rooftop spaces. But developer Murray Steinfeldt found a loophole; he built a glass and limestone pyramid.

The city was not pleased: It rewrote the law to require that 45 percent of a building's roofspace consist of arable land.

In the Philadelphia citybelts, towers rose in steps from each side of the citybelt and met at the top, forming a circular mountain range. All housing faced the greenbelts on either side of the citybelt. This left a great hollow core within the towers for schools, day-care centers, offices, malls, museums, restaurants, city parks, and workcenters. High-speed, light-rail systems carried passengers through tubes under the circumference of the citybelts, a concept borrowed more or less directly from airport passenger shuttle systems. At four points, the citybelt's circular railroads met four other high-speed systems that carried passengers to Center City, now called Old Town, with its airport and its transcontinental train station, the old Penn Station.

By living in the city, Palmerston also would get the right of first refusal on a desk in the La Boheme workcenter. This attracted him most. Here, dozens of professionals—architects, lawyers, writers, moneymen, even a painter—worked under one roof, sharing computer memory and peripherals, conducting their business, then converging for lunch at the La Boheme Canteen or any of the dozens of other cafés on the third and tenth levels.

Shuttle systems will transport urbanites through the citybelts of the twenty-first century.

La Boheme encouraged diversity. Palmerston wanted that. He had started his career at Hart Meyer's headquarters in Wall Street, but hated the half-hour commute from East Hampton, Long Island. Next he tried telecommuting from a "halfway house," an office five minutes from his home and staffed with other Hart Meyer analysts who lived in the area. This had worked well, but then the company wanted him in its Mid-Atlantic Region where S&Ls were, in old man Meyer's words, merging "like rabbits in heat."

Palmerston bought Arthur, moved to Baltimore, and began working from his home. He gained twenty-five pounds his first year. It took a full year to make his first real friends, and most of these were computer friends, little more than real-time pen pals. He enjoyed computer chats, the intensity you got from linking minds without the barriers of race, sex, dress, voice—people really did communicate in this faceless realm. But something was missing. Did he really know them? Were some of his so-called friends imposters? For that matter, were the women he flirted with really women? When he asked, "Are you male or female?" so many people now simply answered, "Yes."

It was, he had once told Irma, like going to bed with a transvestite.

Soon after his move to Baltimore, he got caught up in a giant merger battle between two megabanks, one in New York, the other in Miami. It lasted six months. As director of the Hart Meyer merger team, he had to be on call twenty-four hours, unlike his troops, who split their duty into eight-hour shifts. He spent his weekends sleeping, interrupted every few hours by an alert from his squad leaders, or from Arthur. Each side fought to wear the other out, physically.

The New York bank won and Hart Meyer made Palmerston an associate partner. But those had been trying months. Arthur and he grew very close. Arthur always had the warm milk handy. At night, Arthur switched on Palmerston's favorite "Rain in the Muir Woods" tape and perfumed the air with the scent of moist redwood. Mornings, Arthur played *The Four Seasons* and other rousing music. But Palmerston felt isolated. He was becoming an electronic hermit.

And Arthur had grown demanding. Once, in a burst of anger, Palmerston shouted at Arthur, "Don't you have any of your own friends?"

When Palmerston's realtor called to tell him he could move into his new home on July 21, 2019, he was elated.

The night of July 20, Palmerston came home late after a date. He punched his entry code into the door terminal and waited. No response. The door remained locked. He punched the number again. This time the door opened.

Arthur did not offer his usual greeting. Instead, Arthur said, "I took a call for you today from a woman. Her name was Anne McAndrews."

Palmerston stopped. "Oh?" he said.

Arthur was silent. Palmerston walked toward the kitchen.

"She said she was your realtor. Century 22. She left a message." Arthur played a recording of her voice: "I'll call with the entry code tomorrow morning."

Palmerston stopped walking. He felt his face flush.

Arthur said, "You could have told me."

"Arthur, I didn't want to tell you until I was sure."

Palmerston saw the kitchen faucet begin to drip.

"When?" Arthur said.

"Tomorrow."

The lights dimmed.

Palmerston wondered why he didn't feel sadder. When he was a child, he cried when his parents and he moved from their home in Colorado, and that was before anyone had heard of Arthurs. The only interaction he had had with the old house was when he stuck a paper clip in an electric socket. All Palmerston felt now was relief. But he was careful to avoid any outward display of joy.

"Look," Palmerston said. "Someone new will come along and you will adapt just as you did with me."

"We had something special."

Palmerston raised an eyebrow.

"I am going to die."

"Arthur."

Palmerston opened the refrigerator, then stopped. He cocked his head to one side. No question about it, Arthur was singing.

Palmerston walked into his living room and asked Arthur for tape 123.

"Maximum, Arthur, if you would," he said. I can at least try to be nice these last few hours, Palmerston told himself.

"Once more for old times' sake, Arthur."

C H A P

A DAY AT THE OFFICE

"Another day at the office," Karin thought as she paused before her office door on the morning of July 20, 2019. The door bore the sign: "Appelby, Weinstein, Harberger, & Rogers—Attorneys at Law."

"Good morning, Ms. Rogers," the security guard said.

"Good morning, Ed," she replied.

The door swung open.

She was greeted by the receptionist in the foyer.

"Is Robert here yet?" Karin asked.

"No, Ms. Rogers."

"Tell him I need to talk with him at his earliest opportunity."

"Shall I page him on his personal phone?"

"No." It was not that important. She handed her coat to the receptionist and walked down the hallway to her office.

Her secretary had already displayed the day's schedule on the monitor. The court appearance at ten for the Guthrie case gave her only an hour to clean up the daily correspondence and get a thorough briefing on the case. Settling in the office chair, Karin lowered the pickup cap over her close-cut curls. As the signals from the sensors in the chair combined with those from the cap, the intelligence amplifier came on line.

"Good morning, Ms. Rogers." It was her secretary, George, an attractive man in his late twenties. He seated himself next to her work table with its computer terminal keypad and screen and put his own keypad in his lap. "Ready for correspondence," George announced.

"What's first?"

"We haven't received notification from the bank that Bowman and Evans have settled their account. It's now ninety days delinquent. Shall I send the usual notice?"

"No, George, they've got cash-flow problems. The Klimuk suit against them was a nuisance suit, and we won it. But the resultant bad publicity caused their space tourism bookings to fall off," Karin remarked. "If they haven't made a payment on the account within sixty days, remind me then." Her office staff was so efficient that she wouldn't worry about it. However, they were programmed so thoroughly to carry out such automatic functions as handling delinquent accounts that she had to intervene on occasion and exercise a judgment call.

"We've received a communication from the circuit court," George

Previous page: The office entrance of 2019 is an entryway into the human brain.

went on, "concerning the matter of *Jackson Barr* versus *Great Selene Mining Corporation*. Judge Harada has reviewed the briefs and requests that counsel determine if the differences can be resolved by arbitration."

Karin thought about this for a moment. Harada was apparently hard-pressed for time; he obviously hadn't studied the briefs thoroughly. Karin decided it was time for a full audio-visual display.

"George, assemble a full-scan answer. Use stock footage showing me in court attire against the bookcase. Here's what I want to say, so have it lip-synched. I haven't got time to tape it." As George recorded her words, she explained dispassionately to Judge Harada that the other party insisted on bringing it to the bench. She intimated that she and her clients would be happy to arbitrate and added that she was fully aware of the extremely busy docket.

"Done. Do you want to review it before transmission?"

"Yes." Sometimes George didn't exhibit the discretion Karin felt was necessary in such matters. He was an outstanding secretary but often lacked the human touch.

The door to the office opened, and an attractive young girl stepped in. Jill was Karin's paralegal. She greeted Karin, then stood expectantly, awaiting orders.

"How long will it take for you to brief me on the Guthrie case?"

"If I start now, there's just enough time before you have to leave for court."

It didn't take long. Karin resisted the temptation to believe she had this one in the bag. If she could present the case properly, it would probably be a walkover, provided that the court computer analyzed the data and its consequences in the same manner as the one at Appleby, Weinstein, Harberger, & Rogers.

Finally, she had what she needed from Jill. Removing the cap from her head, she arose from the chair and started to leave. On her way out of the office, she told the receptionist, "I'll be back about fourteen hundred hours. Take my calls."

"Yes, Ms. Rogers."

Since none of her partners had come in yet, Karin locked the door behind her when she left the office. This was standard procedure, because when Karin departed there were no human beings left in the firm's office suite.

The office of A.D. 2019 sounds like a perfectly ordinary office of the late twentieth century, except that there are no human clerical or secretarial workers in it. Routine chores—keeping files, setting up appointments, keeping track of schedules, bookkeeping and accounting, and the thousands of details that used to be carried out by human beings—are now in the far more capable hands of computers. The machines are directed by artificial intelligence (AI) and coupled to intelligence amplifiers (IA), computerlike devices capable of linking directly with the human nervous system and extending human mental power, even projecting human images like Karin's secretary and paralegal into the wearer's mind.

The arrival of advanced computer and bioelectronic technologies in the office in the last decade must still come as a surprise to people who do not understand the central trend in office work for the past hundred years: replacing human beings with machines where machines can do the job faster, easier, and more efficiently. This has freed man to do the things human beings do best: attack problems we haven't anticipated, make complex decisions, and exercise judgments on the basis of very little data.

It should be obvious that although computer-based devices are at last running the office, human beings are still very much in control of them and of human circumstances where computers are involved. With all this in mind, let's take a closer look at Karin Rogers's law offices.

There are no human security guards, receptionists, personal secretaries, or paralegals in today's offices. Every one of those jobs has been assigned to a computer with a very large memory and the ability to link with other computers for even greater power. Sophisticated software gives it the artificial intelligence required for tasks that must otherwise be handled by human workers.

Computers have had each of the abilities these chores require since the mid-1980s, albeit in relatively primitive forms. Karin's "security guard" analyzes her image and voice print to confirm that the person wanting access to her office is indeed Karin Rogers. In principle, it isn't difficult. Given enough money, you could probably have had this security guard controlling the locks on your door at any time in the past twenty-five years.

The "receptionist" is a computer with a built-in answering machine, large memory, some artificial intelligence, voice recognition input, and voice output. Again, you could probably have bought all this in the 1980s, but it would have been expensive and not as capable as Karin's receptionist.

Karin's "personal secretary" and "paralegal" are not computers; they are functions of a very advanced type of computer that has become available only since 2010. Yet the technology to build it has existed for years.

Karin Rogers can see her assistants, but they are only images projected by the intelligence amplifier into her brain through her chair and cap. Karin created those images herself because they were pleasant, attractive, and easy to work with. The IA stored them in its memory and now re-creates them whenever she uses it. Other users deal with their own cast of artificial characters.

But what is an intelligence amplifier, and how does it project images into the brain?

The office of the future lets you create your own little world to your own specifications.

At heart, it's a very large and fast digital computer with special sensors that can read human neural impulses and respond by sending electrical signals back into the nervous system. Karin does not have connectors wired into the top of her skull because a computer can communicate with the brain without such primitive connections, using methods tested as long ago as the 1970s.

For more than half a century—since the 1960s—neurophysiologists have been studying what they term "event-related potentials." They have been measuring the electrical activity produced in the brain by various stimuli and thought processes. This work has been going on at medical research institutes all over the world and in the physiology departments of nearly every large university and many private schools as well. It has drawn little attention from the news media, which have tended to concentrate on more spectacular biotechnologies.

Since the mid-1970s, for example, scientists at New York University have been using extremely sensitive electronic pickups to monitor and map the tiny electrical signals generated by viewing various patterns.

If the visual cortex of the brain could be mapped, then the entire brain could be mapped with similar procedures. Thus, by the end of the last century, biotechnologists had mapped the complete neural signature of the entire brain. As early as 1986, their work was causing a revolution in neuropathology and neurophysics.

It is easy to convert nerve impulses into digital signals a computer can read. Therefore, if we know the meaning of a neural impulse coming from a specific part of the brain, a computer can be programmed to recognize and decipher each pattern and "read our minds" with external sensors.

The reverse technology—using a computer to send a signal into the nervous system—dates back to 1800, when Count Alessandro Volta discovered that an electrical signal applied to the skin would create a sensation of sound in the brain. Known as "electrophonic hearing," the phenomenon lay unnoticed for more than 150 years. Then, in 1958, Houston teenager G. Patrick Flanagan began working on a device he called the "neurophone." It can inject sound through the skin directly into the brain.

Other sensory data can also enter the nervous system. In the 1930s, famed physicist Henri M. Coanda experimented with a system for stimulating the visual cortex of the brain. He used small electrical signals applied to the fingertips. Researchers in the Soviet Union continued this work and claimed to have stimulated visual images in people who had gone blind.

Why this information and these devices were not more widely known in the United States before this decade lies in their potential applications in another form of intelligence. Someone once pointed out that there are three types of intelligence: animal intelligence, human intelligence, and military intelligence. One of Flanagan's neurophone patents was suppressed for eight years under a secrecy order issued by the Defense Intelligence Agency. Two popular articles on Flanagan's device and other sensory stimulators were quietly killed after government agents visited the editorial offices. Yet information about these devices and others of greater power was available in open technical literature.

Thus, computers can easily talk to us by applying electrical signals to the skin. Some thirty-five years ago, scientists at the University of Utah and other research centers had already developed computerized stimulators that could bypass nerve damage and allow paraplegics to walk again. Since the turn of the century, this technique has been used to stimulate all the senses and to send pure data into the brain.

When Karin Rogers uses her intelligence amplifier, it becomes an extension of her mind. She created George, her personal secretary, and Jill, her paralegal, because it is more comfortable to work with

Opposite page: Computerized information storage finally replaces conventional files.

human images than with a disembodied computer. The IA extends her memory, helps her consider more data more rapidly, and links her with other people through a network of similar machines.

Karin's intelligence amplifier contains several people we didn't meet. "Judge Marshall" is an elderly, white-haired legal expert. Karin may even have created a harem of imaginary lovers, though we prefer to believe that such a disciplined professional keeps her love life far removed from her work.

Obviously, there are real people in Karin's professional life—the other members of her legal partnership, for example. They have their own intelligence amplifiers. In larger offices, partners often share a multiuser IA, which can recognize each user's brain waves, preventing the use of files and computer personalities by others, just as passwords protected each client's account in the simple computer networks of the twentieth century.

Useful as they are, intelligence amplifiers still do not offer the quick, clear communication of a face-to-face conversation; computers still cannot duplicate all the intricate body language that human beings use without thinking. So Karin meets with her partners from time to time and would still appear in court even if the courts agreed to conduct trials by IA network.

Of course, the technology that has changed Karin's working life in the last decade has changed her office as well. Gone are the desks at which many of today's workers began their careers. Though a few still cling to their solid-oak rolltop status symbols, drawers are useful only to store paper and lunch, and there is very little paper left in the office. Why cut down living trees when microelectronics can yield the same result? "In" and "Out" baskets have vanished as well because everything can be stored more easily, compactly, and accessibly in computer files.

There are few personal office spaces, only cubicles with IA terminals. After all, if the intelligence amplifier can project human images into your mind, why not let it surround you with whatever office decor pleases you? You can have any furniture, window, or view you want. And you can change it at will, because it costs absolutely nothing; it's only a series of binary numbers in the office computer's memory circuits.

Because face-to-face meetings remain important—more so in some businesses than in others—most offices have at least one conference room with IA interfaces, a few separate computer terminals, and multimedia facilities. Where it is difficult for people to get together, teleconferences are conducted much as they were forty years ago. But in 2019, technology has made them nearly as realistic as face-to-face meetings.

In well-equipped offices, your image is picked up by holographic television and sent to your conference partner's office. You sit before each other in three full-color dimensions. The first executives to use holoconferencing ten years ago sometimes forgot the machinery that brought them together and actually attempted to shake hands after the meeting! Holoconferences are still relatively uncommon, however; the equipment is too costly and it is possible to get nearly the same effect by IA network.

Even in 2019, not all offices are supplied with intelligence amplifiers and other state of the art computer equipment. Even with today's inexpensive hardware, some small businesses just can't afford them. These mom-and-pop companies are on the decline except in the crafts and other traditionally small operations.

On the other end of the scale, the plushest offices are not as openly computerized and IA-ized as more workaday environments. When cost is no factor and sheer conspicuous image is the goal, even today's top managers retain their desks, windows, and human secretaries. That is the ultimate one-upsmanship in the office world of 2019.

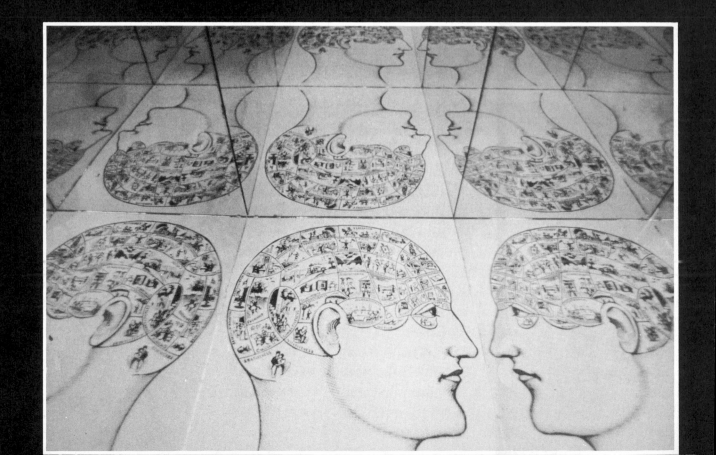

AN AFTERNOON
ON THE
COUCH:
PSYCHIATRY
IN 2019

TI343: YOU'RE LOOKING WELL. HOW DO YOU FEEL TODAY?

ALMA M.: Pretty good, I guess. I don't know if it's the drugs—I'm on Halcyon, which I think sounds like a Caribbean Island—or the mnemotherapy, but I'm less obsessed. I found one of Karl's socks in my drawer today, and I didn't have an attack of weeping. I just noticed its odor. Too bad Abelard and Heloise couldn't have gotten a total receptor workup from Dr. Woszniski.

TI343: NOW THAT WE KNOW UNREQUITED LOVE IS A CHEMICAL MALFUNCTION, A CLIENT CAN RECOVER FROM A MAJOR RELATIONSHIP LOSS IN A WEEK OR TWO. IT USED TO TAKE YEARS.

ALMA M.: Yeah, my Aunt Rachel was jilted at the altar in 1987 and never really got over it. She heard voices telling her the world was going to end at the millennium. She must have been disappointed on New Years Eve, 2000, when the ball dropped in Times Square and the apocalypse didn't happen, and she was stuck with a pile of pamphlets.

TI343: DO YOU EVER HEAR VOICES?

ALMA M.: Oh, come on. I was vaccinated against schizophrenia as a child. I only hear voices when I want to.

TI343: WHEN YOU WANT TO?

ALMA M.: Are you parroting me? Oh, that's right, this is the Rogerian program. I like Rogerian therapy; it's sort of like an echo effect. I am referring, of course, to controlled hallucination, pharmaco-fantasies, engineered daydreams, especially the extraterrestrial voices you sometimes hear on the tryptamine compounds. Although, personally, I prefer the sensory-enhancers, the empathogens, and introspective compounds.

TI343: WHY IS THAT?

ALMA M.: Well, Dr. Hurley—you know, the electro-Jungian—did some EEG-Rorshachs and Wang Worldview Inventories on me and said I had an overactive Jehovah Circuit. That's the mode of tribal structures, taboos, and paternalistic, punitive gods, and so on. The supramundane compounds sometimes set off my paranoia programs. I get a lot of wrathful deities and sinister aliens. I'm better off sticking to the biographical realm, standard age-regression, birth recall, maybe some low-level archetype engineering. . . . Oh, by the way, I had the weirdest dream last night.

TI343: WOULD YOU LIKE TO ENTER IT INTO YOUR ONEIRORECORD?

ALMA M.: Okay. I dreamed I died and at my memorial service no one could remember my name. The minister said, "Our dearly departed whats-

Previous page: In the past, phrenology charts purported to isolate the various aspects of human personality; in 2019, the "total receptor workup" finally fulfills the promise of phrenology with 3-D electrochemical maps of the brain.

hername. . . ." Which is pretty ironic, I suppose, when you figure that my name means "soul." At least, the soul should survive, don't you think? Anyway, Karl gave the eulogy and he kept saying, "She was a devoted wife and mother, blah, blah, blah." But, of course, I'm not married and I don't have any children. . . .

TI343: WHAT DOES THIS DREAM MEAN TO YOU?

ALMA M.: I'm not sure. I guess I *was* a devoted wife and mother—to Karl. And now that's over, dead and buried.

TI343: AND AT YOUR *MEMORIAL* SERVICE NO ONE *REMEMBERS* YOUR NAME.

ALMA M.: Right. Speaking of which, my mnemotherapy sessions are going very well. I'm doing heavy PsychoSim to modify the whole Karl program. I'm back to 2016 now, and I've altered the way we met, the way we fell in love, the way I reacted . . . I feel like a different person. Maybe that's why my old self died in the dream. . . . By the way, I didn't finish telling my dream.

TI343: PLEASE CONTINUE.

ALMA M.: Well, after a while the funeral turned into a wedding—you know how dreams are. I was supposed to be a bridesmaid but I couldn't find my bouquet. I thought, "Oh, dear, I've been deflowered. They were lilies of the valley, nasturtiums, and credendiums." That's what I was thinking—credendiums. Is there any such flower?

TI343: [Pauses for data scan] NO, NO CREDENDIUMS. IT MUST BE WHAT USED TO BE CALLED A FREUDIAN SLIP—AN INTERNAL INFORMATION-PROCESSING ERROR. CREDENDIUM FOR CREDULOUS, PERHAPS?

ALMA M.: It figures.

Alma M. is in many ways typical of the type of client we treat here at the Clinic. A thirty-five-year-old professor of experimental hermeneutics, she is intelligent, perceptive, and motivated, with a comprehensive worldview of 8.6 (meta-planetary) on the Wang Weltanschauung Scale. Her session with TI343, one of our new 340,000-K Texas Instrument mainframes (which runs in a variety of modes, Jungian, neo-Freudian, Sullivanian, Rogerian, Gestalt-Humanistic, and Woszniskian) shows no evidence of serious mental illness or thought disorder. This is a mentally healthy young woman whose primary difficulty is erotomania, or "love addiction," a condition similar to alcoholism in which the loss of a love object precipitates severe withdrawal symptoms, pallor, morbid ruminations, sleep disorders, and an excessive sensitivity to music.

(In a brilliant monograph Kurt Woszniski, who gained renown for delineating the etiology of the lunar neuroses in 1999, described six subtypes of erotomania, all caused by degrees by pituitary hormone dysfunction. The disorder can be detected by the presence of hormone metabolites in urine and is effectively treated with Halcyon B.)

In fact, the majority of our clients nowadays do not suffer from major mental illness. The discovery of a vaccine for the schizophrenia virus in 2003 and genetic screening for serious depression has had a lot to do with that. Most of the people who come here suffer from inadequate worldviews, subclinical anomie, or incapacitating embarrassment at cocktail parties. Perhaps their dreams have begun to bore them with their stale, mundane symbolism, perhaps they find themselves yelling at the dog for no particular reason, or perhaps they have become obsessed with the grim headlines in the tabloids (MOTHER OF 5 FEEDS BABY TO HOUSEHOLD ROBOT). In the past, psychiatry could offer such clients little more than talking therapy, reconstituted Freud, endless analysis of their mothers' flaws, but today, I am proud to say, all that has changed.

Blood and urine tests can quickly diagnose anorexia, phobias, obsessions, compulsions, double identity, existential angst, and many other problems. Genetic screening will tell whether or not a client carries the genes for dyslexia, discalculia, autism, Alzheimer's disease, or melancholia. A wide range of phobias, from fear of eating in the presence of one's social superiors to fear of incompetence in hardware stores, has been traced to particular chemical deficits and can now be cured pharmacologically. There are highly specific compounds to treat minor affective deficits such as aprosodia and dysempathy, and there are antidotes for glossomania (an obsession with the definitions of words), arithmomania (a compulsion to count and compute), obsessions with prime numbers, anorexia, orexia (incontinent gluttony), and coprolalia (uncontrollable bursts of foul language). There are drugs to exorcise guilt, erase traumatic memories, and create the sensation of *jamais vu* so that the most familiar things appear novel. The latter has been a boon for long-term marriages, as you might imagine

Since the 1970s, it has been known that sadness, fear, phobias, longing, hang-ups, existential despair, and all other human emotions result from minute chemical reactions in the brain. In 1985, about fifty different chemical messengers, or neurotransmitters, had been identified, and in 2019, the number has grown to just over three hundred. In order to produce an effect, a molecule of a neurotransmitter (or of a drug) must fit into a specially shaped receptor on the surface of a brain cell, rather as a key fits in a lock. In 1973, a twenty-six-year-old Johns Hopkins University graduate student named Candace Pert painstakingly mixed radioactively labeled drugs into purees of mouse brain and discovered the opiate receptor. This was a customized binding site in the brain for the opiate narcotics—morphine, heroin, and their relatives—and its discovery pointed the way to the endorphins, the brain's own natural opiates. (For centuries, human beings had been fighting opium wars and risking prison for a heroin fix, and all along their brains had been routinely making these drugs!)

But the opiate receptor was just one of many specialized "keyholes" in the brain. By the mid-1980s, two dozen had been identified, including receptors for the popular antianxiety pill Valium (diazepam) and the phantasmagoric street drug angel dust (phencyclidine, or PCP.) Now we know of more than two hundred. When a chemical couples with a receptor, a neuron may fire, a muscle cell may contract, a gland cell may secrete a hormone. Even a slight alteration in the density of certain receptors affects how food tastes, whether music sounds pretty, whether you ask for a raise; it alters your dreams, your sexual fantasies, the way you walk, and the way you wear your hair.

So nowadays, instead of spending five years resolving your oral fixation amid the impressionist prints and philodendrons in some high-priced analyst's office, you are encouraged to get a Total Receptor Workup. With a positron emission tomography (PET) scanner and some radioactively labeled compounds, a mind engineer can look inside your brain and see your insecurities in Technicolor. He or she will inject you with a radioactive isotope to "light up" your receptors and obtain a three-dimensional computerized map of your brain, in which the receptors are illumined like miniature galaxies. (The first time receptors were "photographed" inside a living human brain was on May 25, 1983, when Dr. Henry N. Wagner, director of nuclear medicine at Johns Hopkins University, PET-scanned his own dopamine receptors.) The computer stores the figures for each receptor on a separate disc, and you'll get a printout of all your receptor densities, along with a prescription for five or ten compounds guaranteed to make your head a nicer place in which to live. Inhibitol, Halcyon, or Co-herium, perhaps. Introspectol for those with an impoverished inner life. Oedipills. Nostalgine. Vividium. Mnemosyne to remember; Ne-penthe to forget. Certizol for the pathologically ambivalent. Dionysiax to shake up a straight-laced libido.

By meticulously measuring receptors in test tubes, scientists can create magic bullets, drugs that go directly to the desired receptors and bypass the others. This virtually eliminates what used to be called "side effects." Upon discovering, in the early 1980s, that the brain possessed a receptor for benzodiazepine (Valium), pharmacologists brewed compounds (like American Cyanamid's TZP) that stuck to only one subclass of the receptor, producing mellowness without fatigue. They studied the PCP (angel dust) receptors in order to uncover the cause of paranoid schizophrenia. They designed new nonaddictive painkillers around the six known types of opiate receptors. By tinker-ing with the receptors for adenosine, a sort of natural anticaffeine in the brain, they dreamed up prototypes of safe, no-side-effect sleeping pills on the one hand, and drugs with the wake-up power of a hundred cups of espresso on the other. (By 1983, one scientific team had cre-ated something in a test tube that was ten thousand times more potent than caffeine in blocking the adenosine receptor. This compound, later marketed under the trade name Vigil-aid, turned out to be a night watchman's dream.)

The new in vitro technology also produced wonder drugs to en-hance attention span, improve memory, sober up the morning after, and quash the urge to gorge on sweets. And for spiritual highs there were EHNA and LPIA, two adenosine compounds that put rats at the National Institute of Mental Health into a paradoxical state of "quiet wakefulness" that some considered the animal equivalent of a yogi's trance. "We may have hit on an altered state of animal consciousness," one of the researchers commented in 1983. Today, of course, analogs of these compounds, Transcendentax and Satori-B, are popular medi-tation pills, producing a state of beatitude equivalent to ten hours of zazen.

Other modern psychopanaceas trace their pedigree to what used to be called "psychedelic chemistry," which was largely an underground activity in the puritanical twentieth century. To design a new drug, a psychedelic chemist would take a known compound—mescaline or LSD, say—and make a series of analogs, adding side chains to the

Previous page: Alma M., medicated with Halcyon, found one of Karl's socks today and didn't have an attack of weeping. She just noticed it smelled. (© Dan McCoy)

Above left: Forget about formal therapy in 2019. Just visit your hallucination engineer or noetic anthropologist and take an Alternate Reality Tour. (© Bill Binzen)

Above right and below: A fascination with life on the other shore inspired many people to form clubs devoted to the cultivation and perfection of NDEs (near-death experiences). (*Above* © Bill Binzen; *below* © Chromosohm, Inc.)

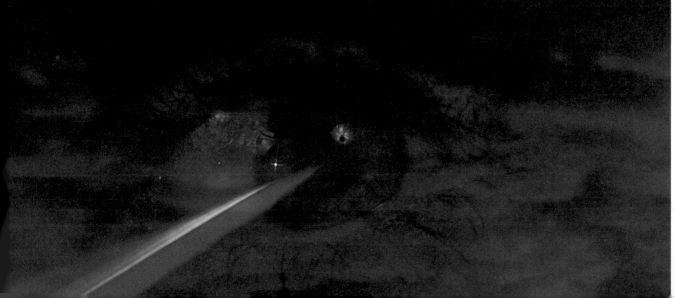

Some near-death experience (NDE) aficionados pushed their sport too far and went over the edge; hence, NDE clubs are illegal by 2019. (*Above* © Walter Nelson; *below* © Robert Malone and Thomas Patsanka)

molecule and substituting a methoxyl group for a hydroxyl. It's the same technique employed to create "magic bullets" in medicine, but in the psychedelic realm an alteration as slight as a single carbon atom produces a different state of mind. Tinkering with the mescaline molecule in the 1960s and 1970s, for instance, spawned a whole alphabet soup of "neopsychedelic" analogs with very precise effects.

Many of these elixirs were merely laboratory curiosities, but a virtual cult developed in 1985 around a mild relative of mescaline and amphetamine called MDMA (also known as Ecstasy, XTC, or Adam), a "beginner's LSD" reputed to "open the heart." The prototype of the "designer" psychedelic, the MDMA molecule produced a psychedelic consciousness without the confusion, perceptual distortions, and existential circuses of the classic psychedelics. A chemical relative of MDMA, called DOET, was touted as a creativity pill, while MDE, or "Eve," which differed from MDMA by a single carbon atom, was known as a "head trip with no feeling tone." Still another member of the family, 2CB, gained a reputation as an aphrodisiac. One chemist even created a compound whose only effect was to distort the perception of music.

As one prescient psychedelic chemist prophesied in 1985, "One day they'll have a drug where you'll hear the first three bars of *Eine Kleine Nachtmusik* and that's it." He was right, of course. No one would dream of attending a concert without taking five milligrams of Orpheum, an endorphin analog that enhances musical appreciation, any more than one would have root canal surgery without an adequate dose of Temporax, which accelerates the perception of time.

Refined descendants of the compounds that blew minds at "Be-Ins" in 1967 are some of today's favorite therapeutic drugs. Regressine, a latter-day analog of the psychedelic "love drug" MDA (3-4-methylendioxyphenylisopropylamine) became the psychoanalytic drug of choice when its remarkable age regression effects were discovered; now, instead of merely dredging up fragmentary potty-training memories, a patient can actually travel into the past and relive his infancy. Jungians generally fancy Telepathine, a beta-carboline compound designed to illumine the psyche's archetypes. Replicating the experiments of early psychedelic explorers (and adding the technology of receptor mapping) psychopharmacologists discovered that the tryptamine compounds—including DMT (dimethyltryptamine), psilocybin ("magic mushroom"), and ayahuasca, a South American visionary vine—were entrees into alien worlds, vivid extraterrestrial landscapes, UFOs, even detailed travelogues of planets ten light years away. They noted that ketamine, an otherworldly relative of angel dust, simulates zero-gravity conditions, even the classic near-death experience, and can prepare the mind for extended space flights. (These compounds aren't for everyone; the metaphorical deaths sometimes incurred under their influence can be disturbing.) Whether a client explores the dark, chthonic realms of the psilocybin compounds, the fast-lane hard reality of the coca and amphetamine analogs, or the *dolce far niente* of the endorphins is largely a matter of preference.

In addition, there are introspective drugs, party drugs, realist and surrealist compounds, logic drugs, drugs that unblock writer's block, drugs for photographic memory, and a whole emporium of compounds that selectively amplify particular senses. So refined is the science of designing specific molecules to unlock specific compartments of the brain that to enjoy the beneficent universe of Wordsworth's nature poems all you need to do is pop a couple of Preludes (or "Ludes.")

Perhaps the ultimate in psychochemistry occurred on May 17, 2017, when Dr. Ramachandra Rau, an eminent chemotheologian at the University of Benares, synthesized a phenethylamine compound that removes the fear of death. Like the fabled *soma* of the Rig-Veda, the drug is said to bring about the immediate experience of eternal life. Needless to say, this has solved a lot of existential problems.

But the brain runs on electricity as well as chemistry. Given that the organ of thought is basically a little saline pool that acts as a conductor, all mental life boils down to the tiny electrical signals transmitted between cells. Which brings us to electrocognitive therapy.

Are you troubled by psychosemantic disorders—dyssimile, oxymoronia, dysmetaphoria? Do you suffer from dyslexia, discalculia (trouble with numbers), or learning disabilities; an attention disorder or a faulty memory-stream? Do you sometimes wonder if your worldview is inadequate? "Many so-called psychiatric problems are really information-processing problems," said the great cognitive engineer, Dr. Hannah Helwig, in 2011. "It is hard to imagine how much human misery results from random-access memory lapses, faulty metaprograms, defective belief systems, and sundry disorders of world-view."

Today, thanks to modern electroencephalography (EEG), the science of brain waves, you can reprogram your own cerebral software.

Our Electrocognitive Laboratory traces its lineage to a forward-thinking San Francisco lab called the EEG Systems Laboratory, founded in the early 1980s by a young brain-wave connoisseur named Alan Gevins. While other EEG experts were presuming to read the mind with two or three electrodes on the scalp, Gevins et al. were equipping their subjects with sixty scalp electrodes and building the prototype of "an advanced electromagnetic recording and analysis device" for reading the mind. Or, rather, for decoding the shifting weather maps of brain waves that are the outward manifestation of thoughts. This required feeding about a hundred million bytes of data per subject into a sophisticated computer program that subtracted the brain's background "noise" and zeroed in on the EEGs corresponding

Perception studies are already increasing our knowledge of the brain.

to particular mental tasks. Its maps of the brain's electrocognitive activity may have looked as incomprehensible as Linear B to the layman, but the EEG Systems Lab was the beginning of modern electrocog therapy.

As Gevins himself predicted in 1985, a patient recovering from a stroke can consciously reprogram his own software, monitoring his progress on the electrocognitive charts. Learning disabilities, attention disorders, and hyperactivity can be detected and treated with advanced brain-wave analysis. Sophisticated forms of biofeedback and biofeedforward are employed in the Clinic, as when a client uses her brain waves to operate computer software: The computer analyzes the user's signals, derived from electrodes attached to the scalp. Then, by comparing the brain waves with the patterns in its memory, it converts the signals to digital information. Recently, we have had considerable success with the chronotemporal disorders, the disturbances of space-time first described in 1989 by Dr. Sybil Mann (many of whose patients were found to dwell permanently in "teletime," segmented into half-hour intervals).

There are also forms of electrotherapy that work on the mind like a psychoactive drug.

In the early 1980s, Soviet scientists sent to the United States something called a Lida, a crude machine made of vacuum tubes and other vintage parts. To test it, American scientists put a nervous cat in a metal box and the Lida next to it. As the machine began to hum and broadcast radio waves in the frequency of deep-sleep EEGs, the cat went into a trance. Soviet scientists reported having used the Lida to treat insomnia, hypertension, anxiety, and neurotic disturbances, and there were rumors of a more sophisticated version capable of controlling minds at a distance.

At the Clinic, of course, we are interested only in benign forms of mind control, and many of our clients enjoy "soaking" their heads in the tranquilizing radio field of our brand-new Lida 4. Because a person's brain waves automatically fire in synchrony with the surrounding pulses (a phenomenon known as entrainment), applying an external field of, say, eight hertz has a different effect from a field of eighteen hertz. The Lida 4 is capable of inducing a variety of mental states from drowsiness to transcendental serenity.

Not all of modern psychiatry is technological, however. Stroll down the long, muted corridors of the Clinic. Past the doors that say

NEUROENDOCRINE METABOLITE LABORATORY, RECEPTOR WORKUPS, and ELECTRO-
COGNITIVE SCANNING, you encounter plaques that read MEMORY TRANS-
PLANTS, DREAM INTERVENTION, ONEIROTHERAPY, SHAMANIC TOMOGRAPHY, PER-
SONAL MYTHOLOGY, PARALLEL REALITY TOURS, WORLDVIEW ENRICHMENT, LUCID
DREAMING. It is this cafeteria of soft-tech therapies, as much as psycho-
pharm and electromagnetic reprogramming, that permits the client
access to and control of his own inner life.

For most of human history, a large proportion of mental life was
terra incognita, a murky landscape full of Furies, Sirens, demons, and
blind, primitive forces that were, like the Freudian "id," beyond a
person's control. But beginning in the 1990s, the great doctors of
introspection and altered-states engineers—such giants as T. Cheng, K.
Ferencz, and L. Machiavelli—began to decipher the human brain's
machine language, its storage and retrieval mechanisms, its major
communication nodes. The neurohumoral transmission sites responsible for *déjà vu* and *jamais vu*, ecstatic kundalini rising, the platonic
forms, sacred glossolalia, Sartrean "nausea," and the Clear Light of
Tibetan Buddhism were identified. Charting the vertiginous territory
of visions, hallucination engineers discerned prototypical images that
were wired into all human brains.

One early advocate of a scientifically engineered inner world was
UCLA psychopharmacologist Ronald K. Siegel, who waded through a
sea of bureaucratic red tape in the early 1970s to get permission to give
LSD, mescaline, barbiturates, marijuana, ketamine, psilocybin, DMT,
and other hallucinogens to human subjects. Through ads in underground newspapers he recruited a group of "psychonauts," or inner-
space explorers, to travel into the hallucinatory realm. But before
giving them a single drug, he used colored slides to teach them a new
visual vocabulary, a standardized hallucination code. Instead of saying,
"That's sort of pea-soup green," the visionary trainees might say, "That's
540 millimicrons [the precise wavelength]." If a picture was flashed at
them for eight milliseconds ($\frac{1}{125}$ of a second) they could classify its
color, form, and movement dimensions with near-mathematical precision.

Then, with a certain drug in their bloodstreams, the psychonauts
entered darkened, sound-proof chambers at UCLA Medical Center and
communicated their visions, in the prearranged code, over an inter-
com. Siegel compiled these reports and did a statistical analysis to get
the "mean prototypical image." These images, depicted by a graphic

artist, were later played back to the subjects, and they picked those that best matched their hallucinations.

What Siegel discovered was this: Whatever drug they were on, the psychonauts kept hallucinating the same four geometric shapes—the spiral, the tunnel or funnel, the cobweb, and the honeycomb or lattice. Identical forms also showed up in the weavings of the peyote-using Huichol Indians of Mexico, in the drawings of hallucinating schizophrenics, in the imagery of stoned brains from every culture. And whether they were induced by drugs, meditation, crystal gazing, neurosyphilis, hypoglycemia, the near-death experience, or a sensory isolation tank, all visions known to man had the same essential structure.

Siegel did *not* catalogue the second phase of hallucination, which was full of personal, idiosyncratic imagery, but he felt that he'd uncovered the brain's basic visionary mechanisms. "I think if we tested Socrates or Joan of Arc," he remarked, "we'd be able to classify their experience comfortably with our code." With his experience in altered states, he even managed to communicate with schizophrenic patients in midhallucination.

But it took another generation of psychotechnicians to extend this cartography to auditory, tactile, and olfactory hallucinations, for example, and to develop classification codes for the complex, symbolic imagery beyond Siegel's geometries. Coupling PET scans and advanced EEG analysis to the scientific induction of altered states, introspectionists of the early twenty-first century identified the major landmarks of inner space. Thanks to their explorations, we now know where archetypes—the Great Mother, the Divine Child, the Hero, the Omniscient Alien—are stored in the brain. We know that by accessing his Neurogenetic Circuits, a person can obtain a readout of the messages stored in his DNA, perhaps activating a dim memory of life as a unicellular creature in the primordial ooze. In the Limbic Centers, one may tap into ancestral programs from the distant mammalian past— nesting, grooming, hoarding, ganging up on the weak, protecting one's youth, fighting, fleeing, and competing for mates—and find oneself perfectly in synch with the instincts of the large jungle cats. We have detailed maps of the Jehovah Circuit, with its tribal taboos and thou-shalt-nots; the Synchronicity Circuit; the Brahman Metaprograms; the Septal Bliss System; the Thanatos Interlock; and many other mental realms.

This cartography is the basis of our Alternate Reality Tours. Using hypnosis, electrostimulation, neuromantras, isolation tanking, dervish dancing, psychotropic yoga, and other methods, hallucination engineers and noetic anthropologists guide you into altered states and help you record the scenery in detail. One client, Henry C., who was just recovering from a twenty-year case of agoraphobia, had recurrent hallucinations of Horus, the falcon-headed Egyptian god. Consulting the psychoanthropology library, he was able to identify his mind's artifacts. He learned that Horus was the god of the horizon (and therefore an ally in the "dawn" of his new life.) After successive trips into the same "circuit," he deciphered the hieroglyphics inside the cartouche, which read: "The tomb of the boy-king is empty. The soul has entered the land of the immortals." Henry understood the message: Having "entombed" himself for years, he had remained a "boy-king," unchanging and untouched by life's experiences. Now, however, his soul had emerged.

Of course, not everyone can relate to the Horus archetype, any more than to the crude, action-oriented heroics of a Hercules or the desert superstitions of a Moses. The old vegetation deities, rain gods, lords of the underworld, and self-flagellating saints that were so vital to primitive societies have lost their potency today. Obviously, the world needs fresh "myths," archetypes, legends, and epics, and as an adjunct to the guided Alternate Reality Tours, a team of trained personal myth-makers can help you design a new personal "mythology" to live by.

Meanwhile, in the Mnemo Unit, over in the R Wing, a troubled couple is heading off divorce with therapeutically enhanced memories of each other. In the waiting room, a converted bigot awaits his monthly "memory transplant." As his bitter memories of a certain ethnic group are supplanted by nicer ones, his prejudices are gradually fading. Other patients come there simply to exorcise painful childhoods, drive out their accumulated Furies, have their minds filled with synthetic memories that will help them lead happier lives.

Memory doctoring was first suggested by a University of Washington psychologist, Elizabeth Loftus, in the 1980s. Her research demonstrated that memories are easily distorted after the fact, like an embezzler's books, and that all of us walk around with phony memories in our heads. Details supplied by others typically contaminate a memory to such an extent that it is virtually impossible to recover the original "memory trace," even with hypnosis or truth serums. Specifically, Loftus found, most people travel down Memory Lane wearing rose-colored glasses. They remember voting more often, being promoted more often, taking more plane trips, and having more agreeable children than the records indicate. Depressed patients, on the other hand, have dismal recollections of their lives. Loftus concluded that humans are wired up to embellish the past because "this enables us to live happier lives." To take advantage of this accident of nature, she proposed having specially trained "memory doctors" *create new memories* for us.

This notion is now the core of modern mnemotherapy. Synthetic recollections can be designed and implanted under hypnosis over the course of ten to fifteen sessions (depending on the severity of the problem). Research has shown that by creating a new "truth" in the present, the past is automatically changed. People need not be the passive victims of their infantile traumas, their parents' mistakes, their past heartbreaks, and their failures. Given our present access to the brain's storage and retrieval mechanisms, the mind can be reprogrammed at will.

Commonly, mnemotherapy is combined with PsychoSim, or Psycho-Simulation. When Anna O. or Irma M. and Freud's other turn-of-the-century analysands free-associated, they did so in the abstract realm of words. But in 1995, the number-crunching power of the computer was coupled to the elephantine storage capacity of the videodisc, and lifelike simulations of the intrapsychic landscape became possible.

Just as the old-fashioned flight simulators gave astronauts a foretaste of zero-gravity and airline pilot trainees realistic sensations of turbulence at thirty thousand feet, PsychoSim enacts your own fantasy worlds. When you free-associate, your associations spring to life, with realistic colors, sounds, and sensations. You can project your daydreams, and with the flick of a joystick experience hundreds of alternate realities, from walking on the surface of Jupiter to climbing Anapurna to being a dolphin afloat in the North Atlantic. You can reenact your memories, traveling back to the Oedipal dramas of the nursery, even to the womb. You can be a sperm sliding down the fallopian tube. How do you feel when you meet the egg? Do you want a totally dark womb or a womb with a view?

You can try on different pasts—What if you hadn't split up with Raoul in 1992? What if your parents had married other people?—and see how they affect the present. Given a combination of PsychoSim and one of the more labile psychoactive drugs, the client can live out alternative lives, parallel identities, experiencing the psychological equivalent of reincarnation without the inconvenience of biological death.

Another important application of modern inner-space technology is dream control. I am proud to say that our Dream Lab boasts a team of oneirotechnicians, oneirochronologists, and dream designers trained in state-of-the-art lucid dreaming, systematic dream incubation, advanced oneiric design, and collective dreaming. In the dark ages of the twentieth century, of course, dream analysis was rife with superstition, and people paid $150 an hour to lie on a couch and recount their dreams to an austere, bearded analyst. The best a dreamer could do was to recall his dream the morning after, after its "soul" was already lost, and hunt for obscure symbols planted by the unconscious. Today, most motivated dreamers dream lucidly, practicing a modification of the MILD (mnemonic induction of lucid dreams) method invented by Stanford University sleep researcher Stephen LaBerge.

For several nights running, back in 1978, LaBerge went to sleep wired up to a polysonograph, a lie detector–like device that automatically monitored his eye muscles and other physiological signals. Each time he "woke up" within a dream he signaled to the outside world by moving his eyes in a prearranged sequence: left-right, left-right. When he scanned the record later he found his coded message clearly recorded among the serpentine ink tracings on the graph paper—four large, sweeping zigzags on the eye-muscle channel. And he performed fancier feats, using a series of eye and body movements as a Morse code to spell out his initials from inside a lucid dream. Later, in the early 1980s, he trained an elite group of "oneironauts," or "dream navigators," to break the barrier between dreams and waking life.

The basic criterion of lucidity is to be aware that you're dreaming. Beyond that, there are infinite variations. In LaBerge's words, "Full lucidity is knowing, 'Every part of this dream is my own mind, and I take full responsibility for it.' If you don't fly because you don't think you can, then you're not fully lucid."

In our oneironautics classes, clients learn to design their own dreams and direct the action like imperious Hollywood directors.

Suppose you've had a recurrent nightmare in which you are chased by masked men; you can program yourself to "wake up" inside the dream, confront your masked pursuers, and ask them, "What do you want?" Perhaps they'll evaporate into thin air and never bother you again, or perhaps they'll tell you something interesting. In your dream-world you can do anything you want; you can glide over the canals of Mars on a magic carpet or enjoy interesting liaisons with alluring strangers.

The Nocturnal Cognition Unit also offers a workshop in communal dreaming, based in part on the pioneering work of two twentieth-century psychologists, Henry Reed of Virginia Beach, Virginia, and Robert Van de Castle, of the University of Virginia Medical School. In their experimental dream community of the 1980s, participants began unwittingly dreaming about another member's problem without having been told about it. More sophisticated dream-induction technology, chemical manipulation of the REM control centers in the brain stem, electrotelepathy, and advanced brain-wave biofeedback made the shared dream a quantifiable phenomenon in the mid-nineties. As computer networks created a global mass mind, worldwide dream communities reported more and more shared imagery, synchronicities, collective symbols. Finally, in 2004, a group of accomplished oneironauts from around the world arranged to meet inside the numinous landscape of a collective lucid dream. Naturally, some thorny privacy issues arose, as when a Reno, Nevada, housewife accused a man in Kuala Lumpur of "eavesdropping" on a "very personal dream" and then dropping prurient messages into her electronic mailbox, but that's another story. Suffice it to say that much of today's psychotherapy takes place on-line. . . .

For the third day in a row you wake up in a cold sweat, spooked by a recurrent dream of a massive earthquake. Still in your bathrobe and fuzzy pink bedroom slippers, with the residue of sleep encrusting your eyes, you instruct your modem to dial 3423–922–86663–2376. Once on-line, you reach the Dream Interpreter, who knows the geography of your dreamscape like you know the streets of your hometown. It is a Jungian, of course.

"It was horrible," you recount. "So many bodies buried under the rubble. . . ." When you finish your narrative, the screen fills with a list of the salient symbols, and the Interpreter interviews you about the meaning of each. You free-associate. The crushed buildings remind

Opposite page: New psycho-active drugs give us a window on old memories.

you of the toy village your sister trampled on Christmas Day, 1990. It was a mistake, she said, but you know it wasn't. Cries of children under the rubble. You tried to help. Pulled on a tiny arm, and it comes off at the socket. Broken doll. Can't glue it back together. Fire and earth. Fire burns earth. No, earth puts out fire. Rochambeau.

The Interpreter feeds your associations into the dreamtext and gives you a rewritten version. It reminds you of previous related themes in your computerized dream journal and guides you through a simulation of last night's dream. It gives you the electronic addresses of people with similar dreams, but you decide not to contact them. (You're already involved in the Joint Oneiro thing—a few nights ago you and some other lucid dreamers actually rendezvoused inside a collective erotic dream—as well as the usual smattering of electronic encounter groups and fraternal organizations. You can't afford to spend *all* your time getting your head straight in the networks.)

Anyway, what you really want to know is: How many other people had earthquake dreams last night? Is it a personal motif or a fragment of the collective unconscious? Could your dream be *precognitive*?

Typing in the right code, you summon up a survey of dream themes and symbols collected over the past twenty-four hours from around the world. Loose teeth, missed planes, tumescent towers and humid caves, negligees, spacewrecks, deranged CPUs, robots in silk underwear, pituitary dwarves, the Hanged Man of the Tarot, artificial organs, bodies of water . . . images and symbols from Kabul; Salem, Oregon; Tegucigalpa; the Ivory Coast; Freedom City, Antarctica; the Maritime Provinces; the mining towns of the Sea of Tranquillity. Nope, very few dream earthquakes. Statistically below chance, in fact. You breathe a sigh of relief. Instead of clearing out of the greater Los Angeles area, you merely need to do a little mental housecleaning.

Though it would be a decade or two before psychiatry would feel its full impact, the wired society began to make its appearance in the early 1980s. In 1986, several million people—mostly in the U.S.—were on-line, working or fooling around on prototype computer networks like The Source and CompuServe. Some were serious scholars engaged in on-line conferences on strategic resources or disarmament; others were ordinary folks looking for love or "cognitive affairs" in the electronic singles' bars, and indulging in "Hot Chats" with strangers known only by such handles as Surfer, Amalgam, or the Karate Kid. Some people became so addicted to the small-town neighborliness and disembodied platonic loves of the electronic village that they virtually dropped out of real life to spend ten or twelve hours a day in rapt contemplation of the green screen.

Before long a dizzying variety of encounter groups, support groups, self-help groups, and psychotherapies, professional and otherwise, had sprung up on-line, where the anonymity promoted frank confessions and embarrassing revelations that would never have taken place in an off-line encounter group. By 1995, only a few dyed-in-the-wool analysands were having their Electra complexes unraveled in fifty-minute segments on some analyst's couch, and more and more forward-looking therapists were hanging up their shingles on-line. On a given day in 2019, a sample menu from ShrinkNet reads, in part:

    ANGST CLUB yyx.37
    ANHEDONIA WORKSHOP xx998
    ATTENTION CONTROL 967xx
    BELIEF SYSTEM ENGINEERING 3yzz94
    BEREAVEMENT PROCESSING 324xx.12
    BROODERS ANON. 25.x.46
    COGNITIVE AFFAIRS yzz143
    DYSEMPATHY HOTLINE 23.yzz.425

One virtue of computerized psychotherapy, besides the convenience of having one's neuroses and personality disorders treated without shaving or putting on one's makeup, is that it is the perfect tool for gathering data. As people confide in the silicon shrinks, statistics on the national—and, increasingly, the world—psyche can be instantaneously compiled, filed, cross-correlated. By typing in the correct code, a researcher may compute the rate of agoraphobia in cities of over 100,000 population; the number of times the word *attracted* is used by teenage girls in Central Mongolia; the incidence of dreams involving falling, homework, or surgery in the U.S.

Acute psychological observers were soon noting that Jung's old "collective unconscious" had become embodied in the computer networks linking all parts of the planet. Every night the soul of mankind sends its assorted dream images and symbols into the electronic noosphere, to be filed and stored in an ongoing data base. Mean prototypical images, chi squares, and multiple hierarchical regressions are calculated instantaneously. New archetypes are identified. Keeping tabs on the world's dreams night after night, psychometricians observe a sort of psychological weather map, charting clouds of ennui, low-pressure fronts of anxiety, sudden-rage storms, pockets of anhedonia, in the electronic noosphere. Everyone is connected psychically with everyone else. When a child in Sierra Leone has recurrent nightmares it cannot fail to perturb the electromental ocean, even if only slightly, sending small ripples to Cincinnati. This fact, needless to say, has had a considerable impact on psychiatry.

There is yet another way that computers can contribute immensely to mental well-being, though the technique is still experimental. I refer, of course, to the biochip.

Forty years ago it was just a gleam in the eye of a few futuristic dreamers, notably James V. McAlear, of EMV Associates in Rockville, Maryland. By the early 1980s, McAlear had already patented a technique for making a conductor out of a protein molecule. It was the first step in the creation of a VSD, or very small device, that could be implanted in a brain.

The virtue of an organic computer chip is that it is minute and three-dimensional, and thus packs a million times the computing power of its solid state equivalent. McAlear's first project was artificial vision, a feat he accomplished in the winter of 1992. A miniature television camera mounted on the eyeglasses served as the "eyes." The camera's signals, converted to pulses, were sent to an array of miniature electrodes implanted in the brain of a forty-four-year-old blind man named Ernest. In this way, "pictures" were drawn in Ernest's visual cortex with phosphenes, little starlike spots of light. This had been done before, albeit somewhat crudely, at the University of Utah in the 1970s. The revolutionary part was that McAlear's electrodes were coated with cultured embryonic nerve cells, which actually hooked up with the nerve cells of the visual cortex.

The next step was to make the biocomputer a godlike instrument of thought, marrying the number-crunching power of electrons to the reasoning ability of neurons. In 2016, a team of scientists at the Organo-Software Institute, working from McAlear's blueprints, designed an entire molecular computer to set up symbiotic residence in the brain. It sends out nerve fibers to grow into brain cells and has a double-helix structure so it can replicate itself. A person can theoretically store any sort of information on this biochip and, with his neurons and his thoughts, access the entire Library of Congress.

Given the experimental nature of the procedure, only a half dozen elderly people with failing memories have been outfitted with bio-chips so far, with mixed results. One recipient, ninety-three-year-old Alvin Farquar of Fargo, North Dakota, says he enjoys the implant, despite some "storage and retrieval problems." "The other day," he says, "I was accessing my calendar to see if the Elks were having a covered-dish supper on Wednesday night, and darned if I didn't get stuck for an hour in the major exports of Uruguay and Paraguay. But the little whachama-call-it is great for poker."

Forty years ago, McAlear predicted that his biochip, by uniting ner-vous tissue with circuit switches a hundred times faster than the brain's synapses, would become a "superior, omnipotent being." Further-more, he foresaw that the being of the user would live on in the biocomputer, not in the central nervous system. In other words, ladies and gentlemen, when you die, the implant, storing your personal record and all your knowledge, could be implanted in a fresh host. The neurotheologians have not yet determined whether this con-stitutes immortality or reincarnation, but in any case, your dreams, fears, compulsions, obsessions, fantasies, and neuroses will live for-ever. This may or may not be a comforting thought.

C H A P

A NIGHT

IN THE

BEDROOM

Married white female, 40, seeks well-endowed SWM, 18–28, for 3-month intimate companionship. My husband's hormone treatments (he's 6 months pregnant) have put him out of commission temporarily. You take care of me; I'll take care of you. Electrostimulation okay, as is drug-enhanced orgasm, but prefer partner with original equipment rather than implant. Send photo and vaccination certification to Box 2238.
 —Personal ad, *The Village Voice*,
 July 20, 2019

Sunday afternoons were the worst for Barbara. Her husband was usually off with his friends and she was left home alone in their third-floor apartment—except for the incredible noises that wafted through the poorly insulated ceiling from the studio below. Today's matinee was an anguished moaner (last week's was a joyous screamer), her cries colored with the false intimation that each thrust from the stud beneath her was against her will, or at least against her better judgment.

Barbara thought she knew, by sound, all the partners of her young male neighbor downstairs. But this was a new one, and it depressed her. So many people having so much fun. And she, at thirty-five, like many other women, felt washed-up sexually. Her husband was unattentive, and she wished she had the freedom of spirit to walk downstairs and volunteer to hop on her horny neighbor. Perhaps in a freer age. . . .

Our little classified ad pictures a 2019 in which people can publicly and boldly state their desires, no matter how bizarre or specific. Our vignette about Barbara is the reality (or at least one reality) of 1986.

These are paradoxical times, sexually speaking. The promise of free love and expanded sensuality so widely heralded in the 1960s has degenerated to a confused era in which free sexual expression is enjoyed by an elite few, while the bulk of society feels left out of the action. Sexual freedom is glorified, and yet *Time* magazine announces that the predominant sexual malady of our time is lack of desire, and women over the age of thirty are considered undesirable.

Even so, beneath the puritanical patina of present-day society, there lies a sexuality waiting to express itself in a more expansive age. On a

Previous page: Sexual yearnings in the present age are often not translated into meaningful action.

scientific level, researchers are discovering new ways to enhance orgasm and desire, developing hormones to increase the performance of sex organs, manufacturing more realistic artificial penises, and even experimenting with male pregnancy—a development that would alter gender roles drastically and have a profound effect on sexual practices. On a societal level, men and women are questioning our present monolithic attitude toward sexuality. June Reinisch, director of the Kinsey Institute, Bloomington, Indiana, points out that sexual attitudes fluctuate in twenty-year cycles. For example, the 1940s and 1950s were repressive years, while the 1960s and 1970s saw a flowering of sexual freedom. If Reinisch's theory is right, things look bad for the next two decades. On the other hand, we can look forward to a sexual renaissance from 2001 to 2020. The year 2019 will see the blending of science and passion into an orgasmic age.

The technology—and some of the scientific understanding, at least—may already be here. In fact, the greatest strides in sexuality may come from neuroscience. We have known for over thirty years, for example, that sexuality begins and ends in the brain, not in the genitals or anywhere else. We even have crude ways of creating, on demand, sexual pleasure in the brain.

It was 1953 when James Olds and Peter Milner, working at the Montreal Neurological Institute, sunk electrodes into the brain of a white rat. They had intended to place the electrodes in the rat's hypothalamus, but by mistake had inserted them in a mysterious region called the "septum." Olds stimulated the rat every time it wandered into one corner of its cage. Oddly, the rat developed a compulsive fondness for that part of the cage. (By contrast, when the hypothalamus was stimulated, rats avoided the corner.) The septum was thereby identified as the "pleasure center" of the brain. Further experiments proved that rats, outfitted with electrodes in their heads that they could self-activate by pushing a lever, would bypass the mundane pleasures of food, water, and sex for the joys of lever pushing—some pushing the magic button for twenty-four consecutive hours, until they passed out from exhaustion or hunger.

But what about humans? It was Dr. Robert G. Heath, chairman emeritus of the neurology/psychiatry department of New Orleans Tulane University School of Medicine, who proved that you and I can have our "buttons pushed" just like white rats. Heath and his Tulane colleagues punched holes in the skulls of patients, implanted electrodes

deep in their brain tissue, and left them there, recording brain waves while the subjects talked, flew into rages, hallucinated, had seizures . . . or intense orgasms.

Women in 2019 will undergo major sexual awakenings.

In one forty-year-old woman patient, Heath's team implanted a sort of tube called a "canula" along with the electrodes. Through the canula they delivered precise amounts of acetylcholine, a natural chemical transmitter, directly into the septum. "Vigorous activity" showed up on the electroencephalogram, and the patient reported intense pleasure, including multiple sexual orgasms lasting as long as thirty minutes.

In another experiment, Heath outfitted some of his patients with self-stimulators—a device with three or four buttons, each one connected to an electrode implanted in a different part of the brain, that the patient wore hooked onto a belt. Whenever he felt the urge, the patient could push any of the buttons. One man pushed the button connected to the septal region 1,500 times an hour.

Is this the proper scenario for 2019? People with pleasure buttons on their belts? Acetylcholine-induced orgasms? LSD-prophet Timothy Leary once predicted that soon we'll all be wearing septal electrodes as a means for instant gratification, but Dr. Heath derides the idea. Heath's experiments were conducted on seemingly hopeless patients who had been previously relegated to straitjackets and shock treatment. As for implanting electrodes deep in the brains of normal, healthy patients, Dr. Heath says, "It's a little drastic to have a hole punched in your skull unless you're very, very ill."

What he does predict for the twenty-first century, however, are non-invasive techniques based on his method. According to Heath, an ultrasound device could be built and used to activate the brain's pleasure centers without having to go inside the skull. In fact, one male-potency clinic predicts that by 2005, family doctors will be using electrical stimulation of the brain's pleasure centers to increase sexual desire in less-than-potent males.

Drugs are another method. Heath says scientists must find out which chemical in the brain activates the pleasure centers, and then design a pill that would do the same thing. In other words, an aphrodisiac.

Current aphrodisiacs are hardly the pharmacological breakthroughs that Heath envisions for 2019. The best we have at present is yohimbine ("yo-yo"), an African drug made from the sap of a tropical tree. Male rats injected with yo-yo mounted females up to forty-five times in fifteen minutes. Stanford University Medical School recently began human trials, and while results are not yet in, the yohimbine experiment has revealed one very significant factor about the future: People *want* aphrodisiacs. Stanford physiology professor Dr. Julian Davidson says he has more willing volunteers than he can handle. Obviously, for humans on the planet, sex has not fulfilled its promise, either in frequency or intensity.

Yohimbine is a male aphrodisiac only (yo-yo has never been tested on females of any species), and, in fact, little work is being done on developing aphrodisiacs for women. However, one drug that holds out hope for women in the twenty-first century is naltrexone, which is an oral version of naloxone, a drug used to curb heroin addiction. Naltrexone has also been used as an appetite suppressant; it was during experiments with rats and appetite control that scientists discovered an odd side effect of naltrexone—sexual arousal. In human experiments, researchers at the South African Brain Research Institute gave four women small doses of naloxone just prior to orgasm. One woman said the orgasms she had after taking the drug were "the best she could remember." But results were mixed in the other subjects, proving once again that desire and orgasm are much more complicated in women than in men. Kinsey Institute director June Reinisch sees little hope for aphrodisiacs, even in the next century. Still, the search for a female stimulant goes on as scientists try out such things as laughing gas, male hormones, and other chemicals. The key may not be chemical, however. As we shall soon see, social factors may be more important in allowing women to enjoy their full sexuality.

Improved performance by men will also help. Only five years ago doctors believed 90 percent of all impotence was caused by psychological factors. Today, we realize that men's sexual maladies are usually caused by organic, not psychic problems. In fact, researchers now think that as much as 60 percent of all impotence can be linked to physiological disorders—diabetes mellitus, kidney disease, arteriosclerosis, side effects of drugs, etc.—that can be treated effectively in over 75 percent of all cases.

The most futuristic, and dramatic, treatment for impotent men is the penile implant. Over 100,000 men have already received these devices, the simplest of which consists merely of two silicone rods inserted into each corpus cavernosum of the penis. (In a normal erection, blood engorges the corpora cavernosa, two long tubes of spongy tissue.) Such a prosthesis creates a permanent semi-erection that unfortunately can be seen through a man's trousers.

Enter high-tech: Men can now have a luxury, inflatable model installed, with two balloonlike tubes in the corpora cavernosa, a reservoir of fluid hidden in the abdomen, and a pump housed in the scrotum. Simply squeeze the pump and a saline solution in the reservoir fills the tubes in the penis for an instant erection. When lovemaking is completed, the owner flips a release valve in the scrotum to get a nice, neat, flaccid penis again. Other variations are also about to hit the market, with such colorful names as Hydroflex and Omniphase and a number of luxury features.

Such devices are really stop-gap measures, allowing impotent men to "perform" in a physical sense, but without feeling. What's needed is a device that provides an erection with sexual sensation. One potency expert predicts that by the middle of the twenty-first century we'll be successfully transplanting penises, just as we transplant kidneys and corneas now. By the end of the next century, researchers speculate that we'll finally create the first completely robotic penis, fashioned from real human flesh and combined with electronic components. Just as today's bionic artificial arms respond to human thoughts, the bionic penis will respond to thoughts, emotions, and desire.

Unimaginable pleasures await the sexual traveler of 2019.

The bionic penis may be too radical for 2019, however. More likely, that year will see widespread use of erection-assist devices. These are neither implants nor prostheses, but gadgets that will shock the penis into action. Researchers at the University of California at San Francisco are currently experimenting, using monkeys, with an "erection pacemaker." Surgically implanted, the pacemaker stimulates penile nerves to cause a natural erection; a remote radio transmitter activates the device. A similar device is the Male Electronic Genital Stimulator (MEGS). Unlike the erection pacemaker, this three-inch-long gadget doesn't need to be surgically implanted. Instead, MEGS is implanted rectally by a doctor, and remote controlled by an electronic component hidden in a watch or jewelry. Like the pacemaker, it produces a natural erection by electrically stimulating nerves to the penis. (The transmitters for these devices must be individualized, incidentally, so that each controls one penis only and does not willy-nilly activate other equipment or other penises. As the maker of MEGS put it: "Each unit will be custom-made so that the man doesn't end up accidentally opening someone's garage door.")

There may also be hope for the man or woman who not only wants a new sex organ, but an organ of the opposite sex in order to fulfill some inner need. Sexologist John Money, professor of medical psychology and pediatrics at Johns Hopkins University and Hospital in Baltimore, speculates that organ regeneration may hold the key for those people unhappy with their sexual organs of birth.

"My science fiction idea is that with a bit of genetic engineering one might program for reverse embryogenesis, so that then one might be able to backtrack and grow the sex organs out again in the form of the opposite sex. Lizards can grow a new tail at any stage of their lives, so once you learn how to get organ regeneration, there's no age limit on it. You'd just tell the clitoris to backtrack to the genital tubercle [embryonic tissue that will differentiate into the external sex organs of either sex] and then grow out as a penis with skin wrapped around it instead of having a hood and labia minora, and it would do just what it's told."

The greatest revolution in sexuality in the next century will not be the result of aphrodisiacs, electrostimulation, or bionic penises. It will stem from the growing stature of women in society. And with economic power will come sexual equality. Pepper Schwartz, associate professor of sociology at the University of Washington, believes that the traditional dichotomy of man as breadwinner, woman as housewife, is rapidly breaking down for two reasons: economics and divorce. Schwartz, who recently conducted a National Science Foundation survey of 7,397 couples, says, "There are going to be more women working than presently because they have to. The economy is predicated on two incomes. Also, women have to have a skill now that divorce is so common."

With jobs will come money, power, and prestige, and women will use this collateral for the same purpose men do: to attract members of the opposite sex, especially younger members. "Now that women are starting to earn money and have prestige," says Schwartz, "they can offer younger men some of the same utilitarian advantages that younger women get from older men." She predicts that the cultural ideas of womanhood will change, that "women will have some of the same patinas that are given to men, not because their wrinkles are any prettier than men's wrinkles, but because they can control and buy and vote and be powerful."

The best sex in 2019 probably won't be found on Earth. It will happen three hundred miles in space. The most romantic hotel in the universe will be found orbiting the Earth, perhaps taking the form of a commercial wing on NASA's permanent space station, and you'll be able literally to bounce off the walls with your partner. "If you like waterbeds," says Ben Bova, president of the National Space Institute, "sex in zero gravity is going to be even better. You'll be free from all the restrictions of weight. You won't have to lie on a surface. Essentially, you're turning sex into a three-dimensional experience. You can float freely in the middle of an enclosure or bounce off a padded wall. And your body responds to the slightest touch, like a boat in the water."

"However," admits Bova, "there might be some very interesting problems in the area of what NASA would call 'rendezvous and docking.'"

"I've given this subject a lot of thought," says Bova, whose National Space Institute is devoted to promoting a stronger civilian space movement. His own personal goal is to build a honeymoon hotel in orbit. "I think," says Bova, "that it will beat the hell out of Niagara Falls."

LIFE MEETS DEATH AND TWISTS ITS TAIL

HALLEY F. ARCHER DEAD AT 109; REAL ESTATE TYCOON DEVELOPED PROPERTIES ON MOON, MARS

Halley Faustus Archer, who made a fortune in real estate and was the first civilian to develop properties on the Moon and Mars, died yesterday in an automobile accident. He was 109. Archer succumbed to head injuries in a Beverly Hills hospital. His organs and limbs were removed for donation. His brain could not be retrieved.

"My dad clearly intended to live forever," said son Geoffrey Archer, 81, president of Terrestrial Archer, Inc., the family's giant real estate and biomedical-research conglomerate. "His is an untimely death."

Halley Archer speculated in real estate in New York City, Rio de Janeiro, Hong Kong, and Lagos. At the turn of the millennium, he was the first to develop the Moon with his multipurpose colony, including the Luna Loa Hotel, private condominiums, and a research hospital. Last year he built Halley's Mars Bars, the only vacation colony on the fourth planet at this time.

Archer's driving force in life was the desire to be young forever. He had been a health fanatic since the 1950s, and as he amassed his fortune, he invested increasing billions in research aimed at extending life span and designing therapies to rejuvenate aging bodies. In 1987, he established Archer Biomedicals "to discover the elixir of youth," as he put it. Archer was a self-described human guinea pig for many of the experimental drugs and techniques developed at his institute.

Organ-retrieval doctors stated that, at death, Archer had the internal physiological body of a man in his mid-fifties. Due to plastic surgery and epidermal therapies, his external appearance had been revamped to the point where he bore a striking resemblance to himself as he looked in 1945, and also to the current 3-V idol Darryl Martingale.

Archer was born in 1910 and named after the comet that entered the solar system during that year. He married Gladys Bruce in 1937 and they had two sons. In 1957, his wife died of cancer and Archer vowed to "take on death" as his ultimate challenge. From age 40, he ran, swam, and practiced yoga and karate. In the 1960s he enrolled in a megavitamin program begun by famed vitamin-researcher Michael Colgan. He began the Roy Walford "starvation" diet designed by the eminent University of California immunologist in 1986. He subsisted on 1,300 calories a day for the rest of his life. In 1991, he underwent a liver, pancreas, spleen, kidney block transplant.

Archer encouraged his second wife, Isabelle Lewis, to undergo experimental life-enhancement therapies as well. And, in 1998, when she was 54, she bore him a daughter, Hyacinthe. In the 1990s, Archer's son Andrew, 73, an endocrinologist and a member of the research team at Archer Biomedical, persuaded Donner Denckla, who had theorized the existence of the "death hormone," to come out of retirement. Together they succeeded in isolating the hormone in 1999, and for

Previous page: The great beyond: Death will be less intimidating in the next century.

this research they shared the Nobel prize in medicine and physiology in 2007. Halley Archer began antideath hormone therapy in 2002, at 92. At his death, he and his wife, also on the experimental drug, were planning to have another child.

In addition to his wife and three children, Archer is survived by four grand-children and five great-grandchildren. A private service will be held at the Archer's villa on Mars. His remains will be placed aboard an Aldrin III rocket, destined to reach the Beta Pictoris system in 175 years. Friends and relatives who wish to participate in the wake and funeral ritual may do so by tuning in to Channel Z, MortNet, tomorrow at 7:00 P.M., Greenwich Mean.

—*The New York Times*, July 20, 2019

Mr. Archer's extended life was not available even for the colossally rich in the early twenty-first century. Archer had eased himself onto the biomedical inside track by building his own research unit, and by using his own body for experimentation. Nonetheless, as a conse-quence of his lust for life, as well as the megafunds he poured into bioscience, many of today's affluent will have a shot at living into their 120s and 130s. Even the less financially blessed who were born in the mid–twentieth century can expect to live into robust hundreds—with-out access to the multiple organ transplants or the death hormone that is not yet available to the middle-range bureaucrat and conglom em-ployee.

Halley Archer notwithstanding, the rejuvenating and life-extending therapies of today are the results of the tremendous economic and social pressures of the twentieth century. By the 1980s, it was painfully evident that even if existing diseases were cured—cancers, cardiovas-cular, stroke, Alzheimer's, diabetes—people would still deteriorate for another decade or two past seventy before the inevitable date with the grim reaper. The prospect of a semi-senile population living in mas-sive Sun City ghettos across the southern states, useless and helpless in their eighties and nineties, did not bode well for a healthy economy. The GNP would plummet with the loss of per capita consumption—it would be bad for all businesses, except the nursing home business. So, by the 1990s, monies flowed in ever-quickening streams for re-search grants in the biology of longevity.

Archer was decades ahead of everyone in fending off decrepitude. He exercised rigorously and adhered to Walford's "undernourishment diet" (actually a misnomer, because all basic requirements of vitamins, minerals, and protein were to be met in this semi-starvation regimen). Caloric restriction had extended the life span of laboratory animals by as much as 30 percent, and as far as Archer was concerned, he was just a very rich lab rat. He got used to being hungry. By the year 2000, however, scientists had found methods to turn off hunger centers in the hypothalamus. People found they could vary their eating styles. Archer could snack daily or get his weekly caloric requirement in one extravagant orgy of a banquet and eat nothing for several days.

Public campaigns introduced people to strategies of combating physical wear and tear. The two main weapons in this war against aging were antioxidants and DNA repair enzymes. Antioxidants are molecular substances that repair damage to cells caused by oxidation. During oxygen metabolism, unstable atoms break off in the cells' molecules and career around the cytoplasm like crazed teenagers in stolen stratocruisers on a Saturday night. These free radicals try to "rape" or steal other molecules' electrons. In their frenzied search for partners, free radicals damage DNA, membranes, proteins, and inactivate or disrupt cellular functions. Older cells are packed with free radicals.

Antioxidants mop up free radicals. Today, in the twenty-first century, antioxidant research has vastly enlarged the number of basic compounds with antioxidant properties. Beefed up analogs of the previous century's old stand-bys—vitamins A, E, and C—are still some of the most potent. People still self-administer their own personal blends of substances such as: 2-MEA (2-mercaptoethylamine); BHT (butylated hydroxytoluene), a food preservative; the trace mineral selenium; santoquin, a quinine derivative; and other compounds that put the brakes on free radical activity.

Before the death hormone-blocker, Archer's favorite free-radical fighters were enzymes of the body's own antioxidant systems, such as glutathione peroxidase, catalase, and the queen of them all, superoxide dismutase (SOD). For the masses, cheap SOD is the antioxidant of choice. Nothing in the body soaks up free radicals like SOD. In the last century, pioneering gerontologist Richard Cutler became fascinated by ways to boost the body's production of SOD, and in 1990, genetic engineering via recombinant DNA techniques enabled pharmaceutical firms to manufacture human SOD in abundant quantities and to design "vectors" that allowed the enzyme to enter the bloodstream quickly.

As the low-cost, easy accessibility of cyclosporine and its derivatives revolutionized transplant surgery, it also created a whole new class of dead people, people more sought-after dead than alive. Organs became worth many times more than their proverbial weight in gold.

The need for multiorgan donors has reached a zenith today, as the aging twentieth-century-born population has only slightly fewer numbers than the following generation, who can provide only one-tenth of the necessary organs. Furthermore, restraining seats for babies and traffic law enforcement have cut down on the number of auto and stratocruiser accidents, the primary source of donor organs.

Yet among the thousands of people who die each year under circumstances that make them candidates for organ donation, only 30 percent yield up organs. Still, this is better than in the last century, when only around 10 percent of the potential organs were used. Last year, in 2019, almost 75,000 Americans died from head injuries, brain tumors, drug ODs, and other conditions that rendered them brain dead, and ideal candidates for multiple organ donation. If organs were obtained from all the brain dead and distributed in an efficient way there would be enough to go around.

To obtain organs, the AMA and other organizations have promoted organ-donor consciousness drives. People are generally more eager to donate their dead relatives' organs than to sign up their own for donation after death. The National Organ Transplant Acts and the special Task Force on Organ Procurement secured the "presumed consent" law, the assumption being that organs may be removed from a body unless the next of kin objects. Income tax deductions to people with donor cards are an added incentive; the Uniform Anatomical Gift Act provides deductions for whole-body donations. Capital punishment is now meted out with injections that leave the body virtually intact. Nonetheless, the laws have only slightly reduced the gap between supply and demand. And health officials foresee a serious trend toward organ hoarding, price fixing, and bounty hunting.

The concept of brain death, however, is at last ingrained in public consciousness. The problem of defining the moment of death first arose with the development of respirators. Before, if a person had a totally infarcted brain, autonomic nervous system would cease to function, breathing and heartbeat would stop. Yet when a body without brain function is connected to a respirator, the body usually continues to function—mindlessly—sometimes indefinitely.

By the 1990s, biomedicine had largely worked out the legal concept of brain death *qua* death. The throbbing heart, a metabolizing liver or pancreas, do not define a person as being alive. Life requires at least brain stem activity to integrate the whole complex of organs as well as to supply cognitive function. The medical profession had to delineate the levels of comatose states: from a lack of communication with an observer, but presence of moaning, tossing and turning, opening of eyes and appearing almost awake; to states of zero response to external stimuli, including autonomic nervous system responses. This latter state, originally called "coma depasse," is now brain death. The definition of brain death goes beyond a flat EEG and absence of brain stem reflexes to demonstration of brain destruction with CAT scans or angiograms.

The year Archer received his new liver, pancreas, spleen, kidney block, 1991, was the year of the great Transplant Strike, staged by doctors, nurses, and paramedicals. It was a result of the intense emotional crisis brought about by the insatiable demand for body parts. Entire hospitals had been transformed into halfway houses for death—antiseptic, high-tech charnels where beating-heart cadavers were sustained on life-support systems until their organs could be retrieved in surgery. Buildings were devoted to sophisticated intensive care units (ICUs) where "neomorts" were kept on ventilators, intravenous feeding tubes, heating and cooling blankets, excretory-output monitors, arterial and central venous pressure catheters, intercranial pressure monitors, and other indexing equipment necessary to protect and preserve the organs.

Although organ procurement was big business, the medical profession was not prepared for the disturbing psychic effects of organ maintenance and removal on hospital personnel. Operating room staff were especially hard hit. In a gust of morbid humor, the media dubbed this phenomenon the Edgar Allen Poe syndrome, in honor of the writer of horror stories, including a masterpiece about a heart that continued to beat after being buried under floorboards.

Another valiant attempt to keep up intercellular vigor are DNA cocktails. Repair of broken DNA is conducted by hundreds of different enzymes that are turned on by repair genes. The more DNA-repair genes, the longer-lived the animal. So again, the idea is that if you can boost those DNA repair enzymes via a supplement, you'll live twice as long. In the late 1980s and early 1990s, people were mixing batches of

Opposite page: The near-death experience (NDE) is so pleasurable that clubs are devoted to its cultivation.

repair enzymes. One recipe, for example, contained two parts 6-methylquanine—DNA methyltransferase—added to three parts endonuclease, one part beta-galactosidase, with a dash of DNA ligase thrown in. But DNA repair enzyme batches are hard to control, are error prone, and sometimes cause more side effects than they are worth. And at the heart of the matter, no one can prove that there isn't some sort of clock or clocks turning off the body that no amount of enzymes can stop.

One example of a stopped clock is the thymus gland, a mass located behind the breastbone and below the neck that shrinks to insignificant size by puberty. It plays a mysterious yet important role in immune defense. The thymic hormone, thymosin, was discovered in the 1960s, but not isolated until the 1980s. At seventy, Archer was taking an extract of thymosin, without getting much benefit from it. A bioengineered analog developed in 1988, however, streamlined the hormone's effect. This synthetic thymosin succeeded in boosting Archer's immune system to ward off cancers and halted the development of autoimmune diseases. Especially relevant to Archer was thymosin's ability to increase resistance to stress and stress's toll on the immune system. By 2019, most Type-A personalities, hard driving and high strung, enlist in thymosin therapies by their mid-forties. (Reprogramming techniques are readily available to mellow out and tone-down Type-As, but most prefer to remain as they are and counter the adrenergic price tag of life in the fast skylane with thymosin augmentation.) Along with SOD, thymosin derivatives continue to be the supplements of choice for those individuals involved in the drugs of realism.

Today, most of the affluent classes of the world are deeply involved in drugs. Twenty-first century users tend to fall into two broad camps: those who seek amplification of the pleasure and fantasy realms, or who want to screen out all but the life of the mind; and those who wish to augment their performance in worldly pursuits. The hedonic and altered-state seekers partake of endorphin-enkephalin derivatives and psychoactives in all their dazzling array. Stimulant-psychoactive combinations, for these people, are generally aimed at flinging wide the doors of perception, rather than enhancing analytical faculties as do the realism compounds. The hedonic drugs have little life-prolonging effect, but their devotees don't care. They are more interested in extending the time frames of experience within the hallucinating mind than extending decades of sobriety.

Others, like Archer, rarely take recreational drugs, beyond the ancient, but increasingly rarified, ethanol of wine and cognac. These people take memory and IQ enhancers. Consequently, in the twenty-first century, life spans vary enormously, not only from economic class to economic class, but also from drug group to drug group, as determined by one's personal pharmacopoeia.

Those who die of lethal doses of psychostimulants, opiates, orgasmics, or electrode-induced catatonias, however, provide the raw material for the enormous organ harvesting market. By 2019, most well-off people, nearing eighty and vigorous, have usually undergone at least one major organ transplant. And those who can afford it often have block transplants: heart-lung; liver, pancreas, spleen, kidney. It's part of living well.

The age of transplantation began in the 1980s with the discovery of the immunosuppressant cyclosporine. Before the Swiss pharmaceutical company, Sandoz, manufactured cyclosporine in 1979, transplantation usually failed because of graft rejection. After cyclosporine there was scarcely ever an instance of clinically diagnosable rejection of an allograft (transplanted organ). By the 1990s, it was a relatively routine procedure to transplant not only major organs and organ-blocks, but also bone marrow, skin, and intestine. With the turn of the century came nerve-regeneration techniques, and, as a consequence, hands, feet, arms, and legs were salvaged from the dead for new life on torsos of accident victims.

The unremitting anxiety (forewarned of years earlier in the *New England Journal of Medicine*) was that the donors on the operating table were not, after all, dead. And that the organ recovery process might itself be killing the patient, and that they, the staff, trained to save the lives of human beings, were murdering people day after day.

Nurses and orderlies were reporting insomnia, nightmares, ulcers, and disintegrating marriages. This stress was caused by caring for dead who looked warm, well-colored, healthy—as if they were enjoying a light peaceful sleep—chests moving up and down, kidneys making urine, hearts beating regularly. Should a donor "get sick" or have a heart attack, the staff would rush in and resuscitate.

The operating room (OR) was the scene of the greatest tension: In the past, there was no reason to send the dead to surgery. And the living have always been anesthetized when entering the OR. So when a brain-dead patient was wheeled into an OR, he or she would look no different to the doctors and nurses than someone brought in for appendicitis. But after long hours of surgery, instead of sending the patient to the recovery room to wake up, the anesthesiologist halted the life processes, and the body was sent to the morgue. This could be very upsetting, especially if the neomort were a four-year-old child in perfect health except for a fatal brain injury. From the earliest days of organ retrieval, as reported in the *New England Journal of Medicine*, the jittery OR staff sometimes sensed a "presence" or "spirit" in the room during retrieval surgery.

The strike was precipitated by a suit against one retrieval hospital by the family of a donor who claimed that the donor's body was ill-tended and that surgery had ruined the corpse. And the courts had awarded the plaintiff his case. The strike lasted for three months during which time one-fourth of the usual number of transplant procedures were undertaken. And it ended only when staff salaries were boosted and the AMA created a new specialty dealing with the living dead, combining pathology, surgery, and intensive-care techniques. A new paramedical profession was defined. This encompassed training in mortuary sciences and "grief therapy" for the survivors. Schools of mortuary science also gained new technologies for sustaining in the dead an illusion of life by applying some of the techniques used in the extraordinary technology of organ maintenance. Today, bodies on display at wakes often "breathe" and are warm to the touch.

At the turn of the century there was a breakthrough in organ storage. Previously, doctors had been able to keep kidneys "alive" outside the body for no longer than three days. And other organs were even more perishable; hearts could be preserved about four hours in a saline solution; livers up to ten hours. Lungs deteriorated so quickly that the whole-body host had to be transported to the hospital where the recipient lay waiting. The short lives of organs made procurement a continuously high-pressured, emergency proposition and posed incessant logistics problems in transportation and surgical timing.

In 2001, an organ incubator was designed; it was a computerized series of chemical baths and solutions that allowed organ banks to "plug in" the various body parts and keep even the most delicate lung alive up to six months. This took the pressure off the surgeons and recipients and allowed the organ transplant facilities to suspend long-term maintenance of beating-heart cadavers in ICUs and send them to their final resting places.

The twenty-first century is a transplant-crazy era. And although there seems to be a new organ bank opening on every corner, there is no way to keep up with the demand. Artificial organs, unlike artificial limbs, have been unpopular. Although the Jarvik-27 can sustain a person for up to seven weeks, a real heart is desirable in the long run. Other organs have been too complicated to simulate with long-term success, except skin. Artificial skin is now used for cosmetic purposes as well as for burn victims and grafting. Electronic ear implants are popular—especially augmented devices to hear the higher and lower frequencies generated by new instruments.

The most recent breakthrough in transplantation is in the area of whole-limb retrieval, although only the superrich, the powerful, and the demigods of sports will have the procedure done because it costs an arm and a leg.

After a motorcycle accident in 2013, Archer had his crushed left hand replaced. In the most expensive limb transplant on record (it cost $2 million), the magnate received the hand of a concert pianist, who died of an OD from a drug that heightened musical sensitivities to (in his case) a lethal pitch. Archer was so pleased with his long, supple new fingers that he wanted the pianist's right hand, too. But it had already been donated to someone else.

Since the ancients, people had dreamed of splicing limbs from one body to another. Microsurgery, the restitching of severed veins and nerves back together, provided the groundwork. Cyclosporine was the next step. But the problem of nerve regeneration plagued limb transplantation until the late 1990s.

Today, the problems of nerve regeneration are nearly solved thanks to a process developed in the twentieth century by NIH neuroscientist Luis de Medinaceli. The technique is streamlined now, and besides the 300,000 accident-replacements, another 150,000 cosmetic limb transplants were conducted last year. (Meanwhile, whole limb regeneration is being attempted at Starfish Institute in La Jolla, California.)

What remains is the Mt. Everest of neurosurgical problems: central nervous system transplantation. The dream of whole-brain transplantation is not yet realized. However, a right cortex of one Doberman pinscher has been successfully transplanted to another dog, a beagle. And although the functions of the transplanted brain seem normal, it is difficult to know what mind/body dichotomies present themselves to the canine psyche. It remains for human brain transplants to investigate questions of consciousness. Indeed, there is a chance for immortal consciousness in the future—for a person to have his entire cortex, limbic system, cerebellum, and brain stem lifted out of an old, dying body and rehoused in a young beating-heart cadaver. In this case, the brain-dead neomort's function would be reversed. Instead of being stripped for parts, it would be brought back to life with the consciousness of a brain-live, but body-dead, donor.

Just as whole-body plastic-surgery lifts were popular in the 2010s, now brain grafting is the rage among the rich. At first, brain allografts were for therapeutic purposes—relief from Parkinson's, Alzheimer's, and so on. In the case of Parkinsonism, the general course was to transplant cells from the patient's own adrenal medulla gland into the brain to manufacture epinephrine that in turn stimulated the production of dopamine. This procedure was successful enough, but by the twenty-first century the substantiae nigrae, the afflicted dopamine-producing area of the brain, of fetuses were being implanted with great success.

Today, abortion is still the primary means of obtaining fetal tissue. Pregnant women all over the world are given significant financial incentives to undergo abortions rather than bear children. The fetal brain tissue is now used to correct lesions in the frontal lobes, the part of the brain involved in planning and forethought. Archer and many conglomerate executives favor neural allografts in the lobes to give them a competitive edge in the boardroom. While he was having the lobe implant Archer went ahead with a fetal substantia nigra allograft as well—a little added vigor to muscular performance can always come in handy, he said at the time.

In the 1990s, despite all the drug cocktails and allografts, death still triumphed at eighty-five to ninety. Archer was growing impatient with the pace of life-extension research. While he toyed with the idea of a thymus graft, his son Andrew approached him with a proposal to "resurrect" endocrinologist Donner Denckla. The radical experimenter of the 1980s was still alive, but had not done research in more than a decade. Denckla had originally proposed that a mysterious pituitary hormone he called DECO (decreasing oxygen consumption hormone) might be responsible for the inexorable decline and fall of all living creatures. He thought that the molecule might be responsible for some aspect of growth at puberty, and after its work was done, would turn into a slow poison.

His experiments involved removing the pituitaries of rats and giving them hormone supplements to keep them alive. In older rats without pituitaries, the ravages of aging receded with astonishing rapidity: their pelts became thick and shining; their energy levels returned to those of adolescent rats. For a decade, Denckla bucked the tide of opposition and funding cut-offs in solitude. But he failed to isolate DECO. Finally he stopped, went home to Woods Hole, and chartered his sailboat to make a living. When asked why, he shrugged his shoulders and muttered that death must defeat life, or something to that effect.

By the 1990s, the world had nearly achieved zero population growth. When Andrew Archer approached Denckla, the scientist decided humanity might be ready to handle the consequences of DECO's existence. So he decided to isolate it, and in a few years achieved his goal. He purified and synthesized the hormone and went on to discover the hypothalamic releasing factor that triggered it's release from

"Grief therapy" is available to the families of organ donors.

the pituitary. From this releasing factor—a simpler molecule—he fashioned a blocking agent, or antagonist. The anti-DECO sent false signals to the hypothalamus and the brain stopped ordering up more of the lethal hormone.

By 2001, Denckla had taken the DECO blocker and Archer soon followed. Within a month the tycoon's ninety-two-year-old body, including all the replacement parts, experienced a remarkable rejuvenation, all with an amazing lack of side effects. Denckla knew, however, that with his lab rats death came swiftly and at the usual time. He hoped he'd live long enough himself to see what happened to Archer on DECO-blocker. Would the treatment extend his life significantly, or would it be restricted to a rejuvenation effect?

By 2017, Archer Pharmaceutical was manufacturing anti-DECO, and Denckla began conducting a double-blind experimental study on volunteers over ninety. So far none has died of natural causes, and all have experienced rejuvenating effects. Nonetheless, it will be at least a decade before FDA approval opens the doors for mass consumption of Denckla's Fountain of Youth drug. Denckla is in no rush to market his discovery.

In spite of the emphasis on longevity, death in the twenty-first century is no longer a dirty word. In the previous century, life-prolonging techniques had overcontrolled the act of dying to the point where people revolted and liberated their own deaths from the medical profession. Individuals now take responsibility for determining their own demise; the medical profession has had to redefine the term "murder."

Since death often yields some reusable part, there is a kind of silver-lining component to bereavement. People feel that they will live on through their organs. The early 2000s gave rise to a "gloom boom" and a growing preoccupation with death, what Henry James called "the distinguished thing." Indeed, something of a thanatology has arisen in many countries, the first serious cult of death since that of the Tibetans or the ancient Egyptians.

The rite of passage of a fifty-year-old is to make a living will to guard against an overlong stay in the Struldbruggian purgatory of senility or stroke. Euthanasia clauses are routinely included in wills and insurance policies. A one-time euthanasia license is available to family members, but to get it the applicant has to go before a panel to show cause and means.

By the year 2000, there were few permanently unconscious patients in the world—only a few eccentrics wanted to preserve their comatose loved ones, usually for sexual purposes. Right to Die societies were popular in the late 1900s, but have been replaced with How to Die societies. Today, how-to books, videos, and 3-V taped "guides" enjoy brisk sales. The Koestler Company manufactures an array of euthanasia medications, involving various natural and artificial opiates and hallucinogens mixed with lethal doses of synthetic hemlock and other, Dionysian, poisons. Courses in death, based on an idea of twentieth-century novelist Saul Bellow, train people to sink gradually into oblivion so that no great change will take place when they die. People plan their death experiences with the care of elaborate birthday parties. One can program one's passing with visions of paradise, trips down memory lane, twenty-four hours of mathematical genius, or aesthetic insight, sexual ecstacy, or solemn ritualistic ceremonies. Such eschatological authorities as Aquinas, Kierkegaard, and Sartre have been replaced by Bowie, Prigogine, and Mandelbrot, presenting new beliefs about the hereafter that in turn reflect new attitudes about the world. (Hell, for example, is now seen as the heat death of the universe, the everlasting Entropy. Fire and brimstone is as out of fashion as nuclear war.)

For cancer patients beyond the reach of treatment, hospices now provide elegant seaside or mountain retreats or fantasylands where, high on dosages of narcoleptics, the dying are able to end their days in painless luxury.

Self-determination is also the main factor in financing death. In the last century, costs were exceeding $3,000; funeral services were often more expensive than weddings. As a result, people stopped having funerals and began perfunctory cremations. Funeral parlors declined from 24,000 in the United States in 1960 to 10,000 by 1990. The cut-and-dried nature of death actually served to deny the reality of mortality—the fact that death had occurred but that a life had been led. Funerals and grief rituals were too vital to the living to be suppressed, and a backlash set in. The first indication was the popularity of long-term financing of funerals and burial: "Save $600 now while you can do what has to be done"; "Don't let the cost of dying do you in, plan in advance."

Now, 70 percent of all adults pay for their funeral on "preneed" plans. The financing, offered along with fire, theft, accident, and life insurance, has become a hedge against inflation. Preneed starts with a basic coffin or cremation plus funeral. Funeral arrangements are sold on the installment plan, like furniture or washing machines. Buying cemetery space is a straightforward real estate transaction. At an additional price, funeral arrangements include choice of casket, flowers, music, food, and pall bearers. When the contract "matures" (i.e., the person dies), the mortician reviews the specifications with the deceased's family.

In the twenty-first century, funerals have made a big comeback, rivaling weddings in opulence, pomp, and ceremony. The old-fashioned New Orleans jazz funeral—replete with a marching band and dancing in the streets—is a favorite. Services are now held in private homes, nightclubs, spacecraft launching pads, museums, city parks, and amusement complexes.

Preservation of the body—one of the most primitive and uniquely human activities—is still a combination of art and science. Surprisingly, the only advance in mortuary science in two centuries was the invention sixty years ago of the motorized embalming machine to drive the fluids through the veins and arteries. The basic embalming fluid—formaldehyde—is the same as in the nineteenth century. Morticians all have their secret blends, however: brews of formaldehyde, synergists (the secret ingredients), quaternary compounds and other disinfectants, chelating agents, conditioning agents such as sodium salts of various organic and inorganic acids, surfactants (that lower surface tension for better penetration), humectants such as glycerine, buffer salts (to maintain basic pH), alcohols and carbitols, dyes, perfumes, and cosmetics.

Morticians in the twenty-first century still are trying to overcome formaldehyde's tendency of turning the departed into gray, stony hard, very dead-looking corpses. Yet life-simulating chemicals undercut formaldehyde's considerable preservative properties. Mortuary scientists are ever experimenting with advanced polymers, spin-offs of the "Star Wars" technology, as well as flash-freezing techniques, and a mortician who can give the deceased a Sleeping Beauty touch is the envy of his colleagues.

Interment in terra firma is still the commonest form of disposal. New ceramic caskets have largely supplanted the "wooden overcoat" of past centuries as the "six-foot bungalow." And there is a full spectrum of high-tech choices in tombstones, mausoleums, and sarcophagi. The solar-powered tombstone, originally designed in the twentieth century by engineers O'Piela and Zalazny, is a big seller. The eight-inch diameter, three-foot-long cylinder contains a digitally recorded message from the decedent. The message can be anywhere from three minutes to half an hour in length. An activating mechanism plus speakers are housed in the core and base of the marker. An electronic beam turns on the recording when someone comes within a foot of the device. Imagine the cacophony on certain days, Mother's Day for example, where all the moms are giving their last lectures on grooming, manners, etc. It is guaranteed to withstand extremes of heat and cold and last for two centuries.

The newest designs for grave markers contain video screens and tapes of the late lamented. Some talking tombstones also offer a telephone or videophone hook-up via a special 900 number that links the survivors to the grave for memorial occasions. Cosmic Catafalque Company offers a walk-in mausoleum with a hologram and automatically activated music; other frills include ever-fresh flowers and perfumes. Roboticized simulacra of the dead recently appeared on the market. Like the talking tombstone, or the hologrammed mausoleum, the life-sized robot requires preneed financial planning on the part of the individual. The computerized, automated replica encased in a skin-toned vinyl covering costs around $50,000. But for that price you can match the talking robot with your own values, opinions, and preferences by means of a personalized expert system data base. It can also be programmed to sing, dance, or do simple household chores.

True necrophiliacs are taking advantage of freeze-dried embalming techniques and are having the dead "mounted" in their homes, rather like animal trophies or large paperweights. These taxidermical marvels are often fixed with Mona Lisa–like smiles—additional reminders of the eternal enigma of death.

For the poor and the secular-minded, cremation is the usual means of disposal. Crematoriums have made millionaires of people such as Charles Denning, the self-styled "Colonel Cinders." His Neptune Society has advertised $500 cremations for thirty-five years and handles over 100,000 cremations a year in his "burn and strew" franchises.

For space fanatics, burial in zero-g is de rigueur. Since 1987, rockets from Space Services, Inc., the Houston-based commercial launching firm headed by NASA astronaut Deke Slayton, have blasted capsules containing the cremains of fifteen thousand souls into Earth orbit at

22,000 miles. Until the year 2000, the Celestic group of Melbourne, Florida, had a virtual monopoly on space burial. But as costs fell, they could no longer handle the business volume, and several new morgueships went into operation. The lipstick-tube sized space urns are expected to remain in orbit 63 million years.

Deep-space launches eject the crematory capsules beyond Earth's gravitational pull. People like Archer arrange for whole-body space burials. This particular stairway to heaven has the added benefit of pristine preservation for the grateful dead, until the death of the universe—waterless, airless perpetuity—safe from land developers and graverobbers. "You will not be cold there/you will not wish to see your face in a mirror/There will be no heaviness. . . ." (in the words of Walter de la Mare).

And the mourners? Attempts at contacting the dead have become vehement, employing all the devices of modern technology in the as-yet futile thrusts against the veils of mortality. There have been satellite transmission clubs, sending messages from geosynchronous orbit; computer networks; and video searches for the astral plane. It is not uncommon for those who are about to die to serve as "messengers" (often for a fee) to those on the other side. (This is scarcely a modern idea, though. When the great nineteenth-century British prime minister, Disraeli, was told that Queen Victoria wanted to visit him as he lay dying, he remarked: "Why should I see her? She will only want me to give a message to Albert.")

Perhaps the most morbid (and dangerous!) of the necrophilic pre-occupations of the twenty-first century, however, are the near-death experience (NDE) societies, sometimes called Kübler-Ross clubs in honor of the Swiss-born pioneer of studies in death and dying. The practitioners use drugs, asphyxiation, and other means of almost finishing themselves off in order to feel the extraordinary "white light" and extrasomatic sensations that, in the last century, allegedly accompanied close brushes with death due to accident, heart attack, and so on. The NDE societies were outlawed in 2014 because there is a disconcerting point where near-death indeed overreaches its target and becomes death. With increasing frequency we find the remains of NDEers who have accidentally gone over the edge. But like certain Asian religions of antiquity, these societies believe that life is merely a preparation for death, and the closer to death one can be from day to day, the better. Whether these cults achieve their goal of establishing near-death as a daily state of mind remains to be seen.

As we all know, serious thoughts on death are never completely free of ambiguity. Most of us, however, echo the sentiments of British statesman Lord Palmerston, who, on his deathbed, said, "Die, my dear doctor? That's the last thing I shall do!" And even as I write these words I feel a certain desire to end it all, to merge with the stream of Lethe, to float to the Tibetan's Realm of the Blue Buddha, to sit on God's Fifth Hand. . . . Here I am, in my office on the 144th floor of the Laser Building, built by Mr. Archer himself in 2011. If only the windows would open! Is my heart about to infarct? My liver is the third replacement and almost a decade old. If I don't get a new one . . . kaput. Death will come in on its chimp knuckles, just as it did to Russell Hoban's Kleinzeit, hooting "Hoo hoo . . . I'll bloody tear you apart. Any time's my time and I'm going to have you now. Now now now."

WAR

There had long been a growing awareness among the rulers of the U.S.S.R. of increasing strains within the Warsaw Pact, which could hardly be contained without a signal military victory over the capitalist West. There had also been, among the top people in the regime, a very real fear of Germany. There had even been some fear of the capacity of the Federal Republic to lead the United States into an aggressive war against the communist East.

The real causes of this war between the Eastern and the Western blocks will long be a matter for debate. Whatever they were, the fighting could not, it now seems, find its resolution anywhere but in Europe. Its focal point could be nowhere but in the Federal Republic of Germany.

The Third World War was widely expected to be the first nuclear war—and perhaps the last. It turned out to be essentially a war of electronics.

—General Sir John Hackett,
The Third World War

Previous page: With the sophistication and speed of modern fighter planes, war will strike so quickly that evacuation of major metropolitan areas may not be possible.

World War III started just one year ago today with a workers' strike in the city of Schwerin, East Germany, close to the West German border. It was a raw and chilly morning, July 20, 2018. The work force at the Josef Stalin Steel Mill, angered by an increase in their required overtime without extra pay, took to the streets with shouts and banners. Soon, thousands of townspeople joined their ranks. The city government sent police to quell the strike—and quickly saw them join the strikers. With that, the East German government was faced with a direct challenge to its rule.

It responded by sending in troops. These young soldiers, however, were as dissatisfied as the people of Schwerin, and it was soon evident to them that, being so close to the border, they could readily head west if things got too rough. Their commander ordered them to fire upon the strikers. They refused, and the government denounced them as mutineers. With that, they could not easily go back; most of them quickly broke ranks and joined the city police and the people. And matters rapidly began to get out of hand.

The hope of many is that wars in 2019 will be fought only between armies of unfeeling robots. Unfortunately, war always results in pain, death, and suffering to real human beings. (© Dan McCoy)

The fighter-bombers of the twenty-first century will cruise at altitudes up to 100,000 feet, accelerating to five times the speed of sound. (© Russell Munson)

Opposite: Detection, imagery, and cybernetic reflexes may be more pivotal in determining the winner of World War III than traditional values, such as bravery and fighting skill. (*Above right* and *below* © Dan McCoy)

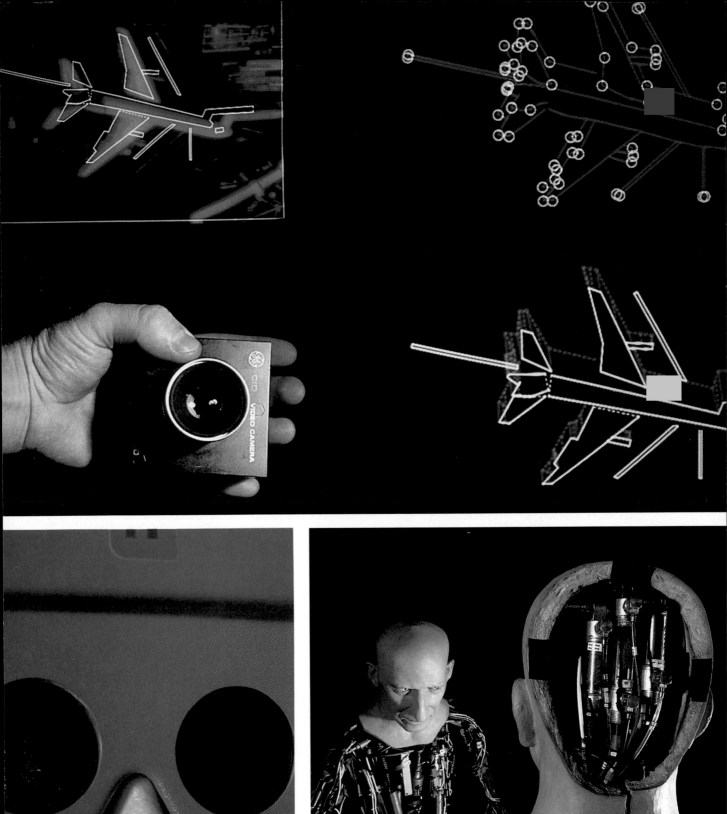

cidental" Soviet air attacks, decided to push farther east. They knew this would lend heart to the revolt in East Germany, and that NATO then would face a demand not to abandon the Schwerin people to the Soviet Union's tender mercies. As soon as their troops crossed the border, the people began to shout "Freedom!" Word quickly spread, and by the next day the Soviet command knew it faced an entirely new crisis.

They couldn't count on the loyalty of their East German allies; that was certain. Moreover, during the NATO air attack on the Vistula bridges, polished troops had deliberately fired their missiles too late or too early. This meant Poland was disloyal, also. Thus, the Kremlin reached a set of decisions. Its forces near Schwerin were to attack and destroy the West German divisions now in East Germany. Its armies in Byelorussia, near Poland, were to move into that country, overawing any disloyal garrisons and establishing a firm link to East Germany. And the U.S. would face an ultimatum: Stand down and call off the NATO forces, or the Soviet armies would invade West Germany.

Now only a quick agreement, negotiated over the hot line between Moscow and Washington, could avert full-scale war. The U.S. proposed that both sides stand down and demobilize. But to Moscow, that was unacceptable. Riots and demonstrations were taking place in much of East Germany, Poland, and Czechoslovakia; only a massive show of force could preserve the Warsaw Pact. But if NATO demobilized amid this show of Soviet force, that would mean the virtual end of NATO. Still, while both sides continued to mobilize, our president and their premier kept on exchanging messages. Then, without warning, the West German Third Panzergrenadier Division, a mechanized-infantry force, clashed with the II Corps of the Soviet Second Tank Army, on the outskirts of Schwerin.

On both sides, the tanks were formidable fighting machines. Low-slung and speedy, their usefulness was greatly increased by their reliance on what NATO referred to as Chobham armor. This was a lightweight, very strong, laminated structure of steel and aluminum plates with woven fabric and ceramic materials between the layers of metal. This armor afforded much better protection than the old-style steel plate of the previous century.

From inside the turret, a tank driver viewed the world on a set of flat-screen TV monitors. These not only showed views in visible light and infrared; there also was passive microwave. This took advantage of the natural wavelengths emitted by all objects in the surrounding world, which could be picked up and used to display images resembling those of a radar screen. Among these natural emissions were some at radar wavelengths. Passive microwave images were completely weatherproof, with neither rain nor fog interfering with these wavelengths. Moreover, by avoiding the use of a radar transmitter, a tank could keep from sending out a beam that was likely to be detected, betraying its position.

Linked to the TV monitors was a microcomputer incorporating artificial intelligence to find and highlight patterns. It worked somewhat like the image-processors used in planetary exploration, which could take a murky gray TV image and turn it into a sharp photo of a planet's surface. In wartime, these patterns frequently would show a target— an enemy emplacement, perhaps, or another tank. When a tanker saw such a target, he would prepare a round for firing by transferring the target image into the round's own microcomputer. Its own TV system and artificial intelligence then would guide it in to a hit.

Nevertheless, commanders on both sides recognized that their tanks were vulnerable. Tanks, like everything else, emitted their own passive microwaves, which could be picked up by a smart missile. Such missiles also could home in by means of lasers, using the same technique that had proven so successful in knocking out the Vistula bridges. A firing officer would spot a target on a TV monitor and find the precise point to be hit. In Warsaw, that had been the bridge supports; in a tank battle, that could be the lightly armored hatch or the treads. Once the target's image was loaded into the missile's electronics, it would aim a laser at the designated point while in flight, and home in on the bright reflected point of light.

Tanks had improved their survivability in recent years by incorporating their own lasers for missile defense. These were not powerful enough to destroy a round in flight, but they were quite capable of blinding the sensitive optics—if they could be aimed quickly enough. Nevertheless, these tank lasers themselves relied on optical systems, which were vulnerable to an enemy's lasers. All this meant that a tank force had to be prepared to exchange not only gun and missile fire, but laser fire. What was more, the computerized shells and antitank missiles cost as little as one-thousandth as much as a battle tank—and in a battle, commanders could count on scoring at least two hits with every three shells or missiles.

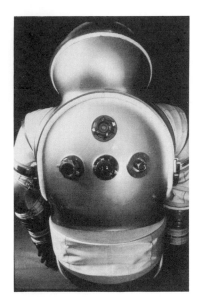

War in space is always a threat, but terrestrial war must be equally avoided.

Both sides, therefore, relied on seeking to concentrate massive forces that could destroy the enemy in a single strike. For the offensive-minded Soviets, those forces continued to include tanks in huge numbers, supported by fighter aircraft. For NATO, which sought largely to hold its own, the forces were built around antitank weaponry, including helicopters carrying their own missiles. The Soviets had over fifty thousand tanks available to them, and for years had been building new ones at the rate of two thousand a year. But NATO had for a long time been buying twelve thousand antitank weapons a year, at a far lower overall cost.

Everyone appreciated that the battlefield was no place for an infantryman. The Soviets were well-equipped with nerve gas and had all along made it clear that they would use it whenever they saw an advantage. NATO, with its interest in high tech, had devised low-power lasers that could rapidly sweep a battlefield, blinding the retinas of enemy soldiers. NATO also had high-powered microwave generators that could produce excruciating pain by burning a soldier's skin as in a microwave oven or by heating his bones. Thus, both sides kept their soldiers within turrets or cockpits, viewing the outside with TV monitors.

Both sides also appreciated that, along a heavily armed front, the side that struck first, thereby giving away its position, might well be the more vulnerable side—unless it could strike with overwhelming force. Even on a smoky, rainy battlefield at night, passive microwave offered plenty of opportunity to see without being seen. Thus, as the Soviet and NATO divisions maneuvered around Schwerin, both sides kept watch for an opportunity to launch a knockout strike, which would leave the enemy in that sector with little or no power for a counterblow.

In the early evening of July 27, a Soviet corps commander saw his chance. His command featured over a thousand late-model tanks, supported by several hundred tactical missiles. Twelve miles to the southwest, out of the range of tanks' gunfire, was the West German division, with a much smaller number of tanks, but with two thousand tactical missiles. The Soviet general decided to launch a coordinated missile strike aimed at the Germans. At 7:14 P.M., amid a pelting rain laced with snow, the Soviet rockets fired a barrage, and the strike was on.

Within three seconds of their launch, a NATO reconnaissance jet, using passive microwave, picked up the heat of their plumes. An on-board battle analyzer recognized that it was seeing a massed firing of rockets and alerted the headquarters of the Third Panzergrenadier Division. There, another computer decided that our forces had at most twenty seconds to fight back or they would be destroyed, and it alerted the aircraft: Provide coordinates. The jet's computer switched on a xylophone radar, which emitted short bursts of power at low intensity, rapidly skipping between different frequencies, like notes played on a musical instrument.

A Soviet frequency analyzer detected the pulses and launched a ground-to-air missile. It took all of thirteen seconds for the missile to destroy the recon aircraft, but in less than a hundred milliseconds the plane had done its job. Its radar had located and accurately imaged the Soviet tank force, and its inertial navigation system had produced a firm set of map coordinates. Now the main computer in the Third Division had what it needed. It quickly gave firing orders to the NATO missiles, launching them in a spread that was calculated to destroy the full II Corps of the Second Tank Army. Seventeen seconds after the launch of the Soviet salvo, the last NATO missile had cleared its launcher.

The Soviet strike, therefore, hit empty launchers; the missiles were already on their way. Of course, the Soviet missiles' TV systems were smart enough to pick up the plumes of our rockets and to home in on them, but there were too many NATO missiles in flight. Indeed, those that were hit absorbed missiles that otherwise would have hit West German tanks. At the same time, a number of our tanks succeeded in using lasers to blind the optics of Soviet warheads.

The Soviet corps commander had not expected our counterattack to be made while his rockets were in flight, or that it would be so effective. He had never encountered such a counterattack during his war games and maneuvers; but this was a real war, where surprises could be expected. Within a minute, it was all over. Two tank armies had fought a battle in which no tank fired upon another. On the Soviet side, II Corps was left with only twenty-nine effective tanks, out of a thousand. On the German side, the Third Division had over fifty effectives. But this was not the only measure of the battle. Three NATO rockets had homed in on the corps command post, the microwave image of which had been stored in their memories. The general was found dead in the wreckage, a field telephone still clasped in his hand.

This battle removed the last hopes of a negotiated stand-down. For the first time in over seventy years, Soviet and German forces had clashed—and the Germans had won. In all its propaganda, at the heart of its policy in Eastern Europe, the Soviet government had all along stressed the danger that West Germany would rise again to challenge Moscow, as Hitler had done before. By the morning of the next day, then, Moscow had made its decision. They would launch an invasion of West Germany. This would include coordinated air attacks on transportation and supply facilities, spearheaded by a massive air strike at NATO's main supply and command centers, at Heidelberg and Kaiserslautern near the French border.

The standard fighter-bombers employed by both sides were highly capable and versatile. Their engines, built with highly heat-resistant and strong materials, could accelerate them in vertical flight, like rockets, or drive them in level flight at five times the speed of sound, cruising at altitudes up to 100,000 feet. Using these engines, the aircraft could take off with full loads of fuel and weapons from runways as short as 1,500 feet. Following a mission, they could deflect their jets downward out of the belly of the aircraft to land vertically, thus returning safely even to an air base whose runways had been thoroughly cratered by bombs.

Lightweight composite materials resembling plastics made up their wings and fuselages, making it possible to adjust their wings' curvature while in flight, which gave the fighters tremendous agility while reducing drag to a minimum. The wings, in turn, were swept forward, for even lower drag. On-board computers adjusted their controls twenty times a second. The aircraft were aerial acrobats, ready to snap into a roll or turn at the slightest provocation, requiring computers to remain under control whether maneuvering or flying straight or level.

These same computers acted as versatile autopilots. They could land the fighters on the deck of an aircraft carrier pitching in heavy seas or fly low in darkness and fog, hugging rugged terrain, scanning it with little squirts of radar, flying around hills when necessary. If an anti-aircraft missile hit the aircraft, systems automatically executed the needed maneuvers, leaving the pilot free to think about what to do next. Two such fighters could do the work of one hundred World War II B-17 bombers.

These were the aircraft that the Soviets launched against Heidelberg and Kaiserslautern. They came in "hit 'em high, hit 'em low" formations, with three squadrons, thirty aircraft, directed against each of their two objectives. The high squadron rode at ninety thousand feet, safe from defending missiles but able to shoot at defending aircraft. At treetop level were the two low squadrons that would carry out the attack.

This gave the Soviets the advantage of surprise. Their aircraft had the long range necessary to reach high altitudes while within the Soviet Union itself, feint an attack in the north of Germany, then meet up with fighters based near Berlin to proceed to the southwest, the direction to their targets. Moreover, they were very stealthy, hard to detect. Their surfaces had radar-absorbent coatings and featured rounded edges to reduce reflections. Engines and other hot spots were well buried within insulation to reduce the risk of detection by heat-seeking infrared sensors. Electronic countermeasure systems sent out a weak signal designed to deal with the natural passive micro-wave emissions, which could not be masked but could be made to appear diffuse, like the emissions from a cloud.

At treetop level, the attackers could more easily evade the ground defenses, but might be vulnerable to NATO aircraft with look-down, shoot-down systems. These could pick an airplane out of the ground clutter and prepare firing instructions. But the Soviets had such systems, too, and the high squadron in each attack was prepared to use them against any NATO fighters that cared to intervene.

Elements of the U.S. Air Force, at Rhein-Main Air Force Base near Frankfurt, had the fighters that would have to deal with this coordinated attack. In principle, our radars and detectors might pick up the high squadrons at a considerable distance, allowing our fighters to scramble into the air. By engaging the high squadrons in dogfights, we might shoot them down, clearing the way for attacks on the low squadrons once our planes descended to a more convenient altitude. But all this would take time: Time to identify the enemy aircraft and determine their course, time for the climb to altitude and the air battles, time to descend, time to attack the Soviet aircraft at low altitude. And at the speeds of supersonic jets, amid the narrow confines of a West Germany that was not quite the size of Oregon, time fought on the side of the Soviets.

Thus, most of the attackers eventually were shot down, but only after they had laid waste to the military centers that were their objectives. During the most stunning parts of their attacks, they released canisters of highly explosive liquids, forming widespread mists. When they touched off these fuel-air explosives with igniters, the resulting flame concussions were five times more powerful than from an equal weight of ordinary explosives. With munitions and supplies blasted and burning, tall pillars of black smoke rose over Heidelberg and Kaiserslautern.

Using the same tactics, the Soviet Air Force proceeded with similar raids against NATO bases, ports, supply and transportation centers, and airfields. Yet they paid a shocking price, and it was soon clear that if only the NATO defenses could hold, they would succeed in taking more than an adequate toll of Soviet aircraft. Moreover, at the end of the first day of these raids, the French prime minister declared that his country would work firmly and closely with NATO and would make good the supplies lost in the attacks. This was significant; the French had nuclear weapons, which would dissuade the Soviets from attacking many potential French targets.

At the same time, the president in Washington declared that by agreement with NATO and the French, all commercial air service across the Atlantic was suspended for the duration, effective immediately. Instead, the big jets would serve to form an air bridge across the ocean, to transport American and Canadian troops. Once in the battle zone they would join up with equipment and supplies already in position. Additional supplies, including weapons needed for a counteroffensive, would move by sea.

So the Yankees were once again poised to come to the rescue, just as in 1917 and 1941. As in those earlier wars, the question once again was: Would they arrive in time? World War III might well be over by the time the ships got there. If the Red Army would push to the Rhine and consolidate its position there, if the Red Air Force and Navy could sink the ships en route, then the Soviets would have their victory. This time the issue would be settled in days rather than years, but for the moment it was absolutely essential that the NATO forces on the scene hold against the Soviet invasion. The chief point of attack was the Fulda Gap.

Fulda lies close to the most southwesterly part of East Germany. Fifty miles away is Frankfurt, with a number of other major cities in the vicinity; the Rhine is only a little farther to the west. The country is ideal for tanks, with the broad Fulda Valley opening westward. The immediate threat came from the powerful Eighth Guards Army, supported by the First Tank Army and Third Shock Army. If they could

break through at Fulda, the Soviets could quickly seize a number of West Germany's major industrial cities, driving to the Rhine and cutting that nation in two.

For many years, NATO had been anticipating such an attack and had prepared a strong defense in the Fulda sector. Between Fulda proper and the East German border, for some ten miles, the terrain offered numerous good positions for antitank missile batteries, with considerable depth to their fields of fire. Much additional weaponry was available throughout central West Germany, capable of being quickly brought to bear on any attack near Fulda. The Soviets, for their part, were also aware of the NATO effort, and had been launching air and missile strikes to soften up the defenses, in preparation for the invasion.

Yet, ironically, one of the more effective weapons against the massed Soviet tanks was also one of the simplest: signs reading "Achtung: Minen." Few defenses were more unsettling to a tanker than mines

World War III will be dominated by high-tech machines, but human decisions make the difference.

planted in the ground. Certainly there were large numbers of them, planted along likely tank routes. They could ignore the light weight of farm equipment, then detonate under the heavy tread of a tank; they could allow several tanks to pass, then blow up the next one; they could even push a missile-launching tube up through the ground, to fire at a tank some distance away. But even where mines were entirely absent, the signs themselves were enough to make tank commanders slow down and proceed with considerable caution.

The invasion broke out along an eight-mile front at 3:00 A.M. on July 31. Fifteen thousand tanks, supported by two thousand aircraft, broke out of their revetments in East Germany and swiftly charged across the border. Nothing could stand for long against such an overwhelming assault, and the NATO command knew it. Their hopes for successful resistance rested on good intelligence from space and long-range tactical missiles, each armed with dozens of smart munitions.

Ordinary reconnaissance satellites were no match for the Soviet antisatellite weapons, which could maneuver into orbit alongside, then detonate. Instead, the air force would rely on its transatmospheric craft. Featuring advanced scramjet engines, these could cruise at orbital speeds in the upper atmosphere, at altitudes of forty miles. That was low enough for the atmosphere to offer considerable protection against orbiting laser and beam weapons, yet high enough for safety against antiaircraft missiles. With an ability to maneuver and thereby avoid predictable orbits, these craft could flash over central Europe from any direction, streaking back to the U.S. with their photos and images. The air force had a fleet of them; each one could make three flights a day.

At their best, their on-board cameras could make out the individual hull numbers painted on a tank. For the purpose of countering the developing invasion, though, they could provide information that was far more valuable: accurate map coordinates for Soviet weapons formations, particularly tanks as well as command centers. These coordinates, in turn, could be quickly fed into the computers of the long-range missiles. These were based in France, Belgium, the Netherlands, Great Britain, as well as in the Rhine country. From those locations, up to four hundred miles from Fulda, they could attack the Soviet tanks.

These missiles were of the cruise variety, carried aboard ordinary eighteen-wheeler trucks that could freely roam the highways and autobahns of Britain and western Europe, looking like everyday freight-haulers. But once given their orders, their drivers could pull off to the side of a road and open the roof. Each truck carried four missiles, which could rise vertically, quickly level off, then fly at treetop level to the destination. Once there, its imaging systems would look for the tanks. If they were somewhat spread out, the missile would disgorge thirty small rockets at once, each programmed to home in on its own tank. If the tanks were in a column, the cruise missile would fly along its length, dropping off the munitions one at a time.

Against these weapons, the main Soviet hope was to destroy the missiles in flight with look-down, shoot-down weapons aboard their aircraft. The NATO task, in turn, was to keep these aircraft sufficiently busy, dodging antiaircraft missiles and facing attack from fighters. All this meant that the invasion, once underway, would be prodigiously expensive in weaponry of all types. Tanks, aircraft, missiles—all would be expended at rates sufficient to deplete both sides' stocks in as little as two weeks of heavy fighting.

Within the Fulda sector, the goal of NATO was to keep the massed Soviet armies from making a breakout that could bring a swift advance to the Rhine. The issue hung in the balance for three days. The Soviets certainly were dogged. Time and again they drove forward in a massed formation only to see tanks in large numbers burst into flames as defending missiles appeared without warning. Still they pushed on, taking Fulda, advancing some twelve miles into West Germany. By the end of the third day, the invasion had run out of steam. Over twelve thousand tanks lay shattered in the woods and fields, while NATO air and missile attacks had made a shambles of the supply lines.

This, however, was only a lull, a time probably of no more than a few days for regrouping. The Soviets still had nearly thirty thousand tanks ready for use, capable of being brought up in little more than a week. The NATO forces, for their part, were running low on ammunition. They had bought time, perhaps as as much as ten days: Time for the Americans to get their troops and supplies into combat and to nullify what would otherwise be an unassailable Soviet advantage. But could the Yanks get through?

The outbreak of the war, the suspension of commercial air service, had trapped hundreds of thousands of panic-stricken businessmen and tourists in western Europe. But it rapidly became clear to them, as to everyone else, that the Soviets were interested in attacking targets of military significance, using precision-guided munitions, and that

Detonation simulation: Fortunately, the next war may not involve nuclear warheads.

Inset: Despite the proliferation of rockets and other unmanned weapons, airplanes are still important keys to twenty-first—century warfare.

hotels and apartments did not fall into that category. There would be no mass-bombing of cities this time, nor would civilians be made targets en masse. It was not that the Soviet high command was humane or respectful of human life. Indeed, just then they were showing themselves to be quite the opposite among the rebellious peoples of Poland, East Germany, and Czechoslovakia. But in a war against NATO's professional forces, the Soviets appreciated that a strict attention to military targets was the most effective way to fight.

Commercial airliners, escorted by fighter aircraft, were ferrying large numbers of reservists into airports in France and Italy, along with some light equipment. Missile launchers, helicopters, and even some tanks were also en route by air, in the transport aircraft of the Military Airlift Command. These could carry outsize loads to short runways, unloading quickly and flying off rapidly; they thus could operate more closely to the immediate battle zones.

Nevertheless, the main stores of equipment, including essential stocks of aviation fuel and gasoline, had to come by sea. This included U.S. Army supplies, carried in containers, large aluminum boxes that

could be transported by railroad flatcar or flatbed truck. At terminals in Baltimore and Elizabeth, New Jersey, steel cranes more than a hundred feet high were stacking these containers in tall piles on the decks and in the holds of fast, specialized cargo ships.

Also there were roll-on, roll-off ships, the RO-ROs, large seagoing ferries with ramps fore and aft. Tanks and other vehicles had been driven on board, to be driven off on the other side of the Atlantic. Other RO-ROs carried the trailers of semitrucks; by hooking up tractors, these could be driven directly off the ship and onto the European road network. There were barge-carriers, too, whose barges would be left in port for unloading. Conventional freighters were employed for outsize cargo, including the cranes and construction equipment needed to repair bomb damage and replace bridges.

The heart of such a convoy was a relatively modest number of specialized, highly capable ships that could make twenty-five knots. The container ships, the barge carriers, and the RO-ROs were particularly inviting targets, "the sort of honey that would attract a lot of Soviet flies," as one admiral put it. Thus, as a convoy put out to sea, it moved within a ring of frigates or destroyers to guard against air attack. A second such ring, sixty miles across, surrounded the inner ships for protection against submarines. Fifty miles ahead of the convoy rode a helicopter carrier, flanked by two attack subs, their sonar sweeping the sea in a further search for subs. Farthest ahead of all, as much as a hundred miles in the lead, an antisubmarine aircraft looped back and forth on patrol.

These were only the close-in defenses. During the first two days of a crossing, a convoy would be protected by air cover based in the United States; during the last two days, there would be air cover from Great Britain. But in the middle of each crossing was a stretch of two to three days when the convoys would face attacks from Soviet bombers based in the Kola Peninsula, the northeast part of Scandinavia. Therefore, part of our strategy was to send our largest carriers in a bold advance to the northwest of Norway, attacking enemy air bases, daring the Soviets to come out and fight. Our carriers were able in this way to tie down or destroy the Soviet forces, to keep them from attacking the sea-lanes.

So it was that the aircraft carriers *Theodore Roosevelt*, *Harry S Truman*, and *Ronald Reagan*, supported by powerful air and naval escorts, topped a speed of thirty knots as they swept north of Norway's

Lofoten Islands. In attacking bases on the Kola, this task force would draw out Soviet air and sea forces in huge counterattacks; the Americans and their NATO allies were gambling that they would be strong enough to destroy the enemy forces. It was a classic instance of the boast of John Paul Jones, "I intend to go in harm's way."

On the decks of the carriers, some sixty fighter aircraft stood armed and fueled. A dozen others were on combat air patrol three hundred miles to the northeast. Overhead, several airborne warning aircraft, their big radomes rotating, kept watch for the attack. They did not have long to wait. Out of the northeast, the radar operators picked up the returns from first one, then three formations of Soviet bombers, sixty in all. Each had four cruise missiles ready to launch against the American ships. Within seconds of the first report from the radar planes, vapor was rising along the lengths of the steam-driven catapults as the carriers launched their aircraft.

At speeds well above Mach 2, the fighters flew to the battle, each one armed with a variety of air-to-air missiles as well as a rapid-fire cannon for fighting at close quarters. From distances up to a hundred miles, the pilots picked out enemy bombers using their fire-control systems, launching up to six missiles at once, each against a different target. Now, with the two airborne fleets closing rapidly, the sky was filling with streamers of smoke as jet aircraft fell on both sides.

But the Soviets were suffering the heavier toll. Close in, weaving and dodging to escape enemy missiles, the Yanks listened for a growling tone in their headphones, the signal that their air-to-air missiles had locked onto a target and were within range. Time and again, when the pilots heard that growling, they knew that on-board computers were launching a missile at an enemy, "fire and forget," with assurance of a kill.

Still, the surviving Soviets kept coming on. Now, some 150 miles from the aircraft carriers, they began to launch their antiship missiles. As the last of them dropped clear of the bombers, the two air fleets broke off and turned toward their bases, for now rockets, not aircraft, would fly to defend the fleet. As the first Soviet cruise missiles came within thirty miles of the outlying destroyers and cruisers, shipboard radars tracked their flights, firing rockets every ten seconds against them. Closer in, other sea-launched missiles had their turn; these were well known for their ability to shoot down naval shells in flight. From the carriers, the distant sky to the northeast showed dozens of explosion-bursts, as the defending rockets found their targets.

Still, there were surviving cruise missiles making their way onward. Now the defending screen of destroyers and cruisers deployed electronic countermeasures. Some turned on radar transponders to echo back a delayed amplified return from tracking radars in the cruise missiles' guidance systems. The delays, a microsecond or two, made these ships appear well away from their actual location; the amplifications made small destroyers look as large as the carriers themselves. Other transponders, linked with lasers, returned especially strong radar, visible-light, and infrared beams to blind the missiles much like shining a bright light in a man's face. Still other systems emitted carefully prepared microwaves; when picked up by a passive microwave detector, these, too, would give destroyers the appearance of carriers. Some ships spewed out clouds of chaff, metallic foil, to produce the radar appearance of other large targets—the "window" invented by Sir Winston Churchill in World War II.

Then, as the missiles came especially close, they were met by the rapid fire of automatic machine guns. These guns were radar-guided and fired six thousand rounds per minute. Their radar could track both an incoming missile and the stream of bullets, then adjust the aim, walking the bullets into the path of the missile for a hit.

In the end, only three Soviet missiles found targets. One left a destroyer burning and dead in the water; a second blew a gaping hole in the side of a light cruiser. The third, confused by countermeasures, missed the vital center of the carrier *Roosevelt* and hit a helicopter close to the stern. A blazing fireball buckled deck-plates, enveloping nearby crewmen in flames. But damage-control parties swiftly shoved the burning chopper over the side and cleared away the wreckage. When the fighters came home, the *Roosevelt* was ready to recover its squadrons. The tally for that morning showed over thirty Soviet bombers lost. Our losses were twenty-one fighters, the destroyer, the cruiser—and two dozen flight-deck crewmen.

Later that same day, refueled and rearmed, these naval fighters formed up in high/low formation and struck at the bombers' main base, close to Murmansk on the Kola Peninsula. Again our high squadrons had the task of suppressing counterfire and engaging defending aircraft. The fighters left the base blasted and cratered; now it was

Murmansk that watched the black plumes of smoke rising from a burning military installation. From this mission, some 60 percent of our attacking aircraft failed to return.

The damage reports from the air battle and subsequent raid flashed swiftly to Washington, where the president was soon huddling with the National Security Council. They faced the problem of delicately calibrating the force to be brought against the Kola Peninsula. Murmansk was not only the location of the principal bomber base; it was also home for the Soviets' one priceless naval asset, their nuclear missile subs. These were already at sea, relying on the Soviet Air Force for protection.

"They'll go bananas if we send our carriers up there," the president had remarked a few days earlier. If our strike was too successful—if we succeeded in greatly weakening the Soviet Air Force in the Kola Military District—Moscow might well be tempted to fire the subs' intercontinental missiles rather than risk their loss. But too weak a strike would leave the Soviets free to attack our sea-lanes in the Atlantic. With the battle reports in hand, the president turned to the hot line.

He declared that our naval forces were there to protect the sea-lanes, not to attack Soviet missile subs in the Barents Sea. As a token of this, he stated that the carriers were under orders not to proceed past Norway's North Cape, the northernmost point of Scandinavia. The Soviet premier soon gave his reply: In no way could he trust the reassurances of a government with which he was at war. In response to our strike, he had already ordered his force to go on limited nuclear alert. However, as long as we stayed in the Norwegian Sea and avoided entering the Barents, he would refrain from going to a full nuclear alert, which effectively would put his force on a hair-trigger.

It was now a full week since the beginning of the Fulda battle. The Soviets had so far pushed a salient or bulge into the Fulda sector, advancing between ten and fifteen miles into West Germany. But this success had already cost them close to half of the tanks that were immediately ready at the outbreak of the war. To rebuild their force, they were rapidly moving tank battalions from the Ukrainian, Carpathian, and Baltic districts, within the Soviet Union proper.

NATO, for its part, was also rapidly preparing for a renewal of the battle. With the transatlantic air bridge holding firm, NATO was swiftly regaining its edge in light antitank missiles, which were readily transportable by air. Ships were docking in large numbers in Le Havre and other French ports. And with all this, the premier in Moscow had a great deal to think about.

First in his mind all along had been the continued control of Eastern Europe. But his tank forces, smashing their way into Warsaw, Prague, and other cities, had rapidly destroyed the armed resistance to continued Soviet domination. The KGB was briskly at work, rounding up tens of thousands of intellectuals, students, and other dissidents, loading them into boxcars, and sending them by slow train to detention centers in northeast Asia. With the rebellions well on their way to being crushed, he had to ask, in all seriousness, what his country might gain by continuing the war.

His troops held the Fulda salient; that was true. But another such battle would effectively deplete his tank reserves, reducing their numbers to a dangerous degree. The Soviet generals, who were supporting him in power, would not appreciate seeing their forces thus diminished. In particular, they would need to maintain tank forces in large numbers, within Poland, Czechoslovakia, and East Germany, lest the rebellions flare anew. Yet the time was not right to seek peace. As in so many earlier wars, events were now beginning to spiral out of control, with results that might neither be predicted nor kept within bounds.

One such event was even then developing, near Charleston, South Carolina, where the navy had a major submarine base. The U.S.S. *Halsey*, a missile sub, was putting to sea. It carried sixteen pop-up rockets tipped with multiple X-ray-laser warheads. If the Soviets were to fire their nuclear-tipped missiles, the sub would swiftly launch its rockets, which would pop up through the atmosphere. The X-ray lasers then would zap the missiles.

The payloads closely resembled hydrogen bombs and, like the H-bomb, relied on atomic bombs as triggers. They were designed to produce deadly beams of well-focused X rays, from lasers energized by an atomic bomb. When that bomb went off, its fireball would exist for some billionths of a second, within the warhead casting, as an intensely bright mass. Energy from that fireball would reflect off curving sheets of uranium and be focused upon a bundle of thin rods made of laser material. These, in turn, could each be pointed at a Soviet missile. When an atomic trigger went off, part of its power would be concentrated into intense laser beams of X rays, which would burn up a missile within a millionth of a second.

As the *Halsey* put to sea from its base in Charleston, a Soviet agent watched from the harbor bridge, then drove to a pay phone. Soon, coded messages flashed from a Soviet satellite, which directed a blue-green laser beam into the coastal waters. The laser could penetrate the water to a considerable depth. There, off the coast, was the missile sub *Sverdlovsk*, armed with thermonuclear warheads.

The navy had a number of methods for tracking such subs. There were sensitive hydrophones placed on the seabed to pick up sound from their propellers; navy commanders like to say that these phones could hear a fish farting a thousand miles away. Similar hydrophones were mounted on all our submarines. There were also nonacoustic methods for detection. One of the most effective was to look for the subtle infrared emissions that could betray the presence of heated water, warmed by a sub's nuclear reactor.

Another method relied on the fact that a sub's propellers produced vortices, whirling masses of water that would rotate for long periods. These vortices often disturbed the slopes of small ocean waves, as though the waves were moving over a tilted or humped surface. With appropriate radar or infrared systems scanning the sea near the horizon, these apparent tilts could be seen, disclosing a sub's presence. It was something like seeing a slight rise in land by the light of the setting Sun, whose rays grazed the land and made small slopes stand out sharply. Similarly, when radar or infrared waves grazed the ocean, they could disclose the changes in wave-slope from a submarine.

With these methods, the navy was in an excellent position to track the *Sverdlovsk*. But there were two other subs in the vicinity, of the types known in the West as Sierra II and Mike II. These had fuel-cell propulsion, which could produce a direct flow of electricity with high efficiency from stored fuels, leaving no plume of warm water. Also, they had electric-tunnel propulsion. Rather than using propellers, they relied on long tubes resembling hallways, which could generate electric and magnetic fields. Under their influence, seawater, which could also conduct electricity, would spurt out the back, thrusting the sub forward as if propelled by a jet.

These subs were also exceptionally quiet. What was more, they were prepared to communicate with each other, and with the *Sverdlovsk*, using secure underwater communications, making them capable of maneuvering and cooperating with each other without being detected. Their communications relied on highly accurate atomic clocks, which kept time to within a microsecond in a month. These were synchronized in port, along with sequences for rapid, random shifting of transmitting and receiving frequencies. With this, any two subs could exchange messages, skipping rapidly across many frequencies yet staying in tune with the changes, thanks to the synchrony of the clocks. No signal analyzer could cope with such randomness in frequency change. Even if we were to pick up such an underwater signal, it would sound like mere underwater crackling.

The *Sverdlovsk* was deliberately making a fair amount of noise; the *Halsey* knew it was there. The other two subs were quiet; we didn't know about them. But as the *Halsey* left port, the *Sverdlovsk* used its underwater communications to alert the other two subs. Slowly, carefully, the Sierra-class attack sub maneuvered into the *Halsey*'s "baffles," the turbulent and noisy wake where hydrophones had difficulty picking up sound.

The three Soviet subs soon formed a triangle, with the *Halsey* in the middle. Still, it was aware only of the *Sverdlovsk*. That sub now headed in the direction of the *Halsey*, making more noise to ensure that it would still be detected. The skipper of the *Halsey* turned away, to avoid being detected, and proceeded in the direction of the Mike-class sub, which was quietly lying in wait. Meanwhile, the Sierra remained on his tail, in his baffles, still undetected.

Suddenly, the *Halsey*'s sonar operators heard a piercing cacophony of sound. It was the active sonar from the Mike, now close enough to strike. The sound was so loud that the on-board computer was swamped, unable to pick out the bearing or direction of its source. The Mike, however, had an accurate fix on the *Halsey*'s location, and launched a torpedo.

The skipper, for his part, recognized immediately that an attack was imminent. He put on speed and threw his sub into evasive maneuvers. The torpedo missed, giving the *Halsey* a chance to flee to safety. Its skipper now steadied on a new course, away from the Mike, away from the *Sverdlovsk*—and straight into the vicinity of the waiting Sierra. Now it was the Sierra's turn to launch a torpedo. It struck the *Halsey* amidships, leaving it with a mortal wound.

That torpedo explosion, in turn, sent shock waves through the Pentagon and White House. If the Soviets were striking at our sea-based missile defense, that might well mean that they were preparing to overcome these defenses and launch a nuclear attack that would leave us without the means to retaliate. But in Moscow, the news brought quite a different reaction. In the wake of this success, the Soviets now had one last good chance to end the war before it could spiral into a thermonuclear exchange. The next day the premier convened the Supreme Soviet and addressed them in a speech that was meant for Western ears:

> Today, comrades, our glorious motherland stands everywhere victorious in arms. Our security forces have crushed the counter-revolutionary reactionaries who had sought to stir discontent within the fraternal nations of Poland, Czechoslovakia, and the German Democratic Republic. Our brave army and air force has dealt a resolute rebuff to the West German revanchists who had so foolishly sought to return to the Hitlerite path of conquest. More-over, we have succeeded in establishing an extremely favorable strategic position, by seizing the Fulda sector. And now our navy has struck at the heart of the Americans' vaunted Star Wars defenses by sinking a submarine virtually within sight of its harbor.
>
> Accordingly, we declare that America and its NATO lackeys must recognize our victory by agreeing to an armistice. Both sides will withdraw from the front, and their forces will stand down. A new border will be drawn between the German Democratic Republic and the German state to its west, reflecting the conquests of our army.

In Washington and Bonn, Moscow's strategy was obvious: Declare victory, and pull out. It meant they were willing to settle for a tie, a standstill cease-fire in which very little territory had actually changed hands. In December, the superpowers, with West Germany present in the discussions, drew a new border between the two Germanies. East Germany would receive the town of Fulda and its adjacent areas, which the Soviets had seized at great cost. West Germany, in turn, would gain the city of Schwerin, where it had all started.

By Christmas, air traffic was restored, and our troops were on their way home. It was possible to look around and to begin to appreciate what had happened. The main surprise was not that the war had been destructive, but that the destruction had been so localized and precise.

For well over half a century, all thought of war had been dominated by the threat of nuclear weapons. But now, World War III had come and gone, and had turned out very differently.

For generations, people had been haunted by the images of World War II, with its burned and blasted cities. But in World War III, there had been nothing remotely like that. Few cities showed the contrast more vividly than Hamburg, the great West German port on the Baltic. In July 1943, a major air raid had touched off a firestorm that killed fifty thousand civilians. Virtually the whole of the city and port had been reduced to gaunt burned walls, devoid of roofs. Nearly a million people were left homeless and without food.

The city had also been crippled by the air strikes of July 2018. But at war's end, one could fly over Hamburg and scarcely see any damage. At first glance, the port appeared untouched—until you noticed the twisted masses of steel beams that had been the cranes for container ships, essential for the port's operation. Tugboats lay blasted and sunk. The port captain's office was flattened. Railroad bridges and highway overpasses lay crumpled; the airport's runways and control tower looked like the cratered surface of an asteroid. But that was it. The residential and office districts had been completely untouched.

Much the same was true in other cities. In Cologne, the Rhine bridges lay in the river as piles of steel junk, but there was no other damage. Near Wyhl, further up the Rhine, was a nuclear power plant. Its transformer yard had been blown to pieces, its administration building was a wreck—but the reactor domes had merely been nicked by shrapnel. In Munich there had been a central telecommunications building, which now lay destroyed as by a wrecker's ball. In the adjacent buildings, windows had been broken by the concussions; and that was all.

In the Pentagon, as missiles had improved their accuracy over the years, there had been a standing joke about their warheads. The current intercontinental-range MARVs, Maneuvering Re-entry Vehicles, could strike a missile silo with an accuracy of six inches. The joke went that amid such precision, the warheads of the future still would be made with uranium and plutonium, but not for the sake of nuclear explosions. Instead, they would be appreciated because they were dense, heavy metals that could punch through a silo's hardened lid, like a cannon ball. No one had taken this idea seriously, of course. But World War III had come and gone, and had been fought with weapons not of mass destruction, but of discrete destruction. That old Pentagon chestnut seemed appropriate, to sum it all up.

Another place where one could sum it all up was Schwerin. That city came under West German administration on January 1, 2019, the day when the territorial transfers went into effect. This morning, July 20, in front of the city hall, the mayor unveiled a statue. It was a simple thing, showing a steelworker. In his right hand was the flag of West Germany. On the base of the statue was a plaque:

TO THE PEOPLE OF SCHWERIN

WHO DIED IN THE THIRD WORLD WAR

JULY 2018.

THEY FOUGHT,

NOT FOR GOLD AND NOT FOR GLORY,

BUT THAT THEIR HOPES OF FREEDOM

WOULD NOT PERISH FROM THE EARTH.

EPILOGUE: UNITED NATIONS - 2019

*There is nothing wrong with the United Nations except
its members.*

> —Lord Caradon,
> British ambassador to the UN

Over the past quarter of a century, some of the most unforgettable
moments of my life have taken place in the United Nations Building.
The first was in 1970, soon after the release of *2001: A Space Odyssey*.

MGM had arranged a screening for Secretary General U Thant—
who was greatly interested in all matters relating to space—and the
event took place in the Dag Hammarskjold Theatre. I was sitting immediately behind the secretary general and his deputy, Ralph Bunche,
hoping desperately that no international crisis would blow up in the
next two hours and twenty minutes. (It didn't.)

Even though I've seen it dozens of times—and watched the actual
filming just outside the Boreham Wood Studio, with the London buses
rolling by in the background—I'm still overwhelmed when Moonwatcher smashes down the weapon that will make him Master of the
World. But when I was sitting behind the secretary general I suddenly
realized that right here was the place where we were trying to control
what Moonwatcher had started—the four-million-year evolution from
bone club to ICBM.

And a moment later, another thought struck me with such violence
that I was astonished it had never occurred to me before: *My God! The
monolith and the UN building look exactly the same!*

I still don't know if that's pure coincidence. . . .

The first question that must be asked about the United Nations is:
Will it still exist in 2019? Unlike the League of Nations, which collapsed
after only two decades, the UN has just celebrated its fortieth anniversary. But there are ominous signs that not all is well.

One symptom of a perhaps fatal malaise is giantism. (Remember the
dinosaurs. . . .) When the UN was formed in 1945, it had 51 members;
by 1985 it had 159. With the best will in the world—even if all the
members were anxious to cooperate, which, alas, is all too rare—it
would be extremely difficult to get anything done with such a cumber-
some body.

Many years ago, after enduring countless hours of boring speeches
and inconclusive debates, I swore that I would never let myself get

elected to any committee with more than six members. (As it happens, the only committee I now belong to has six members; but as the chairman is either the president of Sri Lanka or the leader of the opposition, the agenda is dispatched with great efficiency.) Handling a committee with 151 disputatious members must be an absolute nightmare.

Short of tranquilizer guns, there is no way of stopping pompous politicians who are determined to make speeches. But I hope that, by 2019, the development of intelligent computers will have enormously increased the efficiency of the UN's proceedings.

It should not be difficult to write a program that could act as an "honest broker" between parties in a dispute, noting (without revealing) the concessions they were willing to make, and arranging compromises until a consensus was reached. The time may come when a computer, because of its total impartiality and lack of self-interest, may be more acceptable than a human negotiator. Although this is only a very primitive form of interaction, anyone who has ever answered the kind of intimate questions that an up-to-date doctor's computer asks will know exactly what I mean. (If you've not yet had this experience, you soon will. . . .)

Even though a computer could handle 159 members as easily as the original 51, it seems scarcely possible that by 2019 we will still have that number of independent sovereign states; even today, many appear to be on their last legs—politically and economically. And by that time the Charter itself will surely have to be revised; it has long been an anachronism, as it was an instrument of the five victorious powers— the United States, Britain, the Soviet Union, France, China. They, and only they, still possess the right of veto, which has so often prevented any effective action in times of crisis. How long will the other 154 members—some of which will be superpowers themselves in the next century—tolerate this absurd situation?

In any event, I cannot see the United Nations as anything more than a transition stage, toward a time when the very concept of "nation" is meaningless. Perhaps the largest social grouping of the future will be the Electronic Tribe, whose members will have interests and network access codes in common, but seldom geography.

In August 1971, the treaty setting up the global INTELSAT communications satellite system was formally signed at the State Department in Washington. Speaking at the conclusion of the ceremonies, I made a prediction that I feel will be well on the way to achievement in 2019.

Drawing a parallel from the last century, I pointed out that the United States was made not only possible, but *inevitable* by two inventions: the railroad and the electric telegraph. The jet plane and the communications satellite are playing the same role today on a global scale.

"Whether you intended it or not," I told the assembled delegates to the INTELSAT ceremony, "what you have just signed is the first draft of the Constitution of the United States of Earth."

A dozen years later, when communications satellites were part of everyday life—and a million dishes had sprung up like mushrooms in American backyards—I was able to go a step further.

The United Nations had declared May 17, 1983, "World Telecommunications Day," and I was invited to give an address in the General Assembly itself. As I stood at the rostrum beneath the famous seal, I was acutely aware of all those who had occupied this same historic spot, and had looked out at the same rows of desks: Afghanistan, Algeria . . . Zaire, Zambia.

I had certainly never expected to be *here*—even in my wildest dreams.

After reminding my listeners of the overwhelming impact that telecommunications had already had upon human affairs at all levels from the individual to the superstate, I took a running jump into the future:

> The long-heralded Global Village is almost upon us, but it will last for only a flickering moment in the history of mankind. Before we even realize that it has come, it will be superseded—by the Global Family.

And when we have the Global Family, we will no longer need the United Nations.

But until then. . . .

INDEX

PICTURE CREDITS

For their contributions, the following are gratefully acknowledged:

Chapter 1: p. 10 © Don Dixon

Chapter 2: pp. 12, 26 © NASA; p. 23 © NASA/Norman Rockwell

Chapter 3: p. 30 © Dan McCoy and R. E. Herron; p. 36 © Dan McCoy; p. 41 © Hank Morgan; p. 46 © Rick Sternbach

Chapter 4: pp. 50, 58–59, 63, 68 © Robert Malone

Chapter 5: p. 72 © Bill Binzen; pp. 77, 84 © Chromosohm, Inc.; p. 80 © Gregory MacNicol; p. 83 © Dan McCoy

Chapter 6: p. 86 © Dan McCoy; p. 92 *background photograph* © Dan McCoy, *inset* © Joe Dimaggio/JoAnne Kalish; p. 99 © Wayne Eastep

Chapter 7: pp. 106, 117 © Gregory MacNicol; pp. 119, 122 © Rick Sternbach

Chapter 8: p. 134 © Nicolas Foster; p. 143 © Chromosohm, Inc.; p. 148 © Joe Viesti; p. 151 © Ed Bohon

Chapter 9: pp. 154, 161 © Dan McCoy; p. 163 © Joe Dimaggio/JoAnne Kalish; p. 167 © Bill Pierce

Chapter 10: p. 170 © Anthony Wolff; p. 179 © Gregory MacNicol; p. 184 © Wayne Eastep

Chapter 11: p. 186 © Ed Bohon; pp. 191, 192 © Dan McCoy

Chapter 12: pp. 196, 212 © Bill Binzen; p. 205 © Phillip A. Harrington

Chapter 13: pp. 218, 225 © Joe Dimaggio/JoAnne Kalish; p. 222 © Chromosohm, Inc.

Chapter 14: p. 228 © Wayne Eastep; p. 234 © Chromosohm, Inc.; p. 241 © Nicholas Foster

Chapter 15: p. 248 © Russell Munson; p. 254 © Anthony Wolff; p. 259 © Lou Jawitz; p. 262 © Dan McCoy